ETHICAL ISSUES
in Adult Education

ETHICAL ISSUES
in Adult Education

Edited by
RALPH G. BROCKETT

Teachers College, Columbia University
New York and London

Published by Teachers College Press, 1234 Amsterdam Avenue,
New York, NY 10027

Library of Congress Cataloging-in-Publication Data

Ethical issues in adult education / edited by Ralph G. Brockett.
   p. cm.
  Bibliography: p.
  Includes index.
  ISBN 0-8077-2910-8. ISBN 0-8077-2909-4 (pbk.)
  1. Adult education—United States—Moral and ethical aspects.
2. Continuing education—United States—Moral and ethical aspects.
I. Brockett, Ralph Grover.
LC5251.E77 1988
374′.973—dc19
                                           88-1233
                                           CIP

Manufactured in the United States of America

93 92 91 90 89 88   1 2 3 4 5 6

Contents

Preface

A continuing education program at a small college is faced with strong competition for enrollments from the local state university and the public school district. The director, fearing the possibility of cutbacks, initiates a marketing campaign in which existing courses are repackaged as "institutes." When queried about the lack of a physical location and staff for these institutes, she replies that the name *institute* is used "because it sells."

In attempting to allay fears of students enrolled in a course on public speaking, an instructor relates the experience of Bob Randolph, a student who had taken the course last term and, because of "stage fright," was unable to finish a speech he had begun in front of the entire class. Referring to Bob by name several times, the instructor pointed out that Bob was able to regive the speech at a later time and performed admirably. Thus, students had no reason to fear failing an assignment because of their anxiety about public speaking.

A consultant is hired to evaluate the effectiveness of an adult basic education program. The evaluation reveals that because the size of the program has been declining over the past several years, the program could function without loss of effectiveness with two fewer teachers. Since the teacher who was most recently hired into the program is a close personal friend, the evaluator is faced with the decision of whether to modify the interpretation of results for the evaluation report.

As a field characterized by extreme diversity in both practice and ideology, adult education often serves as a stage for controversy and moral conflict. Regardless of the specific settings in which they practice, adult educators must deal on a daily basis with dilemmas, such as those described in the hypothetical scenarios above, that force them to confront their basic values and beliefs. Whether functioning primarily as a teacher, program planner, counselor, administrator, or researcher, educators of adults must regularly face a wide range of ethical issues. Yet, to date, very little has been written about this most vital area as it relates to the practice of adult education.

At present, the field of adult education is struggling with the question of professionalization. Convincing arguments are being presented both for and against the trend toward viewing adult education as a profession. A quick glance at the literature from several other fields with a strong service orientation, such as higher education, social work, medicine, counseling, and law reveals that the topic of ethics is an important one, for it serves as a basic foundation for effective practice. Furthermore, ethical considerations lie at the heart of discussions about the professionalization issue in each of these fields. The purpose of *Ethical Issues in Adult Education*, therefore, is to promote a greater awareness of the kinds of moral dilemmas that are inherent in the education of adults and to serve as a resource for the examination of ethical issues relative to the practice of adult education. While the contributors offer few prescriptive solutions to specific ethical dilemmas, the volume's goal is to give readers new insights into their own values as educators and ideas that should prove helpful in decision making relative to ethical issues that they face in their own practice.

This book has been developed with several audiences in mind. First, it was written for adult education practitioners, who on a daily basis must address issues or problems that challenge their basic values and beliefs. Second, it is directed toward students and professors engaged in graduate adult education programs. The book should prove particularly appropriate in courses dealing with foundations or current issues in adult education. Third, it is hoped that the book will serve as a resource for researchers and writers, who will use it as a point of departure for further inquiry.

The 13 chapters of the book offer a broad examination of ethical issues within various areas of practice. In addition, several issues that transcend specific adult educator roles are considered. Chapters 1 and 2 provide a basic foundation for better understanding the nature of ethics in adult education. The opening chapter sets the stage for the volume by distinguishing between the study and practice of ethics and by reviewing selected literature on ethics and adult education. In this chapter a model is presented that distinguishes among three basic dimensions of ethical practice in adult education and serves as a framework for the subsequent chapters.

In the second chapter, Carol E. Kasworm reviews literature on moral and ethical development in adulthood. She points out that an understanding of this dimension of adult development serves as a bridge to understanding the adult educator as an ethical decision maker.

The next six chapters address ethics in the context of major roles assumed by the educator of adults. Chapter 3, by Thomas J. Sork, focuses on ethical questions that can arise in the planning of programs for adult learners. He explores such aspects of planning as needs assessment, setting of objectives, and funding of adult education programs.

Marketing is a topic that has sparked much controversy within the adult education field. John H. Burns and Gene A. Roche, in Chapter 4, argue that when used in a responsible way, marketing can serve as a valuable resource for assisting learners in effective decision making.

Burton R. Sisco addresses several ethical concerns in Chapter 5 that confront the administrator of programs for adult learners. The illustrations in this chapter are drawn from the continuing higher education context; however, the issues raised have relevance to administrators throughout the field, regardless of the specific practice setting.

In Chapter 6, Stephen Brookfield addresses ethical concerns that can arise in the evaluation of adult education programs. Using illustrations taken primarily from the evaluation of adult education graduate programs, Brookfield identifies several broad themes related to both the process of evaluation and the utilization of evaluation results.

The teaching–learning situation presents a multitude of opportunities for ethical conflict. Chapter 7, by Rosemary S. Caffarella, addresses issues related to the basic beliefs held by teachers of adults and several ethical dilemmas related to the multiple responsibilities that are so often a reality in teaching adults.

In Chapter 8, Michael J. Day looks at ethics from the viewpoint of the brokering or advising relationship. He points out that adult learning is intimately linked with the notion of choice. Through illustrations from popular literature and film, Day addresses possible consequences of choice and raises questions for those educators who provide brokering services to adult learners.

The next three chapters focus on issues of relevance to the broad field of adult education. Phyllis M. Cunningham, in Chapter 9, explores the link between adult education and social responsibility. She argues that the ethical decisions made by educators of adults are important in the social transformation of society and that adult educators can become more socially responsible through critical dialogue with their many publics.

Exploring questions of ethics relative to adult education research in Chapter 10, Sharan B. Merriam outlines considerations related to the purposes of research and the nature of knowledge, the process of conducting research, and the dissemination of research findings. While ethics is an important topic throughout educational research, Merriam offers illustrations relating directly to the study of adult learners.

The question of whether a code of ethics should exist for adult educators has been and will likely continue to be at the heart of discussions related to the increased professionalization of the field. In Chapter 11, Robert A. Carlson argues that the development of such a code will have negative consequences for the field and, ultimately, for adult learners.

In Chapter 12, Roger Hiemstra provides practical suggestions that adult educators can use to translate their personal values into practical action. He suggests that the development of a personal philosophy statement can be a useful tool in effective ethical practice.

The closing chapter is intended to identify major themes found throughout the previous chapters. In addition, a number of possible directions for future exploration relative to ethics are considered.

A special debt of gratitude is acknowledged to Professor Gordon G. Darkenwald, whose vision and enthusiasm for this project helped to turn the idea into reality. Also, the editorial support of the staff of Teachers College Press, particularly Sarah Biondello and her predecessors in acquisitions, Audrey Kingstrom and Lois Patton, and Peter Sieger in production, is gratefully acknowledged. Additional thanks are due to William M. Freese for his assistance in producing the figure in Chapter 1.

Ethical Issues in Adult Education is intended to be a blueprint for examining concerns that, in one way or another, face all of us who practice as educators of adults. While there are rarely clear-cut solutions to ethical dilemmas, the adult educator who chooses to reflect critically on his or her practice will be able to deal with such conflicts in an *informed* way. If the following chapters serve to stimulate greater awareness or to inspire the asking of questions that have previously been overlooked, the book will have served its intended purpose.

Ralph G. Brockett

ETHICAL ISSUES
in Adult Education

CHAPTER ONE

Ethics
and the Adult Educator

RALPH G. BROCKETT

Aᴅᴜʟᴛ education is a dynamic field characterized by extreme diversity in both ideology and practice. There are few, if any, universally accepted practices or beliefs. In a field that is as action-oriented as adult education, however, it is often easy to become so focused on pragmatic issues inherent in the day-to-day operation of a program that some of the broad questions confronting the larger field can easily become overlooked or relegated to second-ary importance. Regardless of the specific setting in which one practices, it is vital that the adult educator not lose a grasp of his or her basic mission. As de Chambeau (1977) has stated, "the question of *why* must precede questions of *what* or *how*" (p. 308).

Among the most important of these "why" questions are those related to the ethics of practice in adult education. While few would argue that ethics is not an important aspect of adult educa-tion practice, the lack of emphasis on this topic, as witnessed, for example, in the professional literature to date, is most disturbing. The purpose of this chapter is to explore the topic of ethics as it pertains to the adult education field. Specifically, the chapter will offer a brief look at the meaning of ethics, review literature on ethics in adult education, and suggest a model that can be used to differentiate between three aspects of ethical practice relevant to the education of adults.

Adult educators are confronted on a daily basis with the need to make choices. There is too much to be lost from relying on reactive approaches to decision making, such as doing it "the way we've always done it" or "shooting from the hip." More than 20 years ago, Cotton (1964) stated that "adult educators should accept their responsibility to be something more than program technicians"

1

(p. 86). Such a view requires a proactive posture involving critical reflection upon one's actions and a willingness to assume responsibility for those actions. That is what this chapter, and indeed the entire book, is intended to be about.

The Practical Nature of Ethics

Ethics is an often-misunderstood term involving at least two major aspects. First, it is a branch of philosophical inquiry that focuses upon moral questions. In addition, *ethics* refers to a set of beliefs that serve as guides to action. According to Fagothey (1972), ethics, by derivation of the word, is "the study of human customs" (p. 1). However, since customs can include manners, such as fads and fashions, as well as morals, Fagothey goes on to specify that ethics may be defined as "the study of *right* and *wrong*, of *good* and *evil*, in human conduct" (p. 2). Similarly, Singarella and Salladay (1981) distinguish between ethics as a discipline involving *descriptive* observation and examination of moral behavior and the practical use of ethics, involving *prescriptive* selection among competing values. The distinction between the theoretical and applied elements of ethics is further clarified through the concepts of "metaethics" and "normative ethics." Writing from the perspective of social work, Reamer (1982) states that

> questions of metaethics involve an analysis of the meaning and definitions of ethical terms such as good and bad, and right and wrong; normative ethics, on the other hand, involves the application of ethical standards and values in order to judge whether specific actions, institutions, and ways of life are right or wrong, or good or bad. Thus, the question *What is the meaning of the term good?* is one of metaethics, while the question *Should services and resources be distributed among individuals on the basis of need?* is one of normative ethics. (p. 41)

While both metaethics and normative ethics are important to a comprehensive understanding of ethical practice, the focus of the present discussion, because of its exploratory nature, will tend toward the latter emphasis, recognizing at the same time that questions of metaethics will be an important area for future inquiry, particularly by those adult educators with background in philosophical methods of inquiry.

Essential to an understanding of normative ethics is the recognition that ethics is a *practical* endeavor. Fagothey (1972) argues that since the purpose of ethics is to enable one "to act and live rightly," ethics can be viewed as a *"practical* science, standing somewhere between a purely theoretical science and its corresponding art" (p. 5). Finnis (1983) argues that the practicality of ethics can be traced directly to Aristotle, who said that ethics involves the pursuit of practical knowledge. In his analysis, Finnis claims that the idea of ethics as a practical pursuit is often distorted or "watered down" and goes on to interpret Aristotle's idea in the following way:

> He [Aristotle] meant that one does ethics properly, adequately, and reasonably, if and only if one is questioning and reflecting *in order to be able to act*—i.e., in order to conduct one's life rightly, reasonably, in the fullest sense 'well.'" (Finnis, 1983, p. 1)

It is precisely this practical element that makes the examination of ethical issues vital to professions or fields of practice that provide service to others. Indeed, a glance at the literature of other service-oriented fields reveals that ethics has been addressed in such areas as social work (Levy, 1976; Reamer, 1982), higher education (Dill, 1982; Baca & Stein, 1983), counseling psychology (Kitchener, 1984; Goodyear & Sinnett, 1984), and health care (Purtilo & Cassel, 1981; Rosenbaum, 1982). However, relatively little has been written about ethics in adult education. Yet ethics is no less important a concern for the adult educator than it is for those in other helping fields.

Ethical Dilemmas in Adult Education

Wooten and White (1983) have defined an ethical dilemma as "a situation involving choice, encountered by a change agent or client system, which has the potential to result in a breach of acceptable behavior" (p. 18). Similarly, Purtilo and Cassel (1981) state that an ethical dilemma "occurs when acting on one moral 'conviction' . . . means breaking another" (p. 5). Adult educators are clearly in a situation where conflict and controversy can be a way of life. Kreitlow and associates (1981) have addressed several such issues in their volume on controversial issues in adult education. And while issues such as these have been prevalent in the adult education literature since the earliest years of the movement in North America, it has only been recently that authors have begun directly to confront specific ethical dilemmas that can emerge in the education of adults. At present, the majority of literature on ethics in adult education has consisted of general discussions revolving around the topic. In addition, descriptive data from at least one survey are available. Finally, the recent publication of a set of "principles of good practice" for continuing educators raises several questions for consideration relative to ethics. This body of literature is considered below.

Recent Discussions of Ethics in Adult Education

Several authors over the past few years have attempted to distill a number of ethical issues related to the education of adults. For instance, Davies (1981) states that when being assessed, trainees and students have a right to privacy, confidentiality, and reasonable assessment of performance. These, it would seem, are general principles relevant to the entire teaching–learning interaction.

Maidment and Losito (1980) argue that most ethical problems in training and development are not deliberate efforts to abuse responsibilities to clients, but rather grow out of a general lack of understanding about the nature of ethical questions or an overreliance on formal ethical codes. They present what they call "A Faker's Dozen," which outlines 12 categories of unethical behavior sometimes found among training professionals. Among these categories are: "the boilerplater," who relies on a packaged program when clients are led to believe that what they are receiving has been developed specifically for them; "the fancy footworker," who offers little of substance, but does it in an entertaining way; and "the siphoner," who fails to give appropriate credit to others for ideas contained in his or her presentation or handouts. These few types of unethical practices illustrate that the range of questionable behaviors is quite broad and that, in many instances, the line between being ethical and unethical may not be entirely clear.

Lenz (1982) devotes a chapter of a book on teaching adults to the topic of ethical issues. Among the issues she identifies are concerns related to the administration of enrollment-driven programs, including "body counts"; truth in advertising; conflicts of interest, particularly among part-time teachers engaged in other full-time pursuits; and hidden agendas, where self-interests of the teachers can "erode the teaching process" (p. 100).

Singarella and Sork (1983), in what is probably the most comprehensive discussion of adult education ethics in the literature to date, state that personal ethical codes are often in conflict. In such situations, it may be easy to allow personal values to be superseded by self-interest or expediency. Because multiple roles, including change agency, characterize the adult educator, an understanding of ethical principles is crucial. Singarella and Sork do not argue in favor of a formalized code of ethics; rather, they offer 11 questions relative to ethical issues that program planners need to confront. These questions address such concerns as learner needs, learning outcomes, social intervention, mandatory continuing education, confidentiality, program promotion, funding, and evaluation. A further discussion of ethical issues relative to the program planning process is offered by Sork in Chapter 3 of this volume.

Kazemek (1984) has explored the area of ethics within the context of adult literacy education. Drawing from the work of Dewey, Kazemek suggests that adult literacy can serve as a strategy for developing social intelligence in a democracy. Basic to this argument is the belief that individuals are capable of taking action in an intelligent and responsible way.

Brockett and Hiemstra (1985) consider a number of ethical questions that can arise in working with the self-directed learner. Here, ethical dilemmas can arise both within the learner–facilitator relationship and in the policies and practices determined at the institutional level. Questions that need to be addressed relative to the learner–facilitator interaction focus upon potentially detrimental consequences of facilitator intervention and on problems that can surface from jumping on a currently popular bandwagon without adequately understanding the degree of responsibility and effort that need to go into facilitating self-directed learning activities. At the institutional level, the potential for abuse also exists in terms of promoting nontraditional approaches emphasizing learner self-direction without adequately considering the actual needs of the population to be served.

Moody (1985) explores the question of ethics relative to education for older adults. He points out that if education in later life is "good," there must be some criterion for judging such activity. According to Moody, the often-held assumption that education during the later years "is good because it gives old people 'something to do'" should be scrutinized carefully (p. 39). He goes on to suggest that an alternative rationale for justification might be linked to "a vision of old age as the fulfillment of life" (p. 39).

In the area of nursing, Pearson and Kennedy (1985) have addressed the application of principles of business ethics to continuing education programming. They state that providers of continuing education programs have a responsibility to use ethical marketing practices, to ensure that faculty have a clear understanding of the nature of their agreement with the provider, and to avoid duplicating programs or materials developed by other providers without appropriate permission. In addition, Pearson and Kennedy raise the "conflict-of-interest" issue in the selection of faculty who have a commitment to a potentially competitive organization. Finally, they consider the question of program ownership. For instance, under what circumstances should a program and/or materials developed for the program belong to the provider or to the individual faculty member? Pearson and Kennedy conclude their discussion by recommending that ethical standards be developed by accreditors of continuing nursing education programs. Through such a procedure, it would then be possible to deny the approval of continuing education units for providers who violate those standards.

The ASTD Survey

Conspicuous by its absence from the above section is an inclusion of *research-based* literature on ethical issues in adult education. To date, research on ethics in adult education has been virtually nonexistent. One exception to this gap in research is an investigation that was part of a larger study on competencies of training and development professionals commissioned by the American Society for Training and Development (ASTD) (Clement, Pinto, & Walker, 1978).

In this study, a survey pertaining to the roles and competencies of professionals in training and development was sent to members of the ASTD. Included as part of this survey was an open-ended question seeking examples of unethical or improper behavior actually *observed* by respondents. Of the 2,790 ASTD members responding to the survey, 999 addressed this question. A content analysis of responses revealed seven major categories. In order of frequency, these were as follows: lack of professional development; violation of confidence; use of "cure-all" programs; dishonesty regarding program outcomes; failure to give credit (e.g., copyright violations); abuse of trainees; and other improper behaviors (e.g., entertaining rather than teaching, lack of follow-up). In addition,

96 respondents reported that they had observed no unethical behavior.

Based on the above responses, it was concluded that improper or unethical behavior "may occur at all stages of the training and development process" and that these behaviors may range "from very serious breaches of ethical (if not legal) codes" to "unprofessional conduct" and "some simply careless acts" (p. 12). Clement, Pinto, and Walker stress how important it is for training managers to recognize that improper behavior is much more than ineffectiveness and that such behaviors can actually cause harm greater than the potential benefits of training.

Standards of Practice

One of the perennial issues facing the field of adult education is the question of professionalization. Should adult education strive increasingly toward status as a profession in the same way that fields such as social work and nursing have done? This question is an important one, but it is beyond the scope of this chapter, except that a common element of most professions at present is a formally stated code of ethics (e.g., Houle, 1980; Cervero, 1987).

In an effort to provide guidance in the resolution of several potential ethical dilemmas in the education of adults, the Council on the Continuing Education Unit (CCEU) developed a report entitled *Principles of Good Practice in Continuing Education* (CCEU, 1984a). This statement was the result of a three-year project intended to strengthen standards in the field through cooperative efforts among a wide range of noncredit continuing education and training providers (CCEU, 1984b). A background study of noncredit continuing education providers (House, 1983) revealed that 93% of those organizations surveyed believed that written standards aimed at enhancing quality assurance should exist. The CCEU report (1984a) offers 18 general principles and 70 "elements of good practice" in the areas of learning needs, learning outcomes, learning experiences, assessment of learning outcomes, and administration. The 18 major principles are listed in the Appendix.

In April 1984, an invitational conference was held to introduce the CCEU report and to address ways in which the principles could be disseminated and implemented throughout the field. The conference report (CCEU, 1984b) includes quotes from several participants on behalf of the report. For instance, Leonard Brice, president of the CCEU, states that each adult learner "should eventually benefit from the impact of *Principles*. . . . *Principles* brings together in one useable statement the best thinking about planning for quality" (p. 2). William Draves points out that adult learners "need to know how to shop more smartly in the burgeoning marketplace of learning opportunities" (p. 3). And Malcolm Knowles emphasizes that *Principles* is a major breakthrough, since it places emphasis "on the learner, and on getting results." He goes on to say that the next challenge is to "get this into the bloodstream of every educator or trainer of adults" (p. 3). Among the general conclusions of the conference were that an active marketing strategy should be employed to disseminate the *Principles* and that "personal influence" should also play an important role in encouraging educators to implement the principles in their practice settings.

While the conference report indicated strong support for the widespread adoption of the principles, an alternative viewpoint has been presented by Mezirow (1984). His concerns are highlighted in the following statement:

> The fallacy of "Principles" is reductionist; they reduce all significant personal learning needs to expressed personal needs; they reduce all significant adult learning interests to those fostering individual performance and organizational efficiency; they reduce the learning process to content mastery and problem solving; they reduce learning gains to measurable outcomes; they reduce continuing education to a training ground for production and consumption and they reduce adult education to a technology divorced from any responsibility for social change and serving to maintain the status quo. "Principles" are uninformed about the nature of adult learning and misdirected about the purpose of adult education. (p. 28)

The debate sparked by Mezirow's critique encompasses a number of broad issues relevant to the field, such as the purposes of adult education and professionalization of the field. But it also forces a critical examination of whether a single set of standards can adequately serve a field as diverse as adult education. This is an issue clearly worthy of further discussion and debate.

The Literature in Perspective

Recent literature on ethical issues in adult education has considered several aspects of practice (e.g., teaching, training, program planning, administration) as well as a range of program areas (e.g., literacy, gerontology, nursing). While the areas of emphasis and the views expressed by the authors differ considerably, at least three general points can be gleaned from this literature. First, there is a definite need to examine closely the topic of ethics as it relates to the education of adults. Efforts to date provide a foundation for further dialogue but are only a beginning. Ethics needs to be viewed as a priority area in adult education practice. Second, more extensive efforts to study the topic of ethics in adult education are needed. Indeed, the one research study on ethics reported earlier consisted merely of a single question included as part of a larger study. Finally, the code-of-ethics question is not easily resolved. This issue is intimately linked to the question of professionalization; thus, the two concerns are not likely to be understood independent of each other. Carlson elaborates on the code-of-ethics issue in Chapter 11.

All in all, it can be concluded that while few authors have written on the topic of ethics in adult education, the literature that *does* exist has paved the way for a more extensive exploration of this most important area. The following section offers a model that may be useful in dealing with ethical issues as they arise in daily practice.

Dimensions of Ethical Practice in Adult Education

Formal codes of ethics and standards of "good" practice provide prescriptive guidelines for what may be defined by some as "appropriate" behavior. However, these general approaches merely scratch the surface of understanding ethical practice, for they are only concerned with outcomes and do not take into consideration the process individuals go through in ethical decision making. The "dimensions of ethical practice" model presented here is an attempt to describe a process through which adult educators can draw from their own basic values in making decisions related to their practice as educators of adults. It is not intended to provide prescriptive guidelines for "proper" behavior; rather, its purpose is to identify a process that can be used for addressing ethical dilemmas in adult education practice.

It is proposed here that one way of understanding ethics in adult education is to distinguish between three interrelated levels, or dimensions, of ethical practice. At the most basic level is a recognition of one's personal value system. These are the basic beliefs one holds about such concerns as human nature; because they are internalized within the individual, they are the least "visible" in actual practice. A second dimension of ethical practice is the recognition that the responsibilities of the adult educator extend simultaneously in several, often conflicting, directions. This dimension is concerned with the dissonance that can arise when, for example, differences exist among one's personal belief system, the mission of the agency, and/or the needs and preferences of learners. Finally, a third dimension is the way in which values are operationalized. This can include statements of formal codes or standards, but much more important is the ability of the educator to articulate his or her personal position on specific practices and to determine where to "draw the line" on practices that may be unethical. Figure 1.1 is an illustration of this model. Each dimension warrants further elaboration.

Personal Value System

At the heart of ethical practice is one's basic system of personal values. Raths, Harmin, and Simon (1975) have suggested that values are "general guides to behavior" that "tend to give direction to life" (p. 72). Values become particularly important in situations in which there is a need to choose among two or more possible

FIGURE 1.1. Dimensions of Ethical Practice in Adult Education

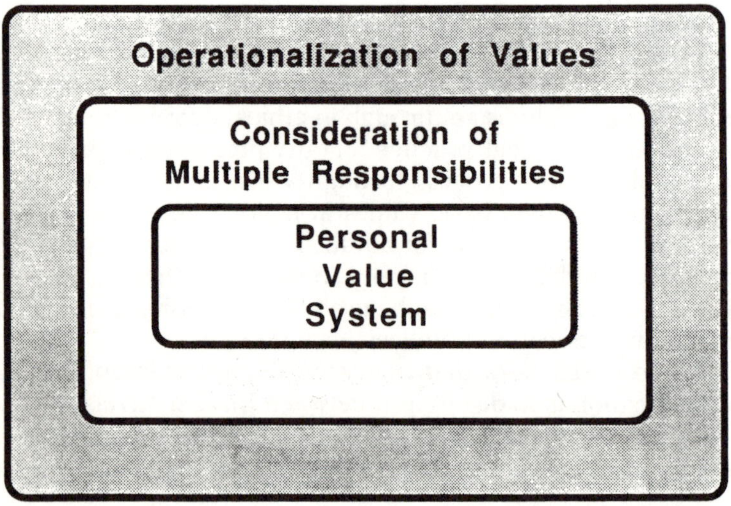

Operationalization of Values

Consideration of Multiple Responsibilities

Personal Value System

courses of action, for they help one to consider the likely consequences of each choice.

A value can be internalized at several levels. In other words, the "strength" with which one adheres to a value can differ from person to person as well as from situation to situation. Krathwohl, Bloom, and Masia (1964) suggest that a value can be internalized at three different levels. The most basic of these levels is an *acceptance* of a value, whereby one holds a tentative belief in a position. At the next level, one shows a *preference* for a value when he or she is willing to actively pursue and be identified with a position. Finally, *commitment* is a very strong belief that is often expressed as conviction, faith, or loyalty. These levels of internalization are most important, since they define the limits of acceptable behavior in a given situation. The ongoing debate that currently exists over such questions as whether adult educators should be engaged in social reform and whether there are situations in which mandatory continuing education is acceptable can perhaps be better understood as dissonance between opposing values. The more deeply committed one is to a particular point of view, the greater the likelihood of polarization when the issue at hand is discussed. An awareness of one's personal value system and the degree to which certain values have been internalized is an essential point of departure in understanding how one will respond in specific situations.

Consideration of Multiple Responsibilities

A second dimension of ethical practice revolves around the question of to whom we are responsible as adult educators. According to Mirvits and Seashore (1979), ethical dilemmas frequently develop "not because roles are unclear but because they are clearly in conflict" (p. 771). The adult educator who is charged with developing a program utilizing a competency-based approach, for instance, will be in a position of role conflict if his or her personal values are not consistent with the underlying assumptions of competency-based education. Similarly, the adult basic education (ABE) teacher in a conservative school district may experience dissonance if students and/or certain community groups envision the ABE program as an opportunity for promoting social and political empowerment.

Adult educators, like those who practice in other service-oriented fields, are responsible to many individuals and groups. In its code of ethics, the National Association of Social Workers (1980) has offered principles related to the social worker's responsibility to self, clients, colleagues, employers and employing organizations, the profession, and society. These categories are equally applicable to the adult educator in terms of resolving conflicts among personal values, addressing learners' needs and desires, working cooperatively with colleagues, serving the mission of the agency, contributing to the larger field of adult education, and promoting the welfare of society. In actively considering one's responsibilities to multiple audiences, the adult educator needs to search for balance. Ultimately, though, this balance necessitates setting priorities based on the anticipated consequences of one's actions and *accepting responsibility for those actions.*

Operationalization of Values

It is suggested above that one's personal value system and the potential for role conflicts combine to provide the adult educator with a foundation for the third dimension of ethical practice: the implementation of ideas to practice. Operationalization can involve the development of a formal code of standards or ethics; however, in adult education, the translation of values into practice has tended to be more informal.

Is there a way to identify general guidelines adult educators can use when putting ethical ideas into practice without needing to subscribe to a formal code of ethics? Perhaps. As an illustration, Sieber (1980) has emphasized four basic principles that constitute ethical norms for practice in program evaluation. These principles—beneficence, respect, justice, and obligations to clients—are equally applicable to adult education.

The first principle, beneficence, refers to the "avoidance of unnecessary harm and the maximization of good outcomes" (p. 54). Adult educators need to be cognizant of the means utilized to reach certain ends and to weigh the potential consequences of such means against the positive outcome that may result. The use of teaching techniques such as role-playing, for example, present the potential for abuse if not well planned and introduced by the facilitator.

Respect refers to a concern for "the autonomy or freedom of persons and for the well-being of nonautonomous persons," such as those who are institutionalized (Sieber, 1980, p. 54). Respect often refers to a nonjudgmental attitude whereby each person is accepted as a unique individual. The idea of respect is analogous to Rogers's (1961) notion of "unconditional positive regard." Adult educators need to recognize the diversity of those whom they serve, as well as the diversity of the field in which they serve. The adult educator who demonstrates respect is unwilling to use his or her position to coerce others to act or believe in a given way or to exploit those who are oppressed.

Justice, as used here, refers to equity. Clearly, this is a vital ethical concern in the education of adults. Certain segments of the adult population can be found to be distinctly underrepresented as participants in adult learning programs. Adult educators cannot afford to lose sight of the question of whom we should be serving.

A fourth principle to consider is the need to offer a statement of obligations to the client. In the context of program evaluation, Sieber states that this refers to showing the client "what must be done to produce both the most favorable and the most honest evaluation possible" (1980, p. 55). The statement of obligations in adult education may refer to an open discussion of the rights and responsibilities of all parties engaged in the transaction. For instance, the adult education consultant needs to state explicitly at the outset what he or she perceives as responsibilities to the agency who has sought his or her services. Similarly, it is important for the consultant to elicit from the agency an understanding of its specific expectations from the consulting agreement. Successful adult learning is not a one-way street. Rather, it is a negotiated process that is most likely to lead to a positive outcome if obligations of all parties are openly addressed from the outset.

The principles stated above are not intended to serve as the foundation for a formalized code of ethics. Nor is it necessarily being argued that these principles be viewed as universally accepted norms throughout the entire field. Rather, these principles have been presented in order to illustrate how personal values and consideration of multiple responsibilities can facilitate ethical decision making.

Conclusion

The model presented above offers a paradigm for understanding some of the complexities inherent in ethical practice. It should not be viewed as a formula for providing simplistic answers to questions that defy simplicity. Rather, it is intended to serve as a tentative guide for understanding a process that can be used by educators of adults in ethical decision making and for clarifying some of the types of questions that need to be asked when examining ethical issues.

Ethics has a definite place in adult education. Whether serving as a program planner, administrator, instructor, or counselor, the adult educator daily confronts questions that force a careful reexamination of one's basic values. While the pace and routine of daily practice can make it easy to relegate such questions to a secondary role, the costs of doing so will likely be great. Adult learners deserve the best that each of us has to offer. Therefore, ethics must lie at the heart, not the periphery, of what we do.

References

Baca, M. C., & Stein, R. H. (Eds.). (1983). *Ethical principles, practices, and problems in higher education.* Springfield, IL: Thomas.

Brockett, R. G., & Hiemstra, R. (1985). Bridging the theory–practice gap in self-directed learning. In S. Brookfield (Ed.), *Self-directed learning: From theory to practice* (New Directions for Continuing Education No. 25, pp. 31–40). San Francisco: Jossey-Bass.

Cervero, R. M. (1987). Professionalization as an issue for continuing education. In R. G. Brockett (Ed.), *Continuing education in the year 2000* (New Directions for Continuing Education No. 36, pp. 67–78). San Francisco: Jossey-Bass.

Chambeau, F. A. de (1977). Why? what? or how? Philosophy as a priority for educators of adults. *Adult Leadership, 25* (10), 308.

Clement, R. W., Pinto, P. R., & Walker, J. W. (1978). Unethical and improper behavior by training and development professionals. *Training and Development Journal, 32* (12), 10–12.

Cotton, W. E. (1964). The challenge confronting American adult education. *Adult Education, 14*(2), 80–88.

Council on the Continuing Education Unit. (1984a). *Principles of good practice in continuing education.* Silver Spring, MD: Author.

Council on the Continuing Education Unit. (1984b). *Principles of good practice in continuing education: Report of the conference.* Silver Spring, MD: Author.

Davies, I. K. (1981). *Instructional technique.* New York: McGraw-Hill.

Dill, D. D. (1982). The structure of the academic profession. *Journal of Higher Education, 53*(3), 255–267.

Fagothey, A. (1972). *Right and reason: Ethics in theory and practice (5th Ed.).* St. Louis: Mosby.

Finnis, J. (1983). *Fundamentals of ethics*. Washington, DC: Georgetown University Press.

Goodyear, R. K., & Sinnett, E. R. (1984). Current and emerging ethical issues for counseling psychologists. *Counseling Psychologist, 12*(3), 87–98.

Houle, C. O. (1980). *Continuing learning in the professions*. San Francisco: Jossey-Bass.

House, R. (1983). *Standards of practice in continuing education: A status study*. Silver Spring, MD: Council on the Continuing Education Unit.

Kazemek, F. E. (1984). Adult literacy education: An ethical endeavor. Cheney: Department of Education, Eastern Washington University. (ERIC Document Reproduction Service No. ED 239 043)

Kitchener, K. S. (1984). Intuition, critical evaluation and ethical principles: The foundation for ethical decisions in counseling psychology. *Counseling Psychologist, 12*(3), 43–55.

Krathwohl, D. R., Bloom, B. S., & Masia, B. B. (1964). *Taxonomy of educational objectives: The classification of educational goals: Handbook II. Affective domain*. New York: McKay, 1964.

Kreitlow, B. W., & Associates. (1981). *Examining controversies in adult education*. San Francisco: Jossey-Bass.

Lenz, E. (1982). *The art of teaching adults*. New York: Holt, Rinehart & Winston.

Levy, C. S. (1976). *Social work ethics*. New York: Human Sciences Press.

Maidment, R., & Losito, W. F. (1980). Ethics and professional trainers. Madison, WI: American Society for Training and Development. (ERIC Document Reproduction Service No. ED 186 980)

Mezirow, J. (1984). Book review of *Principles of good practice in continuing education*. *Lifelong Learning: An Omnibus of Practice and Research, 8*(3), 27–28.

Mirvits, P. H., & Seashore, S. E. (1979). Being ethical in organizational research. *American Psychologist, 34*(9), 766–780.

Moody, H. R. (1985). Philosophy of education for older adults. In D. B. Lumsden (Ed.), *The older adult as learner: Aspects of educational gerontology* (pp. 25–49). Washington, DC: Hemisphere.

National Association of Social Workers. (1980). *Code of ethics*. Washington, DC: Author.

Pearson, G. A., & Kennedy, M. S. (1985). Business ethics: Implications for providers and faculty of continuing education programs. *Journal of Continuing Education in Nursing, 16*(1), 4–6.

Purtilo, R. B., & Cassel, C. K. (1981). *Ethical dimensions in the health professions*. Philadelphia: Saunders.

Raths, L. E., Harmin, M., & Simon, S. B. (1975). Values and valuing. In D. A. Read & S. B. Simon (Eds.), *Humanistic education sourcebook* (pp. 72–81). Englewood Cliffs, NJ: Prentice-Hall.

Reamer, F. G. (1982). *Ethical dilemmas in social service.* New York: Columbia University Press.

Rogers, C. R. (1961). *On becoming a person.* Boston: Houghton-Mifflin.

Rosenbaum, M. (Ed.). (1982). *Ethics and values in psychotherapy: A guidebook.* New York: Free Press.

Sieber, J. E. (1980). Being ethical: Professional and personal decisions in program evaluation. In R. Perloff & E. Perloff (Eds.), *Values, ethics, and standards in evaluation* (New Directions for Program Evaluation No. 7, pp. 51–61). San Francisco: Jossey-Bass.

Singarella, R., & Salladay, S. (1981). Ethical considerations for the biomedical communications professional. *Journal of Biocommunication, 1,* 10–16.

Singarella, T. A., & Sork, T. J. (1983). Questions of values and conduct: Ethical issues for adult educators. *Adult Education Quarterly, 33*(4), 244–251.

Wooten, K. C., & White, L. P. (1983). Ethical problems in the practice of organization development. *Training and Development Journal, 37*(4), 16–23.

CHAPTER TWO

Facilitating Ethical Development: A Paradox

CAROL E. KASWORM

As adult educators, we do not often purposefully focus on how we could influence the ethics of others. Although our work is based on ideas and knowledge, rarely do we see the teaching–learning process from a "values perspective." Yet learning is not a neutral action. By creating a course or a particular evening lecture, we present a perspective or a specific knowledge base that reflects a value stance. We are covertly stating to our learners that a specific set of knowledge and skills will be beneficial for their future actions. It is worthy of their time and interest to consider, if not act upon, this information. In addition, the design of the program, the use of varied teaching–learning strategies, and the projected learning outcomes are also based in value-related decisions and have value impact on the learners.

This chapter will explore one aspect of our ethical role as educators. From varied perspectives, adult development theory and research suggest that significant learning experiences influence the psychosocial development of adults. Adults face an ongoing dynamic tension in their lives. On the one hand, adults continue to seek equilibrium in their lives. They desire to bring their thoughts, feelings, and actions into congruence with the reality of their world. They desire to bring a harmony and wholeness to their daily actions and future goals. This need for stability, congruence, and support is a major theme of additive education: to bring knowledge and skills in support of the adult's current existence. However, due to both external forces and internal changes of the body and mind, adults also face, and often seek out, challenges to their lives. Adulthood is not a period of calm, uneventful living. Recent research characterizes adulthood as a time of transitions, role changes, and psychosocial stresses. These changes occur because of predictable events and purposeful desires for change. These changes also occur because the adult, having significant responsibilities to self and to others, experiences and responds to the social network in new ways. Further, during the course of maturation, each set of new experiences affirms or redefines the adult in relation to both personal identity and the identities of others. These challenges can be transforming. Education can be a catalyst, a facilitator, or the source of new understandings, meanings, and actions. Education can provide a bridge as adults make a transition from a past perspective or life role to a new, unknown way of living and thinking.

In this chapter, three major perspectives of the nature of adult development will be considered. Each perspective will be presented as a journey toward adulthood and will be based in theories of adult development and consisting of both education for stability and education for challenge and transformation. In each journey, significant learning plays a key role in the development of adults, particularly in the evolution of their identities and value structures. A central consideration in the examination of these perspectives is the ethical role of the adult educator, who must encourage learning activities that offer both stability and challenge to the learners. These apparently conflicting aims result in a paradox that will be examined from three major perspectives found in the adult development literature to see what ethical dilemmas are posed for adult education action.

Journey 1:
The Maturing Adult in a Social Context

This first perspective characterizes adult development as a journey with (1) a dynamic maturing, or personal-growth, process, (2) learning based in experiential, powerfully significant environments, and (3) evolving actions that grow in depth and richness, based on respect for others and in support of the social context of the adult. This perspective reflects a diverse group of educators who have grounded their beliefs about education and human development in the originial works of John Dewey (1917, 1938/1969).

Dewey, an early leader in progressive educational philosophy, considered education as the process of continually reorganizing, reconstructing, and transforming. This process of growth, or maturation, occurs within a specific context of democracy. He believed that the educational process is integral to freedom and democracy—that education provides the value context for acts of passing judgment, of evaluating an act or object. This personal evaluation is a tool that grants individuals the "power to frame purposes, to judge wisely, to evaluate desires by the consequences which will result from acting upon them" (Dewey, 1938/1969, p. 64).

In the 1940s, Harry Overstreet expanded on Dewey's concepts of adulthood. He believed that the maturing adult is one who has *linkages* with life that become stronger and richer both in internal development of attitudes and sensitivities to others and in relation to actions and environments external to the adult. Adulthood signifies a journey toward a more personally and socially responsible status. Maturity means accepting that the human experience is a shared experience, "that life's dilemmas are dilemmas for all of us" (Overstreet, 1949, p. 51). This development from immaturity to maturity does not automatically progress with aging. Rather, by significant human involvement in educative acts that link learning to social actions in the world, a cycle of maturing occurs. This maturing, through these involvements, causes change from dependence to independence, helplessness to competence, irresponsibility to responsibility.

To both Dewey and Overstreet, educators and all social institutions are responsible for emulating democratic ideals. They perceived education for adults as necessary for defining, encouraging, and sustaining mature actions and contemplation. Overstreet (1949) characterized an adult who ceased to learn as being like a blindfolded person; he believed this person would be a menace to a democratic community. Thus, to Overstreet, maturing meant becoming a more socially responsible adult, who, in turn, provides the energy and the spirit to democratic ideals.

In recent times, researchers who support these concepts of adult development have more sharply identified the impetus for growth and have broadened the definition of the social context to include a broader world view of diverse value systems (beyond a democratic ethic). These educators and psychologists, including Maslow, Rogers, and Knowles, still view adulthood as a transforming process, but they have focused on a dynamic of adult action based in need motivation or problem orientation. Thus adults mature in an interactive fashion within their social and personal world. However, this development is initiated through a specific and highly personalized focus of concern and need. Learning comes from powerful and unique experiences. As noted by Maslow, "How do people learn to be wise, mature, kind . . . to search the truth, to know the beautiful and genuine . . . ? They can learn from the unique experiences of the heart . . . from tragedy, marriage, having children, success, triumph, death and failure" (Maslow, 1970, pp. 281–282). Knowles (1980), with a similar focus, believes that the life tasks and problem-solving orientation of adults are the key engagement for learning. These perspectives recognize the American value of democratic actions but also support other valuable cultural paradigms of adult learners who view themselves as a part of the world community.

In this particular journey of adulthood, there are several key elements for adult education that influence the value perspective of learners. Significant moral-oriented learning experiences are maturing, transforming experiences, based upon adult needs, motives, and problem orientations. These educational activities are framed in powerful, significant social experiences that responsibly link the adult learner with his or her world. All education experiences are based in a social perspective, premised either in supporting or creating more mature understandings of democratic ideals or in enhancing a world-citizen view for the learner.

Journey 2:
Age-Related Adult Life Cycle

This second journey of adulthood is based on a number of theories that consider the systematic changes in adult lives throughout the life cycle. Broadly categorized, this perspective perceives adult development as including the following elements: (1) the adult develops throughout a life cycle consisting of age-related periods of dominant themes, issues, or tasks; (2) each age-related period has specific tasks or issues that should be addressed and resolved during that age period in order to allow for movement to a new age-related period of new adult concerns; (3) each period has the potential for psychosocial maladjustment due to unsuccessful resolution of age-related concerns; and (4) each period reflects the differentiated forces of biological changes, sociocultural roles/

norms, and personal values and aspirations that influence these age-related changes. These life-cycle changes build upon a person's value system, as well as causing conflict that could precipitate changes of moral perspective for the adult.

Drawing upon foundational efforts of Freud and Buehler, Erikson suggested that growth through the lifespan is a process of meeting and achieving a series of psychosocial tasks. Each task must be successfully resolved before the individual can face the next stage of these psychosocial life demands. The key stages in the adult life as defined by Erikson include intimacy versus isolation, generativity versus stagnation, and ego integrity versus despair (Erikson, 1963). Each of these stages has implications for the development of an ethical standard in adults.

Erikson believed that the stage of intimacy is the most significant one in the development of adult moral values. Each adult must experience and develop a sense of intimacy in order to be able to commit to "concrete affiliations and partnerships" and to develop the ethical strength to abide by these commitments. Erikson believed that individuals lacking this ego understanding of intimacy would seek isolation and possibly would destroy those actions and people who seem to be dangerous or to "invade" (physically and psychologically) their lives. In particular, he believed this stage was significant in determining young adult attitudes toward war and combative politics. Thus prejudice, antagonistic relations, and fear of the unknown play a major role in this unresolved stage. In essence, the successful resolution of this task of intimacy is to commit to intimate friendships as well as sexual love relations, in order to gain an ethical sense of adult responsibilities as a caretaker of significant others and the world (Erikson, 1963).

The next stage, generativity, also has great bearing on ethical development. In this stage, adults focus concern on establishing and guiding the next generation. However, it is more than a concern for survival of a species. This stage also implies that adults establish a true concern and love for the next generation. Adults should assume roles in human organizations that make contributions to future generations. "Generativity is a driving power in human organizations . . . to provide continuity . . . to codify the ethics of generative succession" (Erikson, 1968, p. 139).

The final stage, ego integrity, speaks to the concerns of facing death and reexamining one's life in the context of one's values and life meanings. Adults at this stage must resolve the life task of accepting one's triumphs and failures and viewing oneself as part of the world of humankind. At this stage, one's ethics and morals become the eyeglasses for viewing past life and its meaning.

From a more contemporary vantage point, Gould and Levinson also provide perspectives on understanding the nature of age-related life-cycle developments. Gould (1978) describes adult development as an understanding and overcoming of childhood consciousness through the age-related development of an adult consciousness. He believes that adult lives are constricted by childhood fears and anger; adult development, therefore, means confronting these childhood assumptions that can influence us as adults. In the process of defining ourselves as adults, we must abandon childhood illusions of safety and shed immature beliefs about ourselves. Each age period or era presents specific challenges to assuming an independent adult consciousness reflecting an adult identity and a reality-based involvement in the world. Each of these age-related eras presents conflicting child–adult ethical dilemmas. Of significance in this life-cycle process is the development of an adult consciousness that accurately understands the powers of good and evil in the world, accepts an adult role as a key actor in creating both good and evil events, and, most importantly, accepts these ethical responsibilities.

Levinson and colleagues, in *The Seasons of a Man's Life*, have defined a more clearly age-delineated scheme, with crucial ethical dilemmas faced in each era of a man's life. They suggest that there are stable periods during which an individual is building a life structure, alternated with transitional periods in which the structure is changing. Each period of life is characterized by its own set of developmental tasks. A life structure is formed and reformed around the developmental tasks during these age-related eras. Transitions occur between each of these eras, based on previous life choices, key marker events, the pursuit of goals and values within the structure, and the perception of past conflict with or inadequacy for desired future ambitions (Levinson, Darrow, Klein, Levinson, & McKee, 1978).

Although Levinson's theory is rich in defining multiple dimensions of adult development, this discussion will present a brief overview of his work in relation to moral and ethical development. Levinson theorized that the initial life structure established in the twenties creates a sense of self as well as a sense of relatedness to the external world. This age period establishes the adult foundations of the value structure, preferred roles, and life goals. The age period of the thirties, as defined by Levinson, is the time of settling down and creating deeper commitments and life investments within the life-structure framework. It is an era of order, stability, security, and control. There is a growing intensity of focus in the late thirties as the individual strives to become "one's own man." At this juncture, he attempts to remove perceived forms of restraint or oppression from his life. He also, at this time, desires to be recognized and to focus on the values of the key roles to which he has committed his life. At the close of this era, a key change, the "mid-life transition," occurs. In this transition, he must deal with the disparities between his inner sense of self and his outer life commitments; he must contemplate the fit between the life structure and the self. During the mid-adult years (45–60) a man finds himself at the peak of his career and social status, while also recognizing the possible discrepancies between his original life goals and his current status. This era also entails the recognition of the aging process, an awareness of mortality, and realization of the brief time left to fulfill one's hopes and desires.

These eras of the life structure suggest a man's fairly systematic effort to define, understand, and clarify values. Levinson, however, has provided for a greater understanding of adult development by describing specific transitions and challenges faced in the movement from one era to the next, the reexamination and potential change in the life structure for the man. In this process, "the person forms a stronger sense of who he is and what he wants, and a more realistic, sophisticated view of the world" (1978, p. 195). The adult male gains a greater sense of his separateness and thus can become more autonomous and self-generating, as well as gain the ability to create more intense attachments to the world. At each transition point, the person terminates parts of his past life structure and initiates new structures. Although central values and perspectives may remain, the adult sheds those behaviors, relations, and perspectives that constrict his development toward life goals. This process is based on a reappraisal and evaluation of values, needs, and actions. Each of these life transitions presents developmental crises that jostle the individual's values and moral system.

Levinson reports the most significant moral changes are made in the mid-life transition. At this time, man must grapple with fundamental moral dilemmas focused on aging, mortality, masculinity, and attachment. He must face aging and becoming a member of the older generation, experiencing aging in the physical, psychological, and sociological senses. He must reconcile his own mortality with his life as destructive or creative tool in the world. He must develop a sense of balance, of coexistence between the masculine and feminine part of his identity. This balance reflects his concern for manliness, power, achievement, and toughness versus the desire to reflect, to give sanction to one's feelings, to define oneself as a mentor, and to redefine one's significant love relations. Lastly, he must find ways to integrate the dilemmas of desiring strong attachments to others, while also needing to have separateness in the sense of nourishing one's inner self. Thus this dilemma speaks to defining a new balance in his life between his own inner needs of self and the need to care and relate to others and the society.

These three major age-related adult development theories—as well as other related theories of Havighurst (1964); Lowenthal, Thurnher, and Chiriboga (1975); Neugarten (1976); and Vaillant (1977)—suggest the need for adult educators to consider the nature of age-related issues or tasks in adult moral development. Certain researchers have attempted to create age-specific educative tasks to enhance and support these development-resolution needs (e.g., Havighurst, 1972; McCoy, 1977). Although their perspectives have value, chronological age is often relative, as opposed to a fixed correlation with life tasks. Caution should be exercised in the strict adherence to these specified educational actions in relation to specific age groupings. Although these theories are suggestive of normative standards, there is sufficient research to suggest they reflect cultural, gender, racial, and socioeconomic assumptions. Rather than standards, they should be viewed as one of many sets of guiding landmarks along the journey of adult development.

As with the first journey, this journey in adult development suggests that adult educators must become knowledgeable regarding specific ethical themes, issues, and value conflicts faced by adults in the life cycle. Learning experiences that focus on these ethical issues in the life cycle enhance the adult's ability to be competent and functional in life tasks, as well as to resolve the dilemmas faced in each era of the life cycle. Each of these theories provides insight to the adult educator regarding specific events, tasks, and concerns faced by the adult in various stages of the life cycle. These theories also suggest potential educative experiences that can provide a mechanism for adult reexamination of value structure, life tasks, or consciousness. Significant learning experiences provide the medium for adults to make sense of their aging process, to resolve the dilemmas in their changing world, and to become the adult they wish to be and to lead the life they choose. This particular journey also suggests that inability to resolve these age-related tasks can be problematic for the future development of the adult. Educational experiences can be an important element in the successful resolution and movement of the adult toward effective self-understanding and action in ethical relationships with others and the world.

Journey 3:
Adult Development as a Contextual Transformation

This journey in the development of adults contains certain elements similar to those of the previous journeys. It defines the progression of adult development in periods or stages, and it notes the influence of experiences, both social and personal, in the momentum of change in this process. However, the perspective of this journey is not guided by either the dynamic, social orientation of the first journey or the fixed, age-related periods of the second journey. Chief characteristics of this journey are internal developmental patterns, which are the foundation for the person's contextual judgment base and are altered by transformations in the person's cognitive and value orientation.

The basis of this journey comes from the early work of Piaget in developmental psychology and draws upon the concept of epigenesis, the study of developmental patterns. A key assumption of this journey through adulthood is that moral development occurs through internally organized meaning structures reflected in cognitive and value-related perspectives. In addition, it is assumed that ethical or moral development can be identified through specific stages, each building upon the previous stage, while also exhibiting unique characteristics. These stages are specifically sequenced, representing levels of increasing complexity in form, differentiation of components, and broadening of self–other orientations (Kitchener, 1978). Each stage involves a cognitive understanding of reality as well as a qualitatively perceptual sense of meaning in viewing the world. Although the stages are progressive in pattern, adults follow this path of development at their own rate, often stabilizing at one stage for a number of years, if not a lifetime. Thus development of values is not an age-related concern, as suggested in the previous theories. Values are always part of the adult's sense of making meaning with his or her life. The development process, however, presents the adult with a more complex set of perspectives and interactions between self and others, with progressive stages of development involving an understanding of the actions and ethics of oneself within a broadening view of the world.

Contemporary research on this journey in contextual transformation of the adult experience includes Loevinger's theory of ego development (1976), Kohlberg's theory of moral development (Lickona, 1976), Gilligan's revisionist theory of women's moral development (1982), Perry's theory of cognitive and moral development (1970), and Fowler's theory of faith development (1981). All of these related theories of adult development assume that adults view their world from within a cognitive and perceptual value framework, making judgments and actions based upon these perceptions. Throughout the adult life, each stage brings stability and a sense of congruence to one's life. However, adults also face personal, social, and ethical dilemmas that may activate a contextual transformation to a more complex stage. In this transformation, adults discover that their way of making sense of their world is inadequate, perhaps too simplified or insufficiently sensitive to the diverse concerns external to themselves or to their internal values. In the earlier stages, the adult experiences ideas and meanings as simplistic and unidimensional within a dogmatic context; the later stages reflect complexity and multidimensionality within an ambiguous or conflicting value context. Adults can move in this developmental journey from the frame of significant referent of external orientation (where the individual is dependent on authority of judgment of others) to an inner orientation (where the individual bases responsibility for the consequences on his or her actions). The individual also has a tendency in the early stages to perceive those outside of the immediate group in stereotypic terms and to display a strong self-focus of egocentrism. Progressive stages feature an increasing awareness of individual differences and greater empathy with others. The individual experiences an intermediate stage of conformity to a significant social group and its mores. In the later stages, the individual expands the context of meaning in relation to an expansive interdependence with others in the world (Merriam, 1984; Schlossberg, 1984). To explain this contextual development more clearly, a more in-depth presentation of Kohlberg's and Gilligan's work in relation to the moral/ethical development process follows.

Kohlberg's Stages of Moral Development

Kohlberg's (1981) work focuses on moral reasoning and considers the reasons one gives for what a person ought to do when values are in conflict. In developing his theory, he drew upon situations that presented moral dilemmas and examined the individual's reasoning in determining what is right and wrong. In this theory, six factors are seen as being perceived differently at each level of moral development (Lickona, 1976; Wilcox, 1979):

Concept of person—how the individual relates to oneself and others in the society.

Concept of value of human life—the specific context of considering the worth of a human life.

Role-taking ability—the ability of the person to put him- or herself in the shoes of another person and interpret the thoughts and feelings of the other.

Concept of authority—the person's definition of what it is, where it is housed, how it functions, and how the individual relates to it.

Concept of law—the concept of its function and purpose.

Concept of community—the definition of what constitutes the person's significant referent group, what are perceived as the key structures of that group/society, and how the person relates to these.

These elements are the base of a social perspective on which an individual draws to determine the response of a moral question. Kohlberg's theory draws upon these elements in his presentation of a six-stage cognitive developmental approach (Kohlberg, 1970; Lickona, 1976; Wilcox, 1979).

In this theory, the first two stages are called the *preconventional level* and center upon the individual's concern for egocentric interests. In the first stage the focus is on obedience to authority and avoidance of punishment. Those who are big or powerful exert major influence on the person's moral decision making. In the second stage the individual's moral decisions become more instrumentally oriented. Thus, the concept of moral decision making is based upon utility and equal exchange of goods, favors, blows, or punishments. Obedience is displayed to obtain rewards. Ethics is based upon serving people who are the most useful in giving what one wants in a fair exchange interaction.

The next two stages, called the *conventional level,* are focused upon concern for significant others or society. At these two stages, the individual is able to have empathy for others in relation to self, is able to understand and operate in a societal structure of laws, rules, and mores, and perceives societal roles in relation to contribution to and maintenance of the broader referent group. In stage three, the individual is concerned with his or her own referent group. The good moral decision is based on the "perceived behavior of goodness" as defined by the group and on doing what is valued and approved by significant others. In the fourth stage, the individual moves beyond the context of his or her group to focus on the broader society. At this stage the concern for moral decision making rests with the notion of justice for those who obey the law and who earn the right to justice. Thus duty and obligation for maintaining societal values and laws are of dominant concern. The individual draws upon the standards of the societal group to determine appropriate ethical actions.

In the last two stages, known as the *postconventional, autonomous,* or *principled level,* certain adults may progress to a level of moral decision making that is based on a broader world view. One can stand outside of one's society and cultural values and look at them, along with other cultural norms, from a more objective perspective. Individuals at the fifth stage are no longer concerned with maintaining societal norms; they care about the inherent premise that undergirds these norms—equality of human rights, protection of the individual. The individuals at this stage focus on a notion of a "social contact" based on universal principles of human rights. At this stage, there is emphasis on consistency and rationality in decision making. The last stage, as noted by Kohlberg, is a rarity in adult life. It is reflected in a person who can provide an objective perspective of someone's situation with equity and equality of moral decisions. This person is able to recognize the universality of individual rights apart from societal affiliations. Individuals are viewed as ends in themselves, and not as means to other ends.

Gilligan's Revisionist Theory

In the past ten years, Kohlberg's work has been criticized by researchers who suggest that his orientation, his methodology, and his original base in male samples have created cultural, gender, and socioeconomic bias in his theory. One of his many critics, Carol

Gilligan (1982), has proposed a revisionist theory that eloquently presents the development of the moral understanding of women. She found that Kohlberg's development of an ethic of justice in men featured a development toward maturity focused on the morality of rights, fairness, and equality. This development reinforces the concept of individual autonomy and separateness as a preferred status of a mature individual. Gilligan disputes this notion. In her studies, she suggests that women's moral development reflects an ethic of care and responsibility. It is premised in the concern for connectedness with others and views maturity as maintaining one's ethic in interdependence with ethics of others and emphasizing equity in moral concerns. Gilligan suggests an alternative course for women's moral development. In the first stage, woman's moral decision making is premised on the concern for self in order to ensure survival. In the second stage, it focuses on being responsible, with particular concern for those who are dependent and unequal. Great care is taken at this stage to avoid harming others who have a relationship with oneself. A woman at this stage will sacrifice self to support others, often denigrating her own needs and concerns. At the third stage, the woman views herself, as well as others, as meriting care. Thus her moral decision making now seeks to find an equitable balance between her own sense of self and her relationships with others.

Gilligan suggests that women view moral decision making in terms of attachment, reciprocity, and responsibility to self and others. Men, on the other hand, view moral decision making in terms of rules, rights, and fairness. They are concerned with intellectual detachment in making moral judgments.

For adult educators, this perspective on contextual transformation presents an important basis for creating learning formats and environments. Adults learn from experiences that are congruent with their stage of contextual development or that focus them on the beginning differences of the next stage of development. It suggests that adults at varied stages will have different perceptions, affecting how they view a situation and how they process data for moral decision making. Thus educators, as they deal with learning situations focused on ethical decision making, should consider these perspectives and the current stages of their learners in relation to effective learning formats. In particular, adult educators should be sensitive to triggering changes in a person's perspective on values and on "making sense of one's world." These contextual transformations cause dissonance and are often internally threatening for the individual. Awareness of these learner changes is of primary importance in creating appropriate value-related learning situations.

Paradox of Stability and Challenge

Each of these journeys of adult development suggests that adulthood is synonymous with the desire to be competent and to bring knowledge and skills to bear on one's life. However, all three also suggest that adulthood entails the capacity to change by developing a more in-depth, complex understanding of oneself and one's world. Adulthood implies becoming autonomous from externally imposed authorities while creating a personal value set that reflects one's identity within an interdependent world. It implies reexamining parental and significant other mores and values and validating or creating one's own value structure in that context. These perspectives all suggest direction away from egocentrism and toward a humanitarian world view, bringing reasoning and values to bear on one's life toward others. These three journeys also recognize the drama and conflict of adult life and view learning, which arises from and is intertwined with these significant experiences, as an integral part of the development process.

Adult educators face a significant paradox as they view these perspectives of adult development and integrate them into learning designs. What should be the role of the educator in a learner's psychosocial development and in relation to the learner's value structure? The vast majority of organized adult learning activity is an "additive" experience of building upon established knowledge concepts. This type of education is important in providing the stability necessary for satisfying adult needs. In particular, adults seek equilibrium in their lives and search for information, self-directed projects, seminars, and courses that provide resolution, clarification, and balance to their daily living. This type of additive experience provides greater expertise, broadening of understanding, and a sophisticated application of knowledge to previously unknown areas. It provides the confidence and the harmony for adults to be leaders, decision makers, and contributors to their world. In the mode of additive education, educators should provide opportunities for informed decision making in relation to ethics. Thus, as noted by Brockett in the preceding chapter, we need to respect the current value system of the adult learner and use the principle of beneficence to create learning experiences that are congruent and beneficial to the learner. Often the adult life is a stormy, turbulent passage fraught with internal desires to achieve and with external demands to act in certain ways. Education can provide the necessary ballast and support for competent efforts. It also can prepare us to face a future of uncertainty and change. As noted in the UNESCO report *Learning To Be* (Faure et al., 1972), "for the first time in history, education is now preparing man for a type of society which does not yet exist" (p. 13). It builds upon the foundation of the adult value structure and brings clarity to values in relation to adult actions in the social context; the additive education is vitally important in the day-to-day lives of adults.

However, each of these perspectives suggests that adult development also incorporates internal cognitive, emotional, and value-oriented changes as one gains maturity. For adults to continue their pursuit of life and happiness, they also need to seek challenge through new life-task concerns, complex cognitive insights, and effective resolution of conflicting values within their lives. In this part of the paradox, adult educators also face a crucial role in providing catalytic learning experiences or providing a supportive structure and a stimulus for transformation. There is a need to provide stimulating activities related to unresolved or incongruent life tasks, acceptance of cultural myths, or dysfunctional life structures. In addition, adult educators, according to Dewey and others, have an important role in developing a broader consciousness of the concept of the world citizen who holds responsibility for the future of the world and humanity. Learning experiences are not only person-centered; they are also world-centered.

These journeys of adult development suggest that adults must gain appropriate knowledge sets, develop new affective/perceptual insights, and evolve behavioral strategies to respond effectively to life issues or task concerns. These learning experiences, which are challenging and transforming, are often ego threatening. Great care and sensitivity should be used. In addition, profound learning experiences typically involve a form of perspective transformation, involving the creation of a new sense of meaning to one's life. As suggested by Mezirow (1981), we should also create learning experiences that support "critical reflexivity." This critical reflexivity means that learners should begin to identify their current set of meanings and values in relation to internalized cultural myths. In order to bring challenge and change to one's life, one must learn to be critical of who and what one is and to reexamine the foundations and premise of the personal value structure; in that process, one gains a new sense of perspective and an alternative set of meanings for understanding one's identity and relationship to the world.

In this paradox, great care and respect is given to the learner. A dialogical experience with mutual respect and dignity is established. In this paradox, central issues of equity, equality, justice, truth, obligations, and power are considered. As suggested in the first chapter, this part of the paradox is a morally profound experience as one moves from identifying one's values and meanings to placing them into action in one's daily life.

Conclusion

Adult educators are not merely conveyers of knowledge; they can be reinforcers and transformers of adults' perspectives on life and meaning. They serve an important role in providing both stability and challenge in the lives of adult learners. With each learning design, they are ethically involved in the ongoing psychosocial development of their learners. With their knowledge, expertise, human care, and professional skills, they can facilitate adults' ethical development, both engendering stability and continuity and presenting challenges that can modify or broaden their base for moral decision making.

References

Dewey, J. (1917). *Democracy and education.* New York: Macmillan.
Dewey, J. (1969). *Experience and education.* Toronto, Canada: Collier. (Original work published 1938).
Erikson, E. H. (1963). *Childhood and society* (2nd ed.). New York: Norton.
Erikson, E. H. (1968). *Identity, youth and crisis.* New York: Norton.
Faure, E., Herrera, F., Kaddoura, A., Lopes, H., Petrovsky, A. V., Rahnema, M., & Ward, F. C. (1972). *Learning to be: The world of education today and tomorrow.* Paris: UNESCO.
Fowler, J. W. (1981). *Stages of faith.* San Francisco: Harper & Row.
Gilligan, C. (1982). *In a different voice.* Cambridge, MA: Harvard University Press.
Gould, R. L. (1978). *Transformations.* New York: Simon & Schuster.

Havighurst, R. J. (1964). Changing status and roles during the adult life cycle: Significance for adult education. In H. W. Burns (Ed.), *Sociological backgrounds of adult education* (2nd ed.) (pp. 17–38). Syracuse, NY: Center for the Study of Liberal Education for Adults.

Havighurst, R. J. (1972). *Developmental tasks and education* (3rd ed.). New York: McKay.

Kitchener, R. F. (1978). Epigenesis: The role of biological models in developmental psychology. *Human Development, 21,* 141–160.

Knowles, M. S. (1980). *The modern practice of adult education* (revised and updated). Chicago: Association Press.

Kohlberg, L. (1981). *Essays on moral development: Vol. 1. The philosophy of moral development: Moral states and the idea of justice.* San Francisco: Harper & Row.

Levinson, D. J., Darrow, C. N., Klein, E. B., Levinson, M. H., & McKee, B. (1978). *The seasons of a man's life.* New York: Knopf.

Lickona, T. (1976). *Moral development and behavior: Theory, research, and social issues.* New York: Holt, Rinehart & Winston.

Loevinger, J. (1976). *Ego development: Conceptions and theories.* San Francisco: Jossey-Bass.

Lowenthal, M. F., Thurnher, M., & Chiriboga, D. (Eds.) (1975). *Four stages of life: A comparative study of men and women facing transitions.* San Francisco: Jossey-Bass.

Maslow, A. H. (1970). *Motivation and personality* (2nd ed.). New York: Harper & Row.

McCoy, V. R. (1977). Adult life cycle change: How does growth affect our educational needs? *Lifelong Learning: The Adult Years, 1* (2), 14–18, 31.

Merriam, S. B. (1984). *Adult development: Implications for adult education (Information Series No. 282).* Columbus, OH: ERIC Clearinghouse on Adult, Career, and Vocational Education.

Mezirow, J. (1981). A critical theory of adult learning and education. *Adult Education, 32* (1), 3–24.

Neugarten, B. L. (1976). Adaption and the life cycle. *The Counseling Psychologist, 6* (1), 16–20.

Overstreet, H. A. (1949). *The mature mind.* New York: Norton.

Perry, W. G. (1970). *Forms of intellectual and ethical development in the college years.* New York: Holt, Rinehart & Winston.

Schlossberg, N. K. (1984). *Counseling adults in transition.* New York: Springer.

Vaillant, G. E. (1977). *Adaptation to life.* Boston: Little, Brown.

Wilcox, M. (1979). *A guide to the development of logical and moral reasoning and social perspective.* Nashville: Abingdon.

CHAPTER THREE

Ethical Issues in Program Planning

THOMAS J. SORK

Pᴿᴏɢʀᴀᴍ planning is a complex decision-making process that results in the production of outcome and design specifications for systematic learning experiences. Many of the necessary decisions involve making choices among mutually exclusive ends and means, each of which is associated with a value position. Ethical issues arise in program planning when any of the alternatives under consideration are associated with value positions that may be viewed as unacceptable by society, other practitioners, clients, sponsors, or planners themselves. In making choices and in completing planning tasks, adult educators may engage in conduct that is viewed as improper or unethical. The purpose of this chapter is to identify ethical issues frequently encountered in program planning, to discuss possible responses to each issue, and to explore the consequences for the practitioner, and for the field, of specific ethical choices.

Practitioners devote a great deal of time to designing educational interventions with the intention of bringing about some change in learners' capabilities to act, to understand, to reason, to analyze, to interpret, to influence, and so on. Although this is often done using the learners' best interests as the paramount criterion to guide decision making, practitioners are also influenced by the expectations, norms, and sanctions of the organizations in which they work and by their own value systems. Ethical issues emerge from the program-planning process because evaluative judgments are constantly being made not only about how to proceed with the planning function, but also about the specific character of an educational program. Forrester (1982) reinforces the importance of these judgments:

Among the most important judgments we are called upon to make are evaluations: assessments of the worth of things, actions, and persons. Hardly a day goes by that we do not need to decide what is the right thing to do in a given situation and what is the best procedure for doing it. To this end, we need to appraise objects and actions as good, bad, or indifferent. We must compare them with each other to determine which is better in some respect or other. We must choose, from what is sometimes a vast number of alternative courses of action, how to spend every moment of our lives. At least to the extent that these choices are consciously made, we make them on the basis of which alternative seems better in some way than the others. (p. ix)

Discussing the ethics of practice may increase the probability that these evaluative judgments are indeed made consciously, with full recognition of their philosophical basis and moral consequences.

The content of this chapter is intended to provoke those who plan educational programs for adult learners into reviewing their own practice to identify decisions and actions that may be considered unethical or improper. Such a review is part of a more complex process described by Schön (1983) as "reflection-in-action":

When a practitioner reflects in and on his practice, the possible objects of his reflection are as varied as the kinds of phenomena before him and the systems of knowing-in-practice which he brings to them. He may reflect on the tacit norms and appreciations which underlie a judgment, or on the strategies and theories implicit in a pattern of behavior. He may reflect on the feeling for a situation which has led him to adopt a particular course of action, on the way in which he has framed the problem he is trying to solve, or on the role he has constructed for himself within a larger institutional context. (p. 62)

Although reflection-in-action is a natural accompaniment to thoughtful practice, it can be encouraged or discouraged by contextual factors in the setting in which the practitioner works. The pressure to get the job done, to conform to institutional policies and practices, to accept established norms, and to respond to the needs of clients all make it difficult to question the moral basis for decisions made and actions taken. Lawson (1979) has argued that those engaged in practice "are well aware of the moral issues implicit in the making of decisions about the education of adults" (p. 19). However, he maintains that the service orientation of adult education, and an emphasis on student-centered teaching, allows practitioners to avoid dealing directly with many substantive ethical issues. Discussing the nature of the program-planning process and raising specific ethical issues that are related to that process may provoke the reflection-in-action that Schön considers so important to effective practice.

Program Planning as a Central Function

Planning is the decision-making process through which goals are formulated and the means to achieve those goals are specified. In educational settings, the goals are most often related to changes in human capability that are effected through systematic learning experiences. Organizing a set of experiences to increase the probability that the desired learning will occur is the goal of educational planning.

Planning is a central function in adult education in part because of the wide range of settings, organizations, contexts, and environments in which educational interventions are planned. Unlike formal school settings in which the planning function might be vested in a few curriculum specialists, the function is widely dispersed in adult education. Because planning is carried out at many levels, by many practitioners, in many different settings, the process is diffused throughout the field. It is a central function precisely because it permeates practice.

It is often difficult to draw clear boundaries between program planning and other functions carried out by practitioners. There are clear relationships between program planning, marketing, counseling, administration, instruction, and evaluation—all areas in which ethical issues emerge. But as used in this chapter, the ethics of program planning are limited to the decision-making process and the related information gathering and analysis that is used to determine the outcome and design specifications for an educational intervention.

Decision Making and Encounters with Ethical Dilemmas

As discussed in Chapter 1, adult education is a highly action-oriented field. In the quest to get things done it is easy to make decisions without considering their ethical content. Even those individuals who have received graduate degrees in adult education are unlikely to have encountered courses or textbooks that address substantive ethical dilemmas that a practitioner might confront. One consequence of this action orientation is unreflective choice; decisions are made on the basis of tradition, hunch, organizational press, or other factors rather than on a consistent, defensible philosophical position. Apps (1973, 1985) and Hiemstra (see Chapter 12, this volume) encourage adult educators to develop a personal philosophy to guide their practice and propose frameworks for structuring such a philosophy. A carefully developed personal philosophy should provide a basis for resolving ethical dilemmas encountered in practice. If it does not, then the philosphy is incomplete.

As practitioners reflect on the ethical content of their choices, they will encounter dilemmas that should be resolved. A dilemma in this sense is a choice that has no totally acceptable resolution; whatever decision is made, there will be some negative consequence. In program planning, such dilemmas result from practitioners' attempts to balance their responsibilities to learners with their responsibilities to the organizations for which they work.

One illustration of this point is related to the role of the planner vis-à-vis others involved in the design and delivery of educational programs. One way of viewing this role is *planner-as-maestro*, or conductor of an orchestra. In this view, the quality of the outcome is dependent on the performance of many other people, but ultimate responsibility rests with the maestro. It is the maestro's conception of "good" that guides the collective activities of performers and gives authority to the maestro's directives. Without careful attention to the details of each performer's responsibilities, the quality of the performance suffers and the reputation of the maestro is diminished.

Another way of viewing this role is *planner-as-broker*. In this view, the broker serves as a communication link between a person who is seeking something and a person who may be able to provide it. The broker establishes a relationship between the two parties, but leaves it to the parties to decide how the relationship will develop and how the quality of the relationship will be assessed. Any conception of "good" that guides the design process comes from those who are parties to the relationship. Evaluation of the broker's role is most often based on the number of relationships established, and only rarely on the quality of the relationships.

Each of these views represents different roles, different responsibilities, and different obligations of the planner. In choosing to adopt one role rather than another, the planner accepts or rejects certain responsibilities and obligations. If the *planner-as-maestro* role is chosen, then dilemmas emerge regarding the exercise of power and authority. If the *planner-as-broker* role is chosen, then dilemmas emerge regarding the application of professional knowledge and organizational responsibility for quality control. Many other roles of the planner could be described in this fashion, and their associated ethical dilemmas identified. The essential point is that ethical decisions permeate the planning process from the point at which the planner decides on what role he or she will assume through to the completion of the last planning task. Promoting a more thoughtful consideration of the ethics of planning is what the remainder of this chapter is designed to do.

Ethical Issues: Values and Proper Conduct in Planning

Criteria that are employed to make decisions have their origins in and are moderated by the value system of the individual making the decision. In the language of commerce, we typically make decisions to maximize benefits and minimize costs. What planners consider to be "benefits" and what they consider to be "costs" will be based on their value system. Although many planning decisions are based on empirically verifiable causes and effects, the ethics of planning is concerned with the *moral dimension* of practice, which cannot be empirically verified. More specifically, proper conduct is behavior that can be justified on moral grounds to those who might question the behavior. If an argument to justify the behavior or practice is more compelling than the argument refuting the behavior or practice, then the action will generally be considered ethical by those in a position to make such a judgment. However, actions considered ethical by one practitioner may be considered unethical by another, because each judges the moral costs and benefits of the action using a different personal value system. Understanding the moral as well as the practical justification for planning decisions, and the actions that follow from the decisions, is an obligation of every practitioner who plans programs.

Singarella and Sork (1983) introduced eleven ethical issues relevant to program planning. These issues were presented in the form of questions to be debated, discussed, and answered by practitioners, rather than as prescriptions for behavior. The following selected issues, some of which are based on the work of Singarella and Sork, are intended to stimulate discussion and do not represent an exhaustive list of issues related to program planning. As consideration of the ethics of practice in adult education becomes more refined, additional issues will be identified and discussed. The intention here is to provide some examples of practices that can be justified or refuted on ethical grounds and to suggest some of the arguments that might be considered during the debate.

1. Responding to "felt" or "expressed" needs of adult learners. The concept of need and the process known as needs assessment are ubiquitous in adult education; they are found in literally every program-planning model published since 1950 (Sork & Buskey, 1986). Some programmers may take the position that their primary responsibility as practitioners is to design programs in response to felt needs of adult learners regardless of the content implied by the needs. These practitioners might argue that adult learners are autonomous beings who exercise their free will by expressing their needs and seeking programs they believe respond to those needs. The act of conducting a needs assessment may be interpreted by some as a signal that all needs identified will be addressed. Any effort by the programmer to pass judgment on the appropriateness of a need would be considered unethical because it infringes on the autonomy of the learner. Yet there are clearly situations when a programmer must make these judgments. Some people may wish to acquire knowledge or skills potentially harmful to themselves, to other individuals, or to social institutions. But there is also danger when the planner alone decides which needs receive attention and which do not. Educational institutions may be viewed as parties to a conspiracy to maintain power structures and forces of oppression in society. If there are some needs that warrant a response by the planner and others that do not, then how is the line drawn between the two? What values are reflected by the programmer who makes these decisions? Whose ideology prevails when disagreements arise over allocating resources to meet needs? What justification exists for placing the programmer in the role of arbiter?

2. Basing a program on a need not acknowledged by the learner. Houle (1972) uses the concept of "ascribed" need, and Beatty (1981) uses the concept of "prescriptive" need to label a discrepancy between present and desired capabilities or performance that is asserted by someone *other than* the learner to whom the discrepancy applies. Putting aside for now the practical problems of assuring participation in programs based on ascribed or prescriptive needs, consider the implications of applying the technology of educational planning, and allocating resources required to offer the program, when the learner does not acknowledge that a need exists. Some might argue that it is quite acceptable to plan programs of this sort because it is in the best interests of an individual, an institution, or society for the learner to become more proficient or capable. Others might counter that this practice violates the autonomy and self-determination of the learner and represents unacceptable paternalism. Are there conditions under which developing such programs can be justified? Is it acceptable practice to engage in activities designed to "enlighten" the learners so that they, too, acknowledge a discrepancy in their capability? What values are reflected in a practice that holds the assessment of "others" in higher esteem than the assessment of the adult learner?

3. Basing the planning process on learning "deficiencies" of adults. There is good reason to question the desirability of a planning process that begins with an assessment of deficiencies in capability or performance, especially if that assessment is presented as value-free in character. Critiques of the concept of need have consistently emphasized the value-laden nature of the term and of the process of needs assessment. Reliance on the notion of need as sole justification for planning and as the primary basis for selecting content can be used to argue that a discussion of aims, and the philosophical basis of aims, is irrelevant (Griffin, 1983). The decision to use "needs" as the justification for programs does not, however, absolve the planner of responsibility to consider the ways in which personal, organizational, and societal values influence the reality in which deficiencies in capability are identified. Desired capabilities are not empirical phenomena to be discovered, but are value judgments made in a more or less political process (Griffith, 1978). What are the long-term consequences of continuing to base programs on deficiencies in human capability? What justification do program planners have for continuing this practice? How does an emphasis on deficiencies affect the orientation of programs and the self-esteem of participants? Should the values on which judgments of deficiency are based be made explicit as part of the planning process?

4. Claiming that specific capabilities will be developed by learners who participate in a program. Developing objectives is another planning task that is often completed without consideration of its ethical implications. It can be argued that objectives represent the intended outcomes of a program and that effective planning is dependent upon a clear notion of what outcomes are desired. Without this notion, planning becomes an empty exercise; without clear statements of intention there is no basis for judging the effectiveness of a program. Systematic avoidance of accountability by failing to specify intended outcomes would be considered by many to be unethical practice. It can also be argued, however, that because there are so many variables influencing what is learned during a program, and because adults enter programs with their own ideas of what they should learn, the practice of specifying outcomes misrepresents the complexity of the learning transaction. The act of specifying objectives can preempt the development of other capabilities that might be of more value to the learner. And since objectives frequently change *during* a program, the process of specifying objectives represents a futile attempt to impose structure on a process that is inherently fluid. What obligation does the planner have to describe the capabilities to be developed by participants in a program? Can accountability be achieved without specifying program objectives? Is it acceptable to describe the structure of the program but not the learning outcomes implied by the structure? Is it ethical to design programs for which intended learning outcomes have *not* been specified?

5. Designing programs in which participation is compulsory. An important philosophical battle has continued for almost a decade on the pros and cons of mandatory continuing education (Mattran, 1981; Rockhill, 1981). The focus of this battle has been on legislation requiring those who practice in certain occupations and professions to participate in a specified number of hours of continuing education programs in order to retain their license or certification. This and other forms of compulsion raise important ethical issues for program planners. Those who support, or do not object to, various forms of compulsory attendance argue that attending education programs reduces the probability that practitioners will be using outdated and possibly dangerous knowledge in their work, or that their skills will deteriorate to the point where the patient or client is endangered. They may argue further that those in a profession or occupation have a moral duty to maintain and improve their knowledge and skills for the protection of their clients, and that formal requirements for continuing education are one means to make that duty binding on all who practice. Those opposed to compulsory attendance argue that forcing adults to participate in any educational program is immoral because it violates the autonomy and self-determination of the individual. There is even some question about whether requiring people to participate in programs does indeed increase the likelihood of competent, or even improved, practice. Putting aside the practical problem of dealing with potentially obstreperous participants, the planner is still faced with the ethical issue of whether to apply the technology of planning to the design of programs in which learners are required to participate. Does the fact that an adult is compelled to participate in a program so violate the canons of the field that planners should refuse to apply their talents in such cases? Are there types of programs for which or categories of professionals for whom compulsory attendance can be justified? Do planners have an obligation to design effective programs regardless of the motives underlying participation or the degree of compulsion exerted on the learner?

6. Maintaining confidentiality of information. Planning involves collecting and analyzing information about individuals and social systems. Developing an understanding of the planning context and client system may require collecting potentially sensitive information. If the process of needs assessment reveals serious deficiencies in human capability, for example, the planner is faced with the task of deciding what information should be made public and what information should remain private. A dilemma is encountered when not releasing the information seems to have as many positive and negative consequences as does releasing the information. A responsibility to maintain confidentiality is weighed against a commitment to the public good. Are there circumstances under which it is justifiable to release sensitive information obtained during planning? Does the fact that the planner has made no formal commitment to maintain confidentiality release him or her from the responsibility to do so? At what point does the public good override any commitment made to maintain confidentiality?

7. Selecting instructional and other resources. When the purposes of an educational program become clear, the next planning step involves deciding what human and nonhuman resources will be used to achieve the purposes. Selecting instructors, facilities, equipment, materials, and so on requires making many value judgments that may or may not be ethically defensible. Ideally these judgments should be based on the criterion of how effective the resource will be in helping achieve the objectives of the program. Yet other criteria, which raise ethical concerns, are commonly used. For example, program ideas often originate with someone who wishes to be hired as an instructor. That person contacts a program planner and explores the possibility of offering a program on a certain topic or issue. This is usually done under the assumption that the person who initiates the contact will be hired as the instructor for the course. If the planner has no knowledge of the instructional ability of the person, and yet agrees to hire that person as instructor for the program, then questions could be raised about whether the planner is fulfilling an obligation to select the best possible resources. If, on the other hand, the planner hires someone else as instructor for the program, then the planner could be accused of stealing program ideas. Similar conflicts arise in selection of facilities, materials, and other resources. Some planners may feel obliged to use facilities provided by their own agency, whether or not those facilities are the best ones for a program. Exploring values that are reflected in the criteria used to make these decisions reveals ethical issues. Is a planner justified in using "convenience" rather than "suitability" or "quality" as the overriding criterion when making decisions about program resources? Is it ethically defensible to consider only one alternative when more than one are available? How much energy should responsible planners be expected to devote to seeking out alternatives? Should planners be expected to reveal the criteria they use to make judgments about program resources?

8. Deciding who will be involved in the planning process. It is often recommended in the planning literature that several parties should be involved in making decisions. Most commonly the parties suggested—in addition to the program planner—are content experts and representatives of the learners for whom the program is intended. Others who might legitimately be invited to participate include the following: sponsors of the program, administrators or policy makers with a stake in the outcomes of the program, those who could refer participants to the program, people expert in the type of technology used to offer the program, those familiar with specific instructional techniques or devices used during the program, and those who may hire or otherwise benefit from the improved capabilities developed by participants in the program. Ethical issues arise when the composition of the planning group is decided and when the nature of their participation in the process is established.

One common orientation to planning involves only the program planner and a content expert (instructor). The planner and instructor agree on the topic or title of the program, the dates, duration, location, and other administrative matters, but the details about what content will be introduced, in what sequence, using which instructional or evaluative processes are often left to the discretion of the instructor, who may or may not have knowledge of or experience with the client group. In this case the planner has made two decisions with important ethical implications. The first is that the client will not be directly involved in the planning process. Although many authors extol the virtues of client involvement in planning, conversations with practitioners suggest that such direct involvement is rare. There are practical consequences of not involving clients in decision making, but of concern here is the morality of planning programs *for* rather than *with* adult learners. The second decision made by the planner is that responsibility for deciding the details of instruction is delegated to the content expert. This practice, which is common, raises the issue of professional responsibility for the success or failure of the program. If the program is not successful, the planner can easily attribute the failure to the instructor and thereby avoid accountability for program outcomes.

It is possible to argue that the role of the planner is primarily administrative, thus vesting responsibility for the quality of the instructional component in the content expert. But it is also possible to argue that the planner is the only person ultimately responsible for the overall success or failure of a program, because only the planner has control over all aspects of the design, whether or not he or she chooses to delegate final decision-making authority for some program components. Decisions about who is involved in planning and for what purpose should be carefully considered by the planner. Is direct involvement of the client in planning a moral imperative that should never be violated? Or are there circumstances when involvement of the client is neither required nor desirable? Are there certain forms of "token" involvement that should be considered improper? Are there critical points in the planning process when involvement is required, but other points when involving others is not responsible practice? Is involvement of the learner and others in the planning process used as a means of *avoiding* direct accountability for program quality by distributing the responsibility among several people?

9. Determining fees for programs. Establishing and maintaining a stable financial base for adult education remains a formidable challenge for program planners and agency administrators. In the typical agency that charges fees for programs, the planner usually calculates a fee using procedures specified in an approved pricing policy (Matkin, 1985). Because some agencies or individual programs are subsidized, revenues generated through fees can be lower than the actual costs of offering the program. Other agencies are expected to break even, recovering through fees all direct and indirect costs of offering programs. Still other agencies are expected to make a profit on their programs, generating more revenue through fees than necessary to cover all costs of offering programs. Decisions about pricing and fees are ethically significant because they interact with the learner's ability and willingness to pay for educational programs. Although the decision of whether or not to participate in a program is influenced by many variables, the fee charged is one of the most frequently mentioned factors influencing the decision. Because agencies that do not enjoy subsidies are under constant pressure to generate income, many tend to design programs for those who are most able and willing to pay fees. To a great extent, the nature of the groups served by an agency is determined by the pricing policy of the agency. Yet those who might benefit the most from participation in a program are often those least able or willing to pay a fee. Locating a source willing to subsidize a program for low-income groups takes time and energy that are often in short supply. But is it ethically defensible to set fees using an established pricing policy knowing that those who might benefit the most will be unable or unwilling to pay? Some agencies resolve this dilemma by charging higher fees to those who are most able and willing to pay and then using profits generated on these programs to subsidize other programs for those less able or willing to pay. Yet this practice, known widely as the "Robin Hood principle," raises other ethical issues that seem to have escaped serious debate (Singarella & Sork, 1983). It can be argued that prevailing pricing policies and associated methods of determining fees are restricting participation in programs to those who are most economically advantaged, thereby widening the gap between the educational "haves" and "have nots." Can a pricing policy that results in systematic underrepresentation of the economically disadvantaged be morally justified? Can using profits from one program to subsidize another be defended ethically because it somehow redresses the imbalance created by the original pricing policy? If profits are used in this way, is it an obligation of the planner to acknowledge publicly that this is being done?

These nine issues illustrate not only the moral questions associated with planning, but also the complexity of the decision-making process itself. There are no doubt dozens of decisions made in the planning process that could be analyzed in a similar fashion, but those identified above suggest that although the ethical issues associated with planning can be ignored, they cannot be escaped.

Consequences of Ethical Choices

Unlike the fields of medicine and nursing, where the consequences of unethical actions can be fatal, in adult education the consequences are less dramatic, but may nevertheless be quite serious. One reason that may account for the absence of discussion of ethics in adult education is that the most visible consequences—the primary consequences—are not especially dramatic. But thoughtful consideration of both primary *and* secondary consequences might reveal the true impact of choices that are made. Following are two illustrations of this point.

One of the session titles listed in the program booklet of a recent meeting of a large professional association was "Using Part-Time Instructors Successfully." On the surface, this title seems to address a noncontroversial issue of concern to many program planners—how to recruit, train, and evaluate instructors who are commissioned to teach on a part-time basis. Since many organizations rely on part-time instructors for most if not all programs, providing advice on how to make best use of this resource is quite appropriate. But the title also raises the specter of abusive and unethical policies and practices. Consider, for example, the organization that routinely cancels a large proportion of its offerings due to insufficient registrations. The obvious primary consequences of program cancellation are a few unhappy registrants, a disappointed instructor, and a write-off of any development and promotional costs. None of these three primary consequences seems to be especially problematic for the planner or the organization. But an examination of potential secondary consequences reveals a more troubling scenario. Instructors whose contracts have been cancelled because of insufficient registrations, or new instructors who hear (through the proverbial "grapevine") that a high percentage of programs are cancelled, are not likely to spend much time preparing for courses when cancellation is such a likely event. If this reasoning holds, then over time an increasing proportion of instructors will enter the first, second, or third class session without having made substantial preparations. Ultimately the quality of instruction, or at least the amount of productive time devoted to the topic, will decline, and the learners will receive less for the money and time they have invested in the program. There are other secondary consequences that relate to (1) learners' enthusiasm for enrolling in subsequent program offerings, (2) their long-term participation patterns, and (3) the continued economic viability of the organization. But the primary ethical issues are how part-time instructors are "used" by program planners and the impact that high cancellation rates may have on the quality of programs that are not cancelled.

The second illustration concerns the practice of "borrowing" program ideas from other agencies or organizations, a practice discussed in some detail by Pearson and Kennedy (1985). A planner may read or hear about a successful program being offered by another agency and decide to organize a similar program. Using information gleaned from brochures and from discussions with those familiar with the original program, the planner designs a clone, possibly changing the title and a few program details to avoid being accused of stealing someone else's design. A primary consequence of engaging in this practice is that the person who conceived the original idea, or carried out the needs assessment from which the idea grew, will be chagrined at having the essence of an original and creative program design duplicated without authorizing it or without being acknowledged as the source. In the increasingly competitive marketplace of educational programs, such an occurrence may be viewed as quite acceptable. But, again, the potential secondary consequences prompt questions about the ethics of this practice. Consider the program planner who devotes a great deal of energy to identifying the needs, interests, problems, or concerns of learners, then carefully designs a program based on these findings. If the design of this program is then appropriated without acknowledgment, several responses could be anticipated. One response would be a reduction or cessation of communication between the programmers involved, in itself not an especially traumatic consequence. But if this event is repeated across several agencies or becomes an accepted part of practice, then the field may take on some of the characteristics of highly competitive industries—secrecy, lack of social or professional interaction, predatory practices, and so on. If such practices become widespread, it may not be long until legal action is taken to protect what may be considered proprietary rights to educational program designs. There is now in the courts an action launched by one computer software company against another in which the claim is made that the "look and feel" of the plaintiff's product is essentially duplicated by the defendant's product, even though the details of the code (instructions that guide the operation of the computer) are quite different. Although some may question the appropriateness of the metaphor, it is not difficult to see the similarities between the "product" produced by a computer software developer and the "product" produced by an adult education agency. Adult educators should reflect on the doctrine of "fair use" as found in copyright law and decide how it might apply to educational program designs. If the practices of "borrowing" or appropriating program ideas and designs are not controlled by the personal ethical codes of program planners, then the courts may be asked to provide such controls.

Conclusion

Judging the quality of program planning is often based on such program outcomes as satisfaction of participants, degree to which objectives were achieved, and revenue generated for the agency. It is rare that planning is assessed on the basis of its ethics. This chapter has provided some thoughts on the ethical dimensions of program planning in adult education and has illustrated ethical issues associated with several common planning tasks. Some may view the process of planning as a series of mundane and ethically insignificant tasks required to establish the structure for an educational intervention. The issues presented in this chapter should dispel the idea that planning is ethically insignificant. Although it may indeed be a series of mundane tasks, the reflective practitioner will constantly analyze decisions made and actions taken to uncover and resolve ethical dilemmas.

Historically, adult educators have been concerned with equality, empowerment, justice, freedom, rights, and obligations. If we are to retain, or regain, the high moral ground that characterized the early decades of the field, then greater attention should be paid to the ethics of practice. Professionals of all kinds are clearly being challenged from many quarters to defend the moral basis of their work and to justify the special privileges they are granted by society. Since there is no code of ethics to guide practice, and no prospect of having one any time soon, it is left to individual practitioners to behave in ethically defensible ways. If the issues raised in these pages provoke those engaged in program planning to reflect even briefly on the ethics of their practice, then the objective of the chapter has been achieved.

References

Apps, J. W. (1973). *Toward a working philosophy of adult education.* Syracuse, NY: Syracuse University Publications in Continuing Education.

Apps, J. W. (1985). *Improving practice in continuing education.* San Francisco: Jossey-Bass.

Beatty, P. T. (1981). The concept of need: Proposal for a working definition. *Journal of the Community Development Society, 12* (2), 39–46.

Forrester, M. G. (1982). *Moral language.* Madison: University of Wisconsin Press.

Griffin, C. (1983). *Curriculum theory in adult and lifelong education.* London: Croom Helm.

Griffith, W. S. (1978). Educational needs: Definition, assessment, and utilization. *School Review, 86* (3), 382–394.

Houle, C. O. (1972). *The design of education.* San Francisco: Jossey-Bass.

Lawson, K. H. (1979). *Philosophical concepts and values in adult education* (rev. ed.). Milton Keynes, U.K.: Open University Press.

Matkin, G. W. (1985). *Effective budgeting in continuing education.* San Francisco: Jossey-Bass.

Mattran, K. J. (1981). Mandatory education increases professional competence. In B. W. Kreitlow and Associates, *Examining controversies in adult education* (pp. 46–51). San Francisco: Jossey-Bass.

Pearson, G. A., & Kennedy, M. S. (1985). Business ethics: Implications for providers and faculty of continuing education programs. *Journal of Continuing Education in Nursing, 16* (1), 4–6.

Rockhill, K. (1981). Professional education should not be mandatory. In

B. W. Kreitlow and Associates, *Examining controversies in adult education* (pp. 52–70). San Francisco: Jossey-Bass.

Schön, D. A. (1983). *The reflective practitioner: How professionals think in action*. New York: Basic Books.

Singarella, T. A., & Sork, T. J. (1983). Questions of values and conduct: Ethical issues for adult education. *Adult Education Quarterly, 33* (4), 244–251.

Sork, T. J., & Buskey, J. H. (1986). A descriptive and evaluative analysis of program planning literature, 1950–1983. *Adult Education Quarterly, 36* (2), 86–96.

CHAPTER FOUR

Marketing for Adult Educators: Some Ethical Questions

JOHN H. BURNS

GENE A. ROCHE

Most adult educators in the modern world have little choice about whether or not they will be involved in marketing their programs, but they do have considerable choice in how they will use marketing as a tool. Pejoratively used, *marketing* refers to a series of practices that drive up prices, create false needs, and manipulate learners. An alternative view, however, is that marketing practices inform learners about available opportunities, assist in rational decision making, provide the impetus for the creation of new services to meet learner needs, and help to fulfill the educator's and organization's objectives. In practice, most marketing efforts by adult educators will fall somewhere between these extremes, depending on the institutional and external environment, the populations to be served, the potential programs offered, and other variables.

The importance of marketing decisions to both the learner and the institution range from trivial to vital, depending on the situation, as do the ethical dimensions that must be considered. A successful attorney who is attempting to decide between several different evening courses in woodworking or cabinetmaking makes different demands on an institution's marketing system than does a single parent who is considering investing her life savings in a vocationally oriented course to prepare for a desperately needed job. Institutional demands also differ radically, since the consequences of failure of the marketing effort can range from mild inconvenience to the marketers to the destruction of the institution. Because both the risks and rewards of the marketing process are potentially so significant and because opportunities for abuse are so pervasive, an examination of that process from an ethical, rather than a technical, perspective is important.

Our purpose in this chapter is to provide some practical methods through which individuals can raise—and deal with—some of the ethical issues that surface each day for the practitioner in an educational organization. The remainder of the chapter suggests some tentative positions that could be taken by the adult educator who is faced with determining what constitutes an ethical marketing program. We concentrate on three general stances: (1) development of a sensitivity to the wide range of conflicts inherent in the marketing process; (2) insistence on a planned and systematic approach to marketing, including reflection on the ethical issues, rather than on a haphazard reactive stance; (3) development of a "moral common sense" that will guide the making of daily decisions.

Though often confused with advertising, promotion, or sales, the term *marketing* actually refers to a much broader and more strategic function:

> Marketing is the analysis, planning, implementation and control of carefully formulated programs designed to bring about voluntary exchanges of values with target markets to achieve institutional objectives. Marketing involves designing the institution's offerings to meet the target market's needs and desires and, using effective pricing, communication, and distribution to inform, motivate, and service the market. (Kotler & Fox, 1985, p. 7)

The diversity of adult education as a field of practice, along with the unsystematic adoption of marketing methods, makes the application of such a model difficult. In addition, our analysis avoids some of the longstanding questions that have been posed by philosophers in order to concentrate on some of the practical methods of making ethical decisions in daily practice. Brockett's model, as outlined in the first chapter of this volume, suggests a way of understanding some of the ethical questions inherent in this process. Carrying out the marketing function in an educational organization requires a continual awareness of divergent value systems, an understanding of the dynamic tension between individual and organizational goals, and constant attention to the issues involved in daily decision making in seemingly mundane matters of pricing, publicity, and scheduling.

Identifying Ethical Conflicts

In one sense, the practice of ethics is an exercise in clarifying the nature of conflicting claims. Adult educators can disagree on virtually every element of the educational process—from the appropriateness of research methods to the definition of learning itself. However, before such disagreements can be addressed, much less resolved, the types and points of disagreement must be identified and clarified. In this section we examine some of the major points of departure in ethical analysis of the marketing process. We begin with a cursory look at some basic differences in philosophical thought that have historically helped to shape ethical argument. We then look at some of the value conflicts that exist at the heart of the exchange process itself, before moving on to analyze some of the marketing conflicts suggested by Brockett's model of the dimensions of ethical behavior presented in Chapter 1.

Conflicting Ethical Traditions

While marketing and the problems associated with it are primarily a product of the twentieth century, the perplexing questions associated with the exchange process have been asked for centuries. Philosophers since the establishment of the Greek city-states have been concerned with searching for meaningful definitions of what is right, just, good, and true, both for the sake of better understanding of the terms themselves and for the development of guidelines for appropriate action. An understanding of formal ethical inquiry will not necessarily provide answers to moral dilemmas, but it will provide some method of clarifying the questions, issues, and difficulties that face individuals in the making of ethical decisions.

Many writers on the history of ethics agree that two general philosophical theories have developed in attempts to judge a particular activity. Philosophers from the *deontological* tradition hold that actions should be judged by universal rules or principles of conduct, while philosophers from the *teleological* tradition hold that the degree to which an action is ethical is determined by its consequences or results. Such a fundamental difference in assumptions about the nature of ethical conduct points both to the difficulty in achieving any real agreement on the resolution of a particular ethical dilemma and to the necessity of developing effective methods of clarifying and defining the nature of the ethical differences that come into play in the making of a particular decision. A recent chapter by Martel and Colley (1986) illustrates that an understanding of these major ethical traditions and the subtraditions within them can be applied in problematical situations commonly faced by adult and continuing educators.

Most of the vocabulary, techniques, and basic assumptions about marketing have been developed by results-oriented organizations, prior to being adopted by adult and continuing educators. Consequently, marketing rationales tend to be based on teleological assumptions, suggesting that desirable ends can be identified and measured. Often such assumptions are directly in opposition to those held by individuals dedicated to ideals of individual empowerment and justice and raise serious conflicts regarding the methods that should be used to determine the context of ethical action.

In recent years, many professional organizations and associations, such as the American Marketing Association, have attempted to develop codes of ethics in the deontological tradition as a guide for practitioners. While the results of such efforts are open to question, one of the positive effects has been a general recognition that a higher social order exists and that the actions of the marketer can effect this order. Such codes of ethics generally prohibit actions that would be detrimental to learners, the market itself, the institution, or society in general.

Formal codes cannot replace logical thinking by individual adult educators in individual situations, but they do represent collective and thoughtful efforts by practitioners and scholars to address some of the key ethical questions. As such, they provide valuable guidance, and totally to ignore them is at best imprudent and at worst probably unethical. Adult educators must continually deal with a wide variety of disciplines. Since no one individual can be thoroughly familiar with the diversity of these disciplines, the codes of ethics developed in fields such as marketing, advertising, or public relations can be extremely helpful, even if they do not provide concrete answers in all situations.

Conflicting Needs and Values

If we think of marketing as a systematic process by which an organization's mission is fulfilled by the management of its resources and activities such that the wants and needs of its customers are fulfilled, we realize that "exchange" is central to the marketing process. Beder (1986) points out the importance of understanding the difference between the "tangible product" (the instructors, the materials, and the facilities) and the "core product" (the actual benefits the learner hopes to achieve from the educational experience). In the basic interaction between educational organization and learner, consumers *give up* something of value to them—their time, their money, their energy, or all three—in return for some benefit they believe will be secured from their participation in the educational activity. Since neither the learner nor the institution has unlimited resources, both must exercise some care in determining how these resources will be invested. If marketing is to serve a valuable function in society, the exchange of resources will be conducted such that both the institution and the individual feel that the process has been mutually beneficial.

While the decision to buy a magazine at the checkout counter of a supermarket may be an impulse decision made on the spur of the moment, a more complex process is generally followed by a person considering participation in an educational activity. In a relatively free market, individuals can be expected to make at least three decisions before participating in an educational activity:

1. Is there a problem that can be solved or need that can be met by a particular educational activity?
2. Is that problem or need important enough to be addressed at this time?
3. Which program, from among the available options, is most likely to meet the needs or solve the problem?

Inherent in such a process are many ethical issues and the potential for serious ethical dilemmas that must be addressed. For instance, in what ways are the values different for learners and for educators? How does one define the value system of an organization, which is made up of many divergent individuals? In an educational setting, where does one draw the line between the institution's responsibility to deliver the benefits suggested in the marketing program and the learner's responsibility to participate fully in the process? How can educators working in an imperfect world ensure that the hundreds of individual, practical decisions they make each day are made ethically?

As Brockett's model suggests, some of the greatest difficulties in resolving ethical questions in adult education come about because of the differences in personal value systems and in the degree to which these differences are internalized by educators and by learners. In fact, most adult educators work in the field because they hold certain beliefs about the importance of such participation, beliefs that may not be shared by learners. Particularly in the marketing function, it is important that the divergent value systems be acknowledged, both as the basis for communication and as the basis for understanding why individuals make the decisions they do.

By now it may be understood that our definition of marketing makes one very important assumption: that it is an *organizational* function, critical to the survival of the institution that engages in it. The intensity and the types of marketing efforts will differ greatly among providers, such as major university extension centers, consultants operating as sole proprietorships, literacy centers, or corporate training departments. Nonetheless, the survival of the organization becomes—either implicitly or explicitly—a major goal of the individuals affiliated with it.

The second stage of Brockett's model, consideration of multiple responsibilities, helps to clarify the various constituencies that must be considered in making marketing decisions. Obligations to self, clients, colleagues, the profession, and society in general must all be considered in making decisions and must be balanced against the needs of the institution. In practice, most adult educators will have limited opportunity to make substantial changes in the mission of their organizations, so they must ensure at least some level of compatibility between their own values and that of the organization for which they work, either professionally or in volunteer capacities.

Marketing as a Means of Systematic Inquiry

Many of the issues suggested in this discussion should be addressed in the organization's marketing plan. The term *marketing plan* refers to a comprehensive attempt by organizations to analyze their relationships to their consumers and to outline the strategies, programs, and plans needed to achieve organizational objectives (Kollat, Blackwell, & Robeson, 1972). A comprehensive marketing plan can be the vehicle by which educators may examine their practice from a variety of perspectives. They can acknowledge the diversity of individual values involved in their own decision making and that of learners. They can attempt to reconcile their personal values with those of the organization and to determine strategies for institutional change when needed. Finally, the marketing plan provides a method of examining operational plans to determine in advance what ethical issues will come into play in daily decision making.

Four ingredients are essential in constructing a marketing plan that will meet institutional needs while taking ethical issues into account:

1. *A statement of purpose* clearly outlining the mission of the organization and the current situation
2. *A comprehensive identification* of the consumer needs that the institution seeks to serve
3. *A statement of specific objectives* outlining how the resources of the organization can best be utilized to fulfill its mission and meet identified needs
4. *A strategy* outlining how the program will be developed, priced, and communicated in light of the stated objectives

In practice, marketing plans take a multitude of forms, from a few jotted lines in a notebook by a training consultant after a meeting, to a complex document of several hundred pages developed by a software company planning to distribute a new programmed learning package. Marketing plans that are properly constructed will carefully address questions of value to both the institution and the consumer and will be extremely helpful in clarifying many ethical conflicts arising from pricing, advertising, or design considerations. While the construction of a marketing plan is a time-consuming effort, the time spent in preparing it is valuable, from the perspectives of both effectiveness and ethics.

The methods used to construct the marketing plan will differ widely among organizations, but the process will generally consist of a systematic attempt to answer a series of questions about their relationships to customers and to competitors, as well as about professional and societal concerns. While it is impossible to provide an exhaustive list of questions that provide a basis for examining ethical issues through a systematic market plan, the following will offer some ideas for adult educators who might wish to construct their own lists:

1. What is the purpose of the institution?

Who is currently being served by the institution?
What unique benefits can the institution offer to consumers?
What are the major needs of the institution?

What opportunities exist for the future growth of the institution?
What internal and external constraints have an impact on the institution's ability to meet the needs of consumers in this arena?

2. *What are the needs of current and potential consumers?*

What markets have been targeted?
What are the specific needs of people in the targeted markets?
Is the targeted market one that the institution normally serves? If not, why has the institution not served this market in the past?
Are other institutions better able to serve this market? If not, what do they lack to be able to serve the market?

3. *What are the objectives of the marketing program?*

If the institution's objectives are met, will the targeted consumers' needs be fulfilled?
If the institution's objectives are met, will there be a detrimental effect on either the members of the organization, the learners, or others in the community?
What institutional resources are required? Will this program reduce the resources available to other programs? What will be the effect of such reallocation of resources?

4. *What strategies should be used in implementing this marketing program?*

How should the price for this particular program be established based on organizational pricing practice?
How can the program's benefits be described to enable consumers to judge its value effectively?
What variables must be considered in determining how to deliver the program?
What institutional resources must be invested to communicate the availability of the program to potential consumers?

Since most marketing decisions do not reflect simplistic or easily confronted issues, the construction of a marketing plan encourages the systematic confrontation of all three sources of ethical dilemmas suggested in Brockett's model. The underlying values of the individuals involved are compared with those that define the mission of the organization. The marketing plan also provides an opportunity to identify possible assumptions about the nature of learners and their needs separate from the institutional imperatives to make a profit or to fill empty classrooms.

Ethics in Daily Decision Making

The divergent value systems of the many participants in the educational process and the conflicts between organizations and individuals become reality in the day-to-day decision making of marketers and learners. Many of these decisions are seemingly mundane—what size of type do I use for this brochure? how much should I charge for this course? Taken together, however, these daily decisions define the extent to which interaction between learners and the institution is an ethical or an unethical one.

Let us take an example of how some ethical questions might be faced by the designers of a brochure advertising a new professional program offered in the continuing education division of a large urban university. Since the program contains a number of courses in adult learning and development, the authors feel it is appropriate to list on the cover some of the careers that might be available to students completing these courses. One author suggests that human-resource development (HRD) be listed as one of the options, holding that many jobs in training, counseling, and organizational development require some knowledge of adult learning. Some such jobs may well be available to graduates, and the attractiveness of such jobs will encourage many learners to enroll in the program. Another author contends that to list such information on the cover of the brochure would be unethical, since no graduates of the program have entered human-resource positions. It is noted, in fact, that only a very small number of graduates would actually be able to find such jobs in the geographic area. The sponsor of the proposal agrees that while none of the graduates have taken positions in human-resource management in the past, opportunities certainly do exist for the future. He points out that no effort has been taken to attract learners interested in HRD, resulting in few graduates of the program seeking positions in that field.

A number of general ethical questions emerge, even from the simple decision outlined in this case:

1. Is it ethical to suggest that benefits will be available to learners participating in a program when only a small percentage of the participants will actually receive those benefits? How do the authors determine when such claims are justified?
2. How do we advertise intangible and often immeasurable benefits of an educational experience?
3. How can we ethically determine, prior to the educational experience, what benefits a particular individual might realistically expect to realize from participating in a program or activity?

Answering the ethical questions is not a clearcut or simple process. No one is suggesting outright misrepresentation of the purpose of the institution, false claims, erroneous statements, or blatant lies. The participants in the decision-making process have sound reasons for taking the stands that they do. Yet within the decision-making process, opportunities abound for all sorts of misunderstandings, differences of opinion, limited amounts of data, or misinterpretation. Marketing decisions are perhaps even more difficult in the educational realm than in the case of many commercial businesses. The extent to which the consumer realizes the promised benefits is only partially in the hands of the educational organization, and many variables are in the hands of the learner. What began as a simple decision about one line on the cover of a promotional brochure becomes a thorny ethical question as individuals begin to evaluate the response of consumers to the benefits implied by its inclusion.

Developing Moral Rules of Thumb

Since many, if not most, of the conflicts inherent in the process are difficult or impossible to resolve unequivocally from an ethical standpoint, most adult educators will develop what has been called a type of "moral common sense" to guide daily decision making (Matthews, Goodpaster, & Nash, 1985). Such a sense is sharpened by continued reflection, experience, and application of a skeptical approach to many of the common myths that tend to be accepted at face value.

Ideally, most of these decisions would be addressed in the comprehensive planning process, but in practice such planning is rare. The difficulty of accomplishing an institutional mission with severely limited resources makes daily decision making a pressure-filled process in which expediency can be the primary criterion for judgment if decisions are left unchallenged. The assistant professor on a two-year contract who has a particular program to develop and get off the ground before moving on has little time to initiate an institutional marketing audit, but the ethical questions still must be dealt with. Individual marketers must develop personal guidelines that can be applied to particular situations, based on their own understanding of their institutions and the marketing process.

To prevent expedient decisions from becoming unethical ones, a process of systematic inquiry can be used before implementing individual decisions to help isolate instances of unethical conduct. The following four questions are based on the definition of the marketing process and the four steps in the marketing planning process that we suggested earlier:

1. Does our proposed action conflict with the purpose or mission of the institution as I understand it?
2. Would the proposed action meet genuine consumer needs in the marketplace, as I understand those needs?
3. Is the action consistent with the objectives we have set forth for the program?
4. Is it feasible for our organization to deliver the program with the resources at our disposal?

The following example shows how such questions might be used in the case of the human-resource development brochure headline mentioned earlier: *Is it ethical for the educators to suggest that human-resource development is a realistic career option for graduates?*

TEST ONE: Would such a suggestion or claim conflict with the mission or purpose of the institution? Based on the data available, the mission of the institution would seem to be supportive of the idea of a graduate program to prepare students for entry into positions in human-resource development upon graduation.

TEST TWO: Would such a program meet consumer needs in the marketplace? It would seem that a market would exist in most communities for this kind of program. However, no research has apparently been conducted to determine the extent of that need, so the sponsors of the program can only guess at the extent to which such a need exists and at the degree to which consumers would believe that such a course meets their felt needs.

TEST THREE: Is the claim consistent with the current program's objectives? In the example cited, this is the critical test. The fact that the conflict arises suggests that the program will not meet the students' needs, since it is not designed to prepare students realistically for careers in human-resource development. Further, there is an obvious lack of research to determine if the courses offered in the program do indeed allow graduates to compete effectively in the job market.

TEST FOUR: Is it feasible or practical to suggest in the communications about the program that a future in human-resource development is possible? In this example, it would be quite feasible and practical. All that would be required would be a minor change in the brochure.

In applying this process, the answers to questions one and four were affirmative. No noticeable conflicts were identified. The suggestion to make the career claim, however, would appear to be unethical, since the answers to questions two and three clearly show that the current program is unable to substantiate the claim. Most adult educators would avoid making claims that could not be substantiated. Fram and Clarcq (1978) describe a case in which sound research forms the basis for effective marketing decisions in career and job-related course work. Not only, as they conclude, is direct contact with both learners and employers a key to effective marketing, but it also provides a key to ethical promotion of educational programs.

This process may seem simplistic to some, given the complexity of the issues facing adult educators in such diverse settings as corporate training centers, correctional institutions, literacy programs, and distance education programs. Nonetheless, confrontation of these issues is critical if adult educators are to move beyond the selling concept of marketing and become expert at developing programs that contain genuine benefits to learners in all these settings. Educators who understand and appreciate the possibilities and the limitations of the marketing process, however, will find that confronting these issues with a systematic and regular method will yield a greater appreciation for the complexity of the marketing process. Whatever the setting, adult educators are faced with the necessity for action—always with less-than-perfect knowledge of the needs of learners, with limited access to the resources of their institutions, and with continual competition for scarce community resources.

Conclusion

The majority of this chapter was spent in determining ways in which adult educators, regardless of the size or complexity of their organizations, could use marketing principles to meet the needs of their customers. Of particular concern are the methods by which ethical questions might be answered through the four-part strategy for developing a marketing plan.

Brockett's model provides a helpful method of understanding how ethical questions arise in preparing marketing plans and making marketing decisions for adult education organizations. As in other aspects of adult education, there are no easy answers about what constitutes ethical or unethical behavior. The best assurance of ethical practice by adult educators seems to come from an awareness of the various sources of conflict that are inherent in marketing and in the decision-making process.

References

Beder, H. (1986). Basic concepts and principles of marketing. In H. Beder (Ed.), *Marketing continuing education* (New Directions for Continuing Education No. 31, pp. 3–17). San Francisco: Jossey-Bass.

Fram, E. H., & Clarcq, J. Q. (1978). Commercial marketing techniques in continuing education. *Lifelong Learning: The Adult Years, 2*(1), 16–19, 26.

Kollat, D. T., Blackwell, R. D., & Robeson, J. F. (1972). *Strategic marketing.* New York: Holt, Rinehart & Winston.

Kotler, P., & Fox, K. (1985). *Strategic marketing for educational institutions.* Englewood Cliffs, NJ: Prentice-Hall.

Martel, L. D., & Colley, R. M. (1986). Ethical issues in marketing and continuing education. In H. Beder (Ed.), *Marketing continuing education* (New Directions for Continuing Education No. 31, pp. 91–101). San Francisco: Jossey-Bass.

Matthews, J. B., Goodpaster, K. E., & Nash, L. L. (1985). *Policies and persons: A casebook in business ethics.* New York: McGraw-Hill.

CHAPTER FIVE

Dilemmas in Continuing Education Administration

BURTON R. SISCO

WE live in an interesting and provocative time. There is evidence of turbulence and unpredictability all about us. Almost every waking day brings to light another irregularity or impropriety somewhere in government, business, or medical circles, to name a few. The memory of Watergate has been eclipsed by the recent Iranian scandal in Washington, where the highest officials in the U.S. government appear to have acted immorally, perhaps even illegally, in the sale of arms to Iran. In the financial and investment world, several individuals have been charged with using inside knowledge of the stock market for personal gain. And the list goes on.

From many quarters comes the call for ethical and moral practices. Many people are asking penetrating questions, such as, "how can seemingly intelligent people get themselves in such a pickle?" or "why would they do this?" More importantly, "how could they let this happen to themselves?"

A beginning answer to these and other related questions may be found in an exploration of ethics and moral conduct. For it is here that we find some understanding of what society labels as proper and improper human behavior. Yet what is happening in the federal government and in the investment world can happen in higher education, too. The only difference may be in the scale of impropriety and misbehavior.

In higher education today, there is increasing pressure to behave more as a business and less as a citadel of ideas. With this pressure have come certain dilemmas of purpose and mission. Part of this pressure may be explained by the changing composition of academia, where there are fewer students of traditional age and more students over the age of 25. Another reason may be increased emphasis on continuing professional education as a means of remaining current in a fast-paced world of information production and knowledge transfer; colleges and universities are being asked by the private sector to update curricula that may be outdated before they have been implemented. Still another reason may be increasing pressure from outside providers, who are offering educational programs that were once the sole province of academia. With this pressure has come a kind of schizophrenia in higher education, as well as certain administrative dilemmas. And at the center of this controversy are programs of continuing higher education.

In this chapter, we will explore some of the common dilemmas faced by administrators in continuing higher education today. We will do so first by defining what is meant by a *dilemma* and then by looking at the role and function of continuing higher education programs in the context of the modern college or university. We will follow this discussion with a look at the relationship of ethics to administrative practice. Finally, we will examine several common dilemmas faced by administrators in continuing higher education, illustrating each with an accompanying case study. It is important to note that while some of the dilemmas we will discuss are common to administrative practice in continuing higher education, they also exist in other adult and continuing education contexts, such as adult basic education, training in business and industry, and continuing professional education outside college and university settings.

Dilemma Defined

Life is full of dilemmas. Although most are not of life-or-death magnitude, they can cause us great pain. They are certainly sources of tension. Some people approach these dilemmas with fear and trepidation. Others pass them off callously.

When we use the term *dilemma*, what do we mean? According to *Webster's Third New International Dictionary* (1971), a dilemma may be defined as "a difficult problem: a problem seemingly incapable of a satisfactory solution" (p. 633). To this we might add Good's (1959) observation that a dilemma is "a situation involving a limited number of (usually two) unpalatable alternatives among which a choice must be made" (p. 173). It is synonymous with the word *predicament*.

As we will see, there are many dilemmas that administrators of continuing higher education must confront or deal with nearly every day. These dilemmas grow out of an active tension between the classical mission of the university and the contemporary needs of the marketplace. This perhaps has always been the case, but the lines of tension and turmoil seem to be even more firmly drawn today. Nearly 30 years ago, Burton Clark (1958) described the enterprise of continuing education as marginal to the rest of the university. The intervening years up to the present suggest a similar situation. Part of the reason for this may be found in an exploration of the role and function of continuing education units on college and university campuses.

The Role and Function of Continuing Higher Education

The idea that continuing education is a central part of the academic mission has been slow to gain acceptance. The origins of continuing education in the American context can be traced to the early nineteenth century, when service to the public became an expectation. But it is only recently that colleges and universities have begun to acknowledge the importance of the service function. Part of this can be explained by the marketplace pressure that colleges and universities find themselves in today.

Historically, continuing education activities of an organized kind arose largely outside of higher education and were later brought under university auspices. Some examples of these activities include farmers' institutes, agricultural extension, university extension, and correspondence study. In subsequent years, continuing education programs have proliferated to the point where they are now found on most college and university campuses regardless of size, affiliation, or sponsorship. Despite this growth, Strother and Klus (1982) warn that the situation is far from ideal:

> Many campuses today still see continuing education and extension as an auxiliary enterprise like the bookstore and the food service, useful for supplementing faculty income, improving public relations, or recruiting new students, but academically suspect at best. From the viewpoint of enthusiasts, the rate of change has been agonizingly slow; from the standpoint of staunch traditionalists, the gains have been alarming. (p. 7)

Regardless of which side one is on, the role and function of continuing education may be the source at once of its strength and weakness. For it is here that we find the kind of dilemmas for continuing education administrators alluded to earlier. And what are the role and function of continuing education? More importantly, how do they clash with the role and function of the college or university at large?

Numerous writers have devoted entire texts to the subject of the role and function of educational programs for adults (Bryson, 1936; Dyer, 1956; Apps, 1979, 1985; Strother & Klus, 1982; Boone, 1985). In fact, the field of adult and continuing education is filled with this concern. Lyman Bryson (1936) suggested four functions of continuing education: *expansional,* whereby adults acquire new knowledge and skills continuously as their responsibilities develop and change through the years; *participational,* whereby adults gain knowledge pertinent to local, national, and international issues as well as training and practice in the skills of democratic participation; *integrational,* whereby adults learn to integrate knowledge with experience in order to identify what must yet be learned and to make meaning out of what is already known; and *personal,* whereby adults learn more about themselves as they mature. In an organized sense, Bryson saw continuing education as the means for bringing this about.

Some years later, Dyer (1956) conceived of the role of evening colleges (an older term for continuing education programs) as affording "the individual access to and experience in those intellectual activities which will (1) give him a basis for value judgments based on qualitative thinking, (2) afford a broader base for social thinking, and (3) enable him to acquire a fund of experiences, images, ideas, and behavior patterns which in their totality help to make up the cultured individual" (pp. 157–158). Dyer went on to note that the evening college should not think of itself as contributing much in the field of pure research, but rather should be concerned with service to the community through an emphasis on teaching.

More recently, Kempfer (1979) has identified the following as the central role and function of continuing education:

To help paid workers and volunteers keep abreast of their fields
To help raise one's competence in an occupation to a satisfactory
level

To help maximize one's competence in an occupation
To extend laterally one's range of knowledge and skills
To provide refresher training for occupational re-entry
To help people advance in their lines of work
To help people restore full, well-rounded competence in a licensed
    or certified occupation   (p. 11)

Taking another tack, Apps (1985) examined the aims of continuing education over time. He found a number of recurrent themes, including personal development, remedial education, religious education, cultural criticism and social action education, and education for career development. Peering into the future, Apps suggests that "continuing education will continue to have as its aims (1) education for career development, including improving the competence and performance of professions through continuing professional education activities, (2) remedial education to correct the inadequacy of previous schooling or to teach English as a second language, and (3) education for personal development" (p. 129).

Historically, as we noted earlier, higher education and continuing education have existed apart from one another. Higher education was for youth engaged in pursuing undergraduate degrees after high school, with some individuals electing to pursue graduate degrees. Continuing education was principally a noncredit activity offered by a host of different institutions, including higher education. Continuing education activities offered by higher education institutions were clearly something different from those offered by the rest of higher education. This difference is perhaps no more dramatically illustrated than in the traditional functions of colleges and universities: teaching, research, and public service. Of these three functions, continuing education was located in the area of public service. As a result, continuing education had a different mission, separate funding mechanisms, often separate faculty, and certainly an image different from traditional higher education. In short, continuing education was something to be tolerated but not taken very seriously by the academic community. After all, the kinds of students attracted to continuing education were older, possessed educational motives of a vocational kind, and did not seem to fit the mold of the serious scholar.

Now, with increasing numbers of older students returning to the classroom, we see a blurring of the once-clear distinction between higher education and continuing education. With increased emphasis on continuing professional education, we see more and more adults enrolling in academic programs once reserved for traditional students. The old view of continuing education as offering only noncredit activities, such as basketweaving or bellydancing, is being eclipsed by increasing demand for credit-bearing degree programs responsive to the demands of contemporary society. Perhaps the most sacred of distinctions is being shattered: traditional students 18 to 22 years of age are becoming nontraditional students, and nontraditional students 25 years of age and older are becoming traditional students. The result is a different institution of higher education as well as a mission in flux.

Frandson (1979), one of the most articulate and vocal supporters of university extension, has identified a number of factors influencing the role and function of continuing higher education today. He points out that constituencies inside and outside the institution are exerting considerable pressure on what continuing education programs should be. Frandson trenchantly observes, "Facing a decline in enrollment-based funding, administrative units are suddenly turning their attention to the substantial fee income currently enjoyed by extension and continuing education divisions" (p. 12). More importantly, academic units that have not been involved in continuing education activities in the past now want to be involved and have something to say about their role and function.

Echoing a different but related concern, Berlin (1983) argues that the basic role and function of the university—knowledge and research—has been eroded by a commensurate increase in the number of private providers of education, particularly at the professional level. As a result, higher education is no longer the sole bastion of knowledge and ideas. Berlin further notes that higher education institutions have failed to articulate coherent and defensible policies regarding their continuing education mission and, at the same time, have failed to develop rational organizational models for providing further education. The result is that academia wants to provide continuing professional education, but only on its terms. The professions, displeased with the product offered to them, are looking elsewhere for providers willing to give them what they want, and in the process are finding greater satisfaction. Most administrators of continuing higher education programs are aware of this situation and want very badly to respond, but their marginal position within academia prevents them from doing so.

What we see in the many statements regarding the role and function of continuing education is emphasis on the teaching and service dimensions to the community. While higher education has taken on these functions as well, its central mission has been and continues to be focused on the production of knowledge and research. It is here that conflict over role and function occurs. The trinity of research, teaching, and public service appears in the rhetoric of most college and university mission statements. Yet when they are studied in reality, the research function is almost always positioned at the top, with little more than lip service paid to the latter two. With the marketplace demanding current degree programs of a flexible and responsive kind, as well as teaching excellence, it is little wonder that a kind of schizophrenia exists in continuing higher education today. What appears to make this situation even more difficult now is that the academic units that wish to become involved in continuing education are motivated more by economic gain than by service to the community at large. What may be even more disturbing is that they are moving into continuing education as if it was "business as usual." That is, they are extending to nontraditional populations the same practices offered to traditional students. Professionals in continuing education know it is not business as usual, but they have been overruled. The age-old stigma of marginality and intellectual feebleness play a large role in this impoverished view. The result is the roots of serious dilemmas of a professional and ethical kind for administrators of continuing higher education.

To summarize our discussion thus far, there appears to be an active tension between the public service and teaching mission of continuing higher education and the knowledge and research mission of the university. As long as the marketplace allowed both to coexist, all was well and good. However, as the marketplace changed, so did the demands placed on academia. The once lowly regarded continuing education unit has suddenly been found to be important in the eyes of academic administrators. Yet their motives appear suspect at best. They view continuing education as a means of economic survival, but they wish to proceed with a business-as-usual mentality. Administrators of continuing higher education are at once overjoyed with their newfound popularity and saddened by the prospects of how they will be used. As Berlin (1983) notes, "A rich, elaborate, and highly varied set of continuing education practices and delivery mechanisms, developed over a century, will be most adversely affected" (p. 122). The result is a host of professional and ethical dilemmas facing the administrator of continuing higher education programs. We will take up some of these dilemmas after we look at the relationship of ethics to administrative practice.

Relationship of Ethics to Administrative Practice

Earlier in this chapter, we pointed out that life is filled with a host of dilemmas; some larger than others. The child who enters a candy store with no money in his pocket may be tempted to take a piece when the proprietor is not looking. Similarly, the adolescent who recently received her driver's license may be tempted to borrow the family car without asking for parental permission. The adult who has worked faithfully for a textiles manufacturer for more than 20 years may be tempted to take a sweater home under the ruse that it is owed to her. And so it goes.

At the heart of these dilemmas lie the essence of ethical conduct; for it is here that we begin to find some understanding about what guides human behavior. To some, the scale of the above dilemmas may seem small, and, in fact, they may be. But change the scenarios to life-and-death situations, substantial monetary loss, or falsification of public documents, and the stakes increase considerably.

When we talk about ethics, what do we mean? In the most basic sense, ethics refers to that branch of philosophy dealing with the general nature of morals and moral conduct. Ethics may also refer to any set of moral principles or values that serve as guides to action. Hopke (1968) defines ethics as "the moral obligations and responsibilities which are accepted by a particular group in a society" (p. 131). Ethics may also have a regulatory emphasis as well. In this regard, we might add "the rules or standards governing the conduct of the members of a profession" (*American Heritage Dictionary*, 1981, p. 450). These are, essentially, the distinctions between metaethics and normative ethics addressed by Brockett in Chapter 1 of this volume.

According to Steiner (1977), there are a number of different types of ethics. These types help us understand the multidimensional nature of ethics and how they have been operationalized in decision-making contexts. The most common type is the *philosopher's ethic*, which emphasizes consistency of action. Using this as a guideline, a decision maker faced with a moral problem will act in a way he or she feels is right and just for any other person in a similar situation. Another type is called the *con-*

ventionalist ethic; here emphasis is placed on individual gain so long as it does not violate the law. One of the most popular types in business, government, and military agencies is called the *organizational ethic.* This type implies that the wills and needs of individuals should be subordinated to the greater good of the organization. In other words, be loyal to the organization at all costs. Another ethical type is called the *means–ends ethic.* This age-old principle of decision making stipulates that when ends are of overriding importance, unscrupulous means may be employed to reach them. Another type, which is gaining popularity today, is called the *hedonist ethic.* This ethic is rooted in the belief that there are no universal or absolute moral rules. Thus an individual con-fronted with a moral dilemma will simply act in his or her own self-interest. One of the most widely known ethical types is the *golden rule.* This principle, found in most religions around the world, emphasizes the dictum "do unto others as you would have them do unto you." Here the decision maker tries to imagine how the other party would be affected if a decision or action were taken. A final ethical type is called the *utilitarian ethic.* This type, first espoused by the English utilitarian school, emphasizes the greatest good for the greatest number. In this case, the decision maker must deter-mine whether the harm in an action is outweighed by the good. If the action maximizes the good, then it is the optimum course to take among less desirable alternatives.

Having defined ethics and noted some different types, we might ask what relationship they have to administrative practice in general. More importantly, what relationship do they have to admin-istrative practice in continuing higher education? Finally, what does the field of adult and continuing education have to say about ethical practice as evidenced by its literature base?

In many respects, the first two questions can be treated to-gether. The idea of behaving in an honorable and just way is universal and not unique to administrative practice. People expect fair and just behavior whether they are purchasing a product from the private sector or the public sector. However, what makes a difference is the particular value structure that one brings to a context or situation. A simple illustration may suffice. Suppose I place high value on achievement, monetary gain, organizational advancement, and personal status. My friend, on the other hand, places high value on an active, full life, inner peace, personal freedom, and social justice. In the first case, my value priorities would seem to indicate an organizationally oriented individual. In the second case, my friend would seem to be more socially oriented. If we were both administrators, our value priorities would suggest a certain ethical orientation, possibly similar to one noted above. I might assume an organizational ethic or a means–ends ethic. My friend, however, might adopt the golden-rule ethic as his guiding light. Because of our different ethical orientations, we are going to look at issues, problems, and opportunities that occur as part of our work in a different manner. My problems or dilemmas may be my friend's opportunities, and vice versa. Thus, by looking at the relationship of one's value structure and value priorities to one's ethical orientation, we can also see how administrative practice can be affected as well.

There is one other consideration that should be made when examining the relationship of ethics to administrative practice: one's professional socialization. The hard sciences tend to emphasize a philosophy of empiricism and scientific precision. Instruction is often modeled in a dogmatic, teacher-directed manner. Moreover, experiments are typically carried out in the laboratory under controlled circumstances.

In the social sciences, on the other hand, a philosophy rooted in the human condition is the norm. Instruction can be equally dogmatic, but is often reflective of social needs. Research is typically not carried out in the laboratory under rigorous conditions, but rather in the context being studied, such as the voting precinct, classroom, or workplace. Often the subject under investigation is a human being. This presents certain ethical dilemmas in its own right, such as those discussed by Merriam in Chapter 10 of this volume. If one's professional socialization emphasizes a more scientific approach, as opposed to a more humanistic approach, then this will have a strong bearing on administrative practice. If one's professional socialization emphasizes knowledge production versus vocational preparation, this, too, will have a profound impact on administrative practice. Thus the combination of ethical orientation and professional socialization serve as powerful indicators of how a person will behave as a practicing administrator.

In the field of adult and continuing education, professional socialization tends to be more humanistic and learner-centered. Students are the central unit of analysis, and their satisfaction is a key goal. As a result, programs are typically developed from the ground up, beginning with the needs of the learners rather than the needs of the sponsoring institution. Moreover, an applied and utilitarian orientation tends to mark the work of adult and continuing educators. In part this grows out of the entrepreneurial character of the profession, but it is also related to the operating conditions placed on adult and continuing education programs by sponsoring institutions—such as little or no academic status, fiscal self-sufficiency, and marginal plant facilities. Still, under such conditions, adult and continuing educators are successful despite the odds. It is little wonder that educators of adults, particularly in higher education settings, face certain administrative dilemmas when their professional socialization, rooted in consumer advocacy and learner responsiveness, is tested by operating strictures that emphasize consumer dependence, authoritarian submission, and business efficiency.

In addition to one's ethical orientation and professional socialization, many professions and associated groups have attempted to provide a means of ensuring ethical practice. Some, such as law and medicine, have developed formal codes that specify proper and improper conduct. Many others do not have formal codes, but they operate under a set of unstated assumptions. Also, many professions have assumed responsibility for monitoring and sanctioning behavior. Evidence of some attention to ethical conduct has been one way of distinguishing between a professional group and an amateur group, although this distinction is not always clear or precise.

One of the most authoritative writers on the professions and the professionalizing process is Cyril Houle. In a work on continued learning in the professions, Houle (1980) identified 14 characteristics that characterize the professionalization process. One characteristic in particular—ethical practice—stands out in relation to the field of adult and continuing education. Houle suggests that established professions have a tradition of ethical practice that is sometimes reinforced by a formal code. Professions such as medicine and law are good examples of this. In the business world, there is a substantial body of literature on the topic of ethics and moral conduct. The reasons for this involve such matters as consumer protection, competent performance, and uniform accountability. In the field of adult and continuing education, however, there is no established code of ethics, due largely to the diversity of agencies and organizations offering educational activities for adults. Add to this the multiple roles, suggested by Brockett in Chapter 1, that educators of adults must perform—such as teacher, administrator, counselor, and program planner—and the prospects of such a code are challenged even more. This situation poses a threat to the continued development of adult and continuing education as a bona fide profession in its own right, although there have been several recent attempts to develop such a code (Mason, 1979; Council on the Continuing Education Unit, 1984; Commission of Professors of Adult Education, 1986). It may also be a source of certain dilemmas for the continuing education administrator, since he or she does not have an established code to work from. This issue is addressed more fully by Carlson in Chapter 11.

In the field of adult and continuing education, we find only a cursory examination of ethics and moral conduct, as witnessed by the lack of professional literature on the topic. One notable exception to an otherwise sad state of affairs is a 1983 article by Singarella and Sork, in which the authors argue that educators of adults should be concerned with ethical matters, just as professionals in law, business, and medicine are required to be. They point out that personal codes of ethics for individuals are often in conflict with the demands of the workplace. Given the multiple roles that educators of adults are expected to perform, their advocacy orientation, and utilitarian philosophy, Singarella and Sork argue for a critical examination of ethical principles and practices. They go on to note that although the infancy of the adult and continuing education profession may have mitigated such disciplined study in the past, this can no longer be tolerated. They cogently ask, "Should there be guidelines for the development of the field of adult education, and what part does ethics play in this development?" (p. 246).

In our discussion thus far, we have reviewed the role and function of continuing higher education today. We have looked at its mission and the mission of higher education in general and have found the seeds of conflict for the continuing education administrator. We have probed at some depth as to the nature of ethics and its relationship to administrative practice. We will now look at several common dilemmas facing the administrator of continuing higher education programs and illustrate each with a brief case study. As noted earlier, these dilemmas may also apply to administrative practice in other adult and continuing education settings.

Common Dilemmas Facing the Administrator of Continuing Higher Education Programs

There are a number of dilemmas common to the work of continuing higher education administrators that, we have suggested, grow out of an active tension between the mission of continuing education and the mission of higher education, as well as the personal value structure of the individual and his or her professional socialization. These include such questions as: Should the administrator strive to meet the needs of the client group or the needs of the institution? Should the administrator provide programs only to groups that can pay for them, and in the process, exclude those who cannot? Should the administrator knowingly withhold the results of program evaluations? In the following pages, we will look at these three dilemmas in more detail through the use of hypothetical case studies.

Dilemma #1
Meeting the Client's Needs Versus the Institution's Needs

Thomas Cave has worked as director of development for the division of continuing education at the University of Smartland for the past six months. He came to Smartland fresh out of graduate school with a Ph.D. in adult and continuing education. Prior to that, Cave had worked for five years in a nontraditional community college that emphasized individualized learning.

Smartland is a medium-sized public university in the East, located in a metropolitan area of approximately 200,000 people. The university has been involved in continuing education for some time, but recently the division of continuing education has received increased attention from the president, who is interested in finding ways of offsetting declining enrollments. It seems the university's full-time student population has fallen by 50 percent in the past two years, and the likelihood of a continued decline is very high. The president is hopeful that the division "can pull Smartland out of it's temporary affliction" and "get it back on it's feet." The president has charged the dean of the division, John Franklin, with this task.

One of Dean Franklin's first moves was a complete reorganization of the division. He maintained the evening and summer programs, but added the outreach office as a means of developing new business. Thomas Cave was subsequently hired to direct the office.

Cave had not been long on the job when Dean Franklin told him about a call he had received recently from a local investment firm looking for help in getting their employees trained in the use of computers. The dean asked Cave to follow-up on the matter and report back to him with the results one week later. Cave thanked the dean for the tip and hurried off to find out more about how he and the division could help the investment firm.

Cave called a Mr. Brinkley, Vice President of Employee Affairs for Eastland Guaranty and Trust, and scheduled an appointment for that afternoon. He was excited about the prospects of working with Eastland, the largest investment firm in the city. He remembered how, as a graduate student, he had learned to operate computers. One thing stood out in his mind: the computer business had changed considerably during recent years, as had the training needed to operate them.

Cave met Mr. Brinkley at the agreed-upon time and, after exchanging pleasantries, got down to business. He mentioned to Brinkley his conversation wth Dean Franklin and asked how he might help. Brinkley started by saying that the investment world had changed rapidly, to the point where the use of computers was essential for nearly all employees in the firm. His boss and board had authorized him to institute a computer training program, beginning with upper-level management. Brinkley said he was familiar with some of the computer brands on the market but did not know where to begin or what level of training was required. All he knew was that a friend at a competing firm had told him, "Whatever you do, don't go to the computer science department at Smartland. They'll have you go through a bunch of unnecessary hoops, and you still won't get what you want. My advice is to call the folks at the division of continuing education; they'll know what to do."

Cave listened intently, and once Brinkley finished said, "It sounds like your friend has had some experience with our computer science department. I think we can help you out and get the training you're looking for." That reassurance seemed to help relieve some of the obvious tension that Brinkley had felt, and the two of them spent the rest of the afternoon discussing what was needed, for how many, and what type of delivery mechanism would be best. By the day's end, Cave knew what Eastland wanted and offered the following feedback to Brinkley: "It sounds as though you need training in what is known in the continuing education business as 'computer literacy.' This involves an introduction to computers and computing, some of the basic terms, equipment, and various products with applications to the investment business. You then will probably want some help in learning how to operate computers and what software you will need for the company. Finally, it sounds as though the best time to offer this training would be in the early morning hours, say 7:00 to 8:30 A.M. so as to accommodate the busy schedule of management personnel. That's a quick overview based on what we have talked about. How does that sound to you?" Mr. Brinkley, smiling, exclaimed, "Great! It sounds like that's just what we need. If you could put together a proposal addressing what we talked about, and get back to me by early next week, then I will take it to my boss for review and authorization to proceed. Do you think you can do that, Dr. Cave?" Cave told Brinkley he could, and, over the next three days, he developed a proposal to share first with his dean and then later with Brinkley.

Cave met with Dean Franklin as requested, and in his hand was a proposal for meeting the computer training needs of Eastland. The dean scanned it quickly and then looked up. Cave could tell that all was not well. Franklin started by saying, "It's obvious that you have spent some time on this proposal, and there are some good things about it. However, I see some *real* problems." Cave felt queasy inside and retorted, "Thanks for the vote of confidence, but what's the problem?" Dean Franklin replied, "Your proposal recommends the use of an outside consulting firm called Computer Solutions, which is familiar with the banking and investment business. Why did you do this? Aren't you familiar with the university's policy that prohibits the use of outside people when we have qualified faculty to do the job? I realize that some of the departments are too academic, but we don't have much choice in the matter. My recommendation is to go over and see the folks in the computer science department and see if you can't work something out. Who knows, they may surprise us!"

Cave left the meeting feeling awful. He had proposed an excellent plan, one sure to meet the needs of Eastland. He remembered the warning Brinkley's friend had given about Smartland's computer science department and felt even worse. Being a good employee, however, he did as Dean Franklin asked and went to talk with the head of the computer science department that afternoon.

Cave described Eastland's problem to Dr. Everett Baily, head of the computer science department at Smartland. Baily listened half-heartedly, frequently interrupting Cave. When Cave finished, Baily offered the following: "We can do the job. My recommendation is that we start by having the Eastland folks enroll in our introductory computer science course, and three of our language courses, and then . . ." Cave got the picture quickly. He patiently listened to Baily's recommendation and left soon thereafter with this reply, "Thanks,

Dr. Baily, for your help. I don't think Eastland wants to take a major in computer science, but I'll let you know if they do. Good-bye."

Cave returned to his office and reported to Dean Franklin what had transpired. Franklin was equally incredulous, but said, "Cave, our hands are tied. The university's policy is firm. It's never been changed before, and I doubt it will be over this matter. If we have qualified faculty, then we have to use them. Go see Brinkley and tell him what we are up against. See if he is interested in what Baily suggested. If not, tell him we can't help him; he'll have to go elsewhere. Maybe he should contact that consulting firm directly?"

Dilemma #2
Providing Programs to Paying Customers Only

Brookwood College, a small but prestigious independent liberal arts institution located in the Midwest, had recently inaugurated a new president. With the new president came fresh ideas and the hope for continued excellence. It seems that the college had experienced recent financial problems that had nearly sealed its doom one year earlier. But the new president had come from industry, with a background in finance and management. One of the first changes the president made was to appoint Dr. Gerald Brown as vice president of finance. (His friends called him "Squeak" because of his penchant for saving money; they claimed he was so tight he squeaked.) Dr. Brown's charge had been simple: get the college out of the red and into the black as soon as possible.

What Brown did is probably what any good administrator in his position would do: he took stock of the college's financial position, looking for cost centers and revenue producers. As he looked about, he noticed that the academic units were costing an unusual amount to run, as was the athletic department. However, one unit in particular caught his eye: the continuing education program, known as PACE (Program for Adult and Continuing Education). Brown noticed that, other than food service, this unit was the only one making money for the college and resolved to find out more about it. Brown called the director of PACE, Ms. Helen Mathews, and scheduled a meeting the following week. He instructed Mathews to come prepared to discuss the origins of PACE, who it served, in what ways, and how it was financed. He also asked for some recommendations as to how revenue could be increased.

Helen Mathews had been at Brookwood for the past eight years. She first came as assistant director, but had been promoted to director three years ago at the firing of her former boss. Before coming to Brookwood, she had served in the Peace Corps in Malaysia; more recently, she had completed a master's degree in continuing education at a nearby university. She was active in her church, had served as honorary chairperson of the United Way the year before, and volunteered as a tutor at the local adult literacy center one evening a week. Mathews had a special fondness for community service, particularly in serving the less fortunate, and this was one of the attractions for her of work in continuing education. She had organized several "cluster groups" for displaced homemakers and financed these through profits from other PACE programs. Her efforts did not go unnoticed, as she received the "Continuing Educator of the Year Award" from her state adult and continuing education association.

Mathews spent the week preparing for her meeting with Dr. Brown. She reviewed the origins of PACE, which had been started twelve years earlier, principally as a noncredit operation. In the intervening years, the program had expanded to include credit offerings, conferences and institutes, correspondence study, and a special-projects office. As to whom the program served, Mathews was proud to note that not only were the highly educated and affluent represented, but also minority groups and many older students attending college for the first time. The program had been financed largely through tuition revenue, although a few grants to support special projects had been received as well. She thought about ways of increasing revenue, as Brown had asked her to do, and felt the best way would be to offer degree programs during evenings and weekends, rather than the customary daytime schedule. As the meeting time approached, Mathews felt particularly good about PACE and all that had been accomplished. She was optimistic about the future and looked forward to her meeting with Dr. Brown.

In the meantime, while Mathews was preparing for her meetings, so was Dr. Brown. He had done some checking with one of the college's most highly regarded faculty members about his perceptions of PACE. Dr. Wilson Ward, professor of chemistry for the past 30 years at Brookwood, had seen the development of PACE. As far as he was concerned, the students in the program were marginal at best. A few of them had been in his classes, and all they were concerned about was getting through the course to make more money. Dr. Ward felt PACE was a waste of college money and chided Mathews for her pet projects, such as the "Women's Reentry Center." He felt such projects hurt the reputation of the college more than it helped. "After all," he announced to Brown, "isn't this college for the best and the brightest *young* minds? Don't we have a responsibility to serve them first and foremost? It seems to me that we are getting away from the old Brookwood mission and setting ourselves up for a sure fall. If I were in your shoes, Dr. Brown, I'd put a stop to all this silliness."

Brown had done some further checking as well. He had a graduate school friend who had later become dean of a continuing education unit in a large land-grant university in the Southeast. Brown called his friend for advice about trends in continuing education and what he should be looking for when Ms. Mathews made her presentation. His friend told him that continuing professional education (CPE) activities are particularly strong since they are major money-making ventures. The high-status professions, such as medicine and law, should be targeted and nurtured. His friend advised him to look out for high-cost/low-return ventures, such as minority programs. "These may have some political merit," his friend said, "but they certainly don't have any fiscal merit. Besides, you're a private institution, so you don't have to worry about the political fallout anyway." Brown's friend threw out one other cautionary note: "I've been in the continuing education business for the past ten years and have gotten to know a good deal about those who are in it. In my view there are two kinds. The first are folks like ourselves who have doctorates in legitimate disciplines, who bring some academic integrity and business sense to the task. Then there's the second kind. These are folks who come out of the ranks of education, maybe get a degree in adult and continuing education, and bring little or no sense of academic integrity to the job. They are bleeding-heart liberals, have poor if any business sense, and, worst of all, don't have any idea of what a university or college should be. My advice, Gerry, is be tough and go with what your gut tells you to do. After all, isn't that the best way to proceed anyway? If I can help you with anything else, don't hesitate to let me know." Dr. Brown thanked his friend for his advice and hung up. He thought to himself, "Now I've got enough information to evaluate PACE objectively."

The time had come for Helen Mathews's meeting with Dr. Brown. He greeted her warmly, explained the purpose of the meeting, and asked if she was ready to proceed. She said she was. Mathews recounted the history of PACE, its mission, who it served, and how. She explained that the program was self-sustaining and had continued to show a profit for the college. She finished her report by saying, "I believe PACE is in an excellent position to develop further and continue the close relationship we now have with the community. I am especially proud that Brookwood has reached out to minority groups, the disenfranchised, and people who have been labeled high-risk students. We can do even better, though, by expanding our daytime degree programs to evenings and weekends. I am sure you will agree with me, Dr. Brown, that PACE is an important member of the Brookwood College community."

Brown thanked Mathews for her report, noting that he, too, had spent some time investigating the PACE program. He acknowledged that PACE was an important part of Brookwood, but had a different view of its potential. He asked Mathews if the program had targeted any professional groups, such as lawyers or physicians, and if so, what the extent of the offerings was. More importantly, he wondered if all activities were self supporting. For instance, he asked, "Is the Women's Reentry Center and the cluster program for displaced homemakers self-supporting?" Mathews listened intently to Brown's questions and could tell he had a pointed agenda. She responded, "No, Dr. Brown, we have not targeted any specific professional groups. We do offer several conferences for the local accounting and real estate associations, but beyond that, most of our offerings are for career and vocational advancement. Most of our programs are self-supporting, but not the Women's Reentry Center and the displaced homemakers' cluster program. The women who are a part of these programs can't afford what we charge, and their numbers are small. So as a result, we must use the profits from our other programs to support these. As I mentioned to you earlier in my report, I feel that is part of our responsibility." Dr. Brown shot back heatedly, "Ms. Mathews, where did you get the idea that Brookwood is a welfare institution? We are a liberal arts college and have a reputation to uphold. We cannot continue to operate in such a manner. Besides, I have it on very good authority that continued learning in the professions is big business these days. Professions such as law and medicine are involved in continuing education and are natural audiences for us to court. I want you to come back here one week from now with a plan for how we are going to develop such programs. I also want you to disband those costly women's programs. We can no longer afford to subsidize one program at the expense of another. We don't do that with our regular academic programs, and we certainly aren't going to do that with PACE. Besides, if you feel you can't do what I am asking, I have a friend who would be more than willing to do the job. Do you understand me?"

Mathews could not believe her ears. She thought she had represented PACE well and was not prepared for the reaction she got. She wondered to herself, "What am I going to do? I love it here at Brookwood. I have invested eight years of my life in this institution. I have a house and friends to think about. My professional training is being questioned. My personal beliefs are being threatened. My job's on the line. What am I going to do?"

Dilemma #3
Withholding Results of a Program Evaluation

Jim Baker had worked in the division of continuing education at State University for the past 15 years. He had worked his way up through the ranks of the division and three years ago was appointed dean. While working for the division, he had taken a leave of absence to complete an Ed.D. in adult and continuing education at a large land-grant university in a neighboring state. Baker was well liked at his institution and had an excellent working relationship with the College of Agriculture and the School of Education. This relationship was not coincidental, since many of the credit programs were offered jointly with Agriculture and Education. Baker also held a joint appointment with the School of Education and offered an administration course in postsecondary education twice a year.

The division of continuing education at State University had its roots in the 1920s, when it became responsible for the summer program for teachers and school administrators. Since that time, the division has grown to the point where it now had a conference center, several outreach offices throughout the state, and a television and radio production facility. The division has five major responsibilities, including evening credit programs, summer school, conferences and institutes, public broadcast, and noncredit services. The evening program was by far the largest and had grown significantly during the past ten years, as more and more older students had started or resumed their educational pursuits. The evening program was also Baker's favorite, since he had directed it until being named dean of continuing education.

Things were progressing fairly well for Baker and the division. Enrollments were up substantially, as was the amount of revenue received. The university central administration had authorized exploration of a telecommunications bridge to be used throughout the state. An uplink and downlink satellite system was being studied and would later be brought under the division's control once specifics were worked out. In addition, several cooperative ventures with private industry to provide on-site training, which would continue to enhance the division's image, were nearing final stages of agreement.

While the image of the division was generally good, a small problem had emerged that had the potential of seriously damaging the equally good relationship that had developed over time with the School of Education. This problem involved Baker and his director of evening programs, Cathy White, whom he had hired three months earlier.

The problem had to do with an evaluation policy of the evening program. As was the custom, an evaluation was conducted at the end of each course. This was done to check on the success of the course and to determine if the instructor should be used another time. The evaluation process consisted of an outside person (usually an evening program staff member) administering the instrument while the instructor remained out of the classroom. Once the evaluations were completed, they were given to the proctor, who returned them to the evening program office for typing. Soon after the instructor turned in grades for the class, the anonymous evaluations were returned to the instructor for review. This process was used to ensure that the results of the instructor's evaluation had no bearing on the final grades. A copy of the evaluation results were also retained by the director of evening programs. Upon review, an instructor who had received poor ratings more than once would automatically be disqualified from further teaching.

Cathy White, following established policy, had reviewed course evaluations at the end of the term. She had noted that one instructor in particular, Dr. Roland Smith, had received an extremely poor rating. She checked Dr. Smith's file to see how he had been evaluated before and found similar results. In fact, there was not one poor rating; there were seven. Dumbfounded and concerned, White decided to see Dean Baker for advice about what to do.

Baker welcomed White to his office and asked what he could do for her. She told him about the poor evaluation of Dr. Smith and about recently finding more evaluations of a similar kind in his file. She asked him, "How could this happen? We have a policy that says anyone having two or more poor evaluations will be prevented from teaching for us again. I'm sure I checked that file earlier this semester to see if Dr. Smith had prior evaluations, and I didn't see any. Maybe I just missed them. I thought about calling the dean of the School of Education to see if he had any information, but wanted to speak to you first. What do you think we should do about this matter?"

As White spoke, Baker twitched a bit inside, and after she finished he offered the following explanation. "Cathy, I'm glad you came to see me about this first before calling the dean of the School of Education; that could have caused some real problems. It's really a long, unpleasant story, but if you will bear with me, I'll try to give you the gist of the situation. It all goes back about eight years, when Dean Scott (dean of the School of Education) first came to State University. He wanted to establish good ties with the local school district, so he courted the superintendent of schools, Dr. Roland Smith, who had previously had poor relations with the university. Dean Scott convinced Dr. Smith to open the schools for student teacher placements and research projects. In return, Smith asked if he could teach a course on school administration once a year. Dean Scott agreed, unaware that Dr. Smith would be a terrible instructor. He contacted my predecessor (Tom Jennings) and me about this venture and enlisted our help. Over the years, we have seen the terrible evaluations and have subtly tried to convince Dr. Smith to have somebody else do his course. But he persists, and I'm afraid that we feel his support for the School of Education and the university is more important than his poor teaching performance. I agree with you, Cathy, that this shouldn't be tolerated, but in this case the ends justify the means. Besides, if we didn't have to keep up our close working relationship with the School of Education, you can be assured that I would see to it that Smith would never teach for us again. But we can't as long as the central administration insists we operate as a servant to the rest of the university. Sometimes we have to do things we don't like and this is one. Can I count on you to keep this between you and me? Oh, the reason you didn't find the poor evaluations is that I removed them from the file before the semester started and replaced them recently. I didn't want you to get upset before we had a chance to talk. Okay?"

Cathy White listened increduously to Dean Baker's explanation. She mulled over this dilemma in her mind quickly, wondering what other deals had been struck. She mumbled privately to herself, "I guess this is what the business of continuing higher education is all about." In the end, she told Baker that her lips were sealed: "You can trust me to keep this matter between you and me. Thanks for filling me in. Sometime, I'd like to talk with you more about a project I'm working on dealing with ethics in continuing education. Okay?"

Conclusion

This chapter has explored certain administrative dilemmas in continuing higher education. We have pointed out that the mission of continuing education is often at odds with the mission of higher education and that this, in part, explains the roots of such dilemmas. We have also looked at the interplay between one's ethical orientation, value structure, and professional socialization in adult and continuing education, and have further noted the power these orientations have on administrative practice. Finally, we have offered several case studies as a means of illustrating some common dilemmas facing administrators in continuing higher education.

Ethics play a key role in the conduct of decision makers at any level. In adult and continuing education, however, they play even a greater role, given the advocacy and social justice philosophy that has characterized so much of its heritage. It is easy in a time of hurried expectations to lose sight of these fundamental virtues. Perhaps one way to keep these clearly in our sights is to think of those we are serving: the learners. If we do this, our dilemmas may be much easier to handle and, in the process, we may find it easier to live with ourselves.

References

American heritage dictionary of the English language. (1981). Boston: Houghton Mifflin.

Apps, J. W. (1979). *Problems in continuing education.* New York: McGraw-Hill.

Apps, J. W. (1985). *Improving practice in continuing education: Modern approaches for understanding the field and determining priorities.* San Francisco: Jossey-Bass.

Berlin, L. S. (1983). The university and continuing professional education: A contrary view. In M. Stern (Ed.), *Power and conflict in continuing professional education* (pp. 117–133). Belmont, CA: Wadsworth.

Boone, E. J. (1985). *Developing programs in adult education.* Englewood Cliffs, NJ: Prentice-Hall.

Bryson, L. (1936). *Adult education.* New York: American Book.

Clark, B. R. (1958). *The marginality of adult education.* Chicago: Center for the Study of Liberal Education for Adults.

Commission of Professors of Adult Education. (1986). *Standards for graduate programs in adult education.* DeKalb, IL: Author.

Council on the Continuing Education Unit. (1984). *Principles of good practice in continuing education.* Silver Spring, MD: Author.

Dyer, J. P. (1956). *Ivory towers in the market place: The evening college in American education.* New York: Bobbs-Merrill.

Frandson, P. E. (1979). The politics of continuing education. *Continuum, 43*(4), 12–14.

Good, C. V. (1959). *Dictionary of education.* New York: McGraw-Hill.

Hopke, W. E. (1968). *Dictionary of personnel and guidance terms.* Chicago: Ferguson.

Houle, C. O. (1980). *Continuing learning in the professions.* San Francisco: Jossey-Bass.

Kempfer, H. (1979). What is continuing education? *Lifelong Learning: The Adult Years, 3*(2), 11, 23.

Mason, R. C. (1979). Managerial role and style. In P. D. Langerman & D. H. Smith (Eds.), *Managing adult and continuing education programs and staff* (pp. 45–89). Washington, DC: National Association for Public Continuing and Adult Education.

Singarella, T. A., & Sork, T. J. (1983). Questions of values and conduct: Ethical issues for adult education. *Adult Education Quarterly, 33*(4), 244–251.

Steiner, J. F. (1977). *Focus on ethics.* Santa Monica, CA: Salenger Education Media.

Strother, G. B., & Klus, J. P. (1982) *Administration of continuing education.* Belmont, CA: Wadsworth.

Webster's third new international dictionary of the English language, unabridged. (1971). Springfield, MA: Merriam.

CHAPTER SIX

Ethical Dilemmas in Evaluating Adult Education Programs

STEPHEN BROOKFIELD

A T first thought, the act of evaluation may seem to those involved in this activity to be remarkably free of ethical dilemmas. Evaluation, so they may argue, is simply the value-free ascertainment of whether or not certain predefined objectives have been achieved. To the extent that certain performance behaviors are exhibited or certain quantifiable indicators of accomplishment are present, the program can be judged successful. For example, a library education program might be thought successful if the number of library users increases in the program's wake. Similarly, a word-processing program could be considered successful if the learners are able to write and edit a page of text after a morning's session.

This notion of evaluation is grounded in a particular model, derived chiefly from the work of Ralph Tyler (1949). Tyler believed that "the process of evaluation is essentially the process of determining to what extent the educational objectives are actually being realized. . . . [S]ince educational objectives are essentially changes in human beings . . . then evaluation is the process for determining the degree to which these changes in behavior are actually taking place" (p. 106). Judging the success of a program by the extent to which predefined objectives are attained is appealing to practitioners beset by external, political, and institutional pressures, in particular the demand for "hard" (that is, quantifiable) results. The Tylerian model has an apparent precision and scientism that is attractive to educators immersed in the complex psychosocial reality of a learning group. As I have suggested elsewhere, the unambiguous and unequivocal nature of the model means that it serves "as a navigational device to assist seasick practitioners to chart a course through the storm-tossed waters of daily practice" (Brookfield, 1986, p. 267).

According to literature reviews of evaluation in adult education (Stakes, 1981; Brookfield, 1982) the Tylerian model still holds conceptual sway as the preeminent model of evaluation in this field. In adult basic education, training and human-resource development in business and industry, staff development in health education, continuing professional education, and military education, to take just five areas of practice, very few alternatives to the Tylerian model exist. In community development and social action efforts, formative and participatory models are more common. Within institutionally provided adult education, however, evaluation is generally synonymous with the checking of whether or not previously specified objectives have been attained.

The apparently unequivocal nature of this model of evaluation seems to preclude any consideration of ethical questions, for what could be more straightforward than recording whether or not a program achieved the goals established by its organizers at its beginning? In terms of ethical questions, however, this straightforwardness is illusory, if seductive. As soon as we begin to think about the actions, decisions, and justifications of those involved in an evaluation, we realize that this activity has much more ethical ambiguity than at first sight might appear to be the case.

For example, what if an evaluator employed in a given situation considers the original goals to be morally bankrupt? What if the subjects of the evaluation object to the methods used to check whether or not they are exhibiting the desired performance behaviors? What if the program head refuses to make explicit to the subjects concerned the criteria governing an evaluation study? Worse still, what if the results of an evaluation study are kept private, despite requests from the subjects concerned for this information? It is apparent, then, that one can conduct a flawless evaluation of a program according to the predetermined objectives model yet be faced with a number of ethical questions.

In recent years a number of writers have recognized that evaluation is a value-laden and ethically ambiguous venture. When one evaluates an educational activity, one is making some judgment concerning the relative desirability of that activity. Scriven (1967) argues that even if all program objectives are fully achieved, a program itself cannot be considered successful unless the objectives attained are intrinsically worthwhile. Guba and Lincoln believe traditional evaluation models based on checking the attainment of behavioral objectives to be bankrupt "because they do not begin with the concerns and issues of their actual audiences and because they produce information that, while perhaps statistically significant, does not generate truly worthwhile knowledge" (1981, p. ix).

Stufflebeam defines evaluation as "the act of examining and judging, concerning the worth, quality, significance, amount, degree, or condition of something. In short, evaluation is the ascertainment of merit" (1975, p. 8). Hence, for a program to be considered fully educational, the learners must pursue purposes that are generally agreed to be morally worthwhile. What is defined as worthwhile is, of course, culturally and historically variable. In a democratic society, however, if we train people to be exemplary concentration camp guards, perfect bigots, or highly successful exploiters of minorities, we cannot regard these as educationally worthwhile activities even though the end results are what the program organizers desired. The methods used in evaluation are also of crucial importance, and several writers have suggested that a fully adult educational evaluative approach is one in which criteria and methods of evaluation are negotiated by participants, facilitators, and evaluators (Lindeman, 1955; Forest, 1976; Kinsey, 1981; Nottingham Andragogy Group, 1983).

One last point that needs to be made regarding the nature of evaluation concerns its essentially political nature. Every evaluation study is, in its own way, a political drama in which the different actors concerned are trying to secure a favorable verdict regarding their contributions. Guba and Lincoln (1981) advance the concept of "stakeholders" to describe those who have a self-interest in securing a favorable evaluation. Stakeholders try to influence the evaluator to give good reports of their activities. For example, if an evaluation is conducted for the purpose of deciding which of several departments or programs will receive further funding, then the evaluator will be flattered, cajoled, wooed, nudged, and stroked by the various department and program heads involved.

Those who rely on employment as freelance evaluators or evaluation consultants are likely to be under pressure to produce favorable evaluations. Since their livelihood depends partly on referrals from satisfied clients to institutions looking for evaluators, they will not wish to acquire reputations as "hard" evaluators responsible for loss of funding and program closures.

Case Studies of Ethical Dilemmas in Evaluation

The following ethical dilemmas all spring from real life. They have been reported to me, orally or in writing, during my teaching courses on program development and evaluation in adult education over the last decade. I have personalized many of these and turned myself into the protagonist in order to preserve the anonymity of the students and colleagues involved. Hence, although these dilemmas are often presented in the first person, they actually represent typical dilemmas faced by others.

As part of the program development courses I teach, participants are asked to explore a number of typical theory–practice discrepancies they have experienced in their practice of adult education. In particular, they are asked to relate ethical dilemmas they have faced in their development and evaluation of programs. Some of these dilemmas have surfaced in seminar discussions, some in the context of written assignments, and some in the course of reporting critical incidents through in-class exercises or course assignments. This last technique may be of particular interest to those who have not tried it before, since it produces short narrative descriptions of events that are usually concrete, specific, and detailed.

In a critical-incident exercise, participants are asked to reflect back on their last few months of practice and to think about those events they recall as being of particular significance. In the present case, participants are asked to relate an occasion in which they felt caught in an ethical dilemma regarding how they should behave during the conduct of an evaluation. In recording descriptions of these events (for example, when and where they occurred, who was involved, and what aspects of the dilemma were most unsettling) participants supply a rich collection of narrative statements concerning typical ethical dilemmas. Readers will no doubt have their own examples of dilemmas to add to the following list, and one hope is that the following collection will prompt further analysis and discussion of this issue.

Dilemma #1. Should evaluators always declare their identities to subjects at the outset of an evaluation, or is covert participant evaluation ever justified for the accuracy of the data it produces?

This is a familiar dilemma to all kinds of qualitative researchers. It springs from the common-sense realization that once people are aware of an evaluator's identity, they adjust their behavior. Hence, "normal" (that is, habitual) ways of behaving are replaced by actions that will endear those being evaluated to their evaluator. This makes it virtually impossible for the evaluator to gain a sense of the typical behavior of the person or persons concerned in the particular situation.

In my own experience I have been faced with this dilemma in my attempts to improve a noncredit continuing education program with which I was involved. I was working as an adult education organizer at an adult education center in England. In order to gain a sense of how participants new to the center were treated, I enrolled in what I thought was a typical discussion course without informing the instructor concerned of my identity. My reasoning was that if the instructor was aware of my identity, then his performance would be altered significantly. My contributions might be granted more legitimacy than they deserved, my questions might come to dominate the group's agenda more than was desirable, and the instructor would not feel wholly at ease until my approval had explicitly been granted.

I was faced with a real dilemma. Should I conceal my identity and pretend to have no affiliation with the center in which the course was running? At worst, this would be lying to the instructor concerned. At best, it would be equivalent to concealing relevant information. My decision was to conceal my true identity for the sake of evaluative integrity. I simply did not feel that I could gain some sense of how an adult learner new to the center was treated if my identity as an employee of that center was revealed. In my opinion the temptation for the instructor to pay special attention to my contributions, to be overly welcoming to my attempts to contribute to the discussions, and to be less than wholly critical of those contributions was too great to ignore.

At the time I could not rid myself of a feeling of dishonest sneakiness for not being completely open with the instructor. I did not feel comfortable with the situation and kept reminding myself that I was, in effect, breaking with generally agreed-upon rules of conduct within groups in concealing what might well be relevant information about myself. I was not sure, and still do not know, whether my actions were justified, but I did know that I was caught in an ethical dilemma regarding my attempts at evaluating activities within my own institution.

Dilemma #2. Are evaluators ethically bound to share the findings of evaluation reports with the subjects of those reports, or can a case be made for limited distribution of the results to those in positions of institutional power?

Perhaps the most common instance of this dilemma is in the form of performance appraisals of employees. A frequently identified dilemma concerns the need for program directors or department heads to decide upon the appointment, promotion, or reappointment of adult instructors. In making this decision, a performance review is generally called for, which may well include reviews of the instructor concerned by his or her peers as well as superiors. Since continuing education directors are engaged in a continual process of hiring and firing part-time teachers, the question of how to conduct these kinds of reviews is one of particular importance to them.

Sometimes these reviews are made completely available to the employee concerned, and sometimes they are even generally accessible to public scrutiny. Frequently, however, they are kept private, being for the director's eyes only. The justification usually given for this is strictly operational; that is, that continuing education directors could not function in their jobs if they were faced with continual cases of aggrieved instructors complaining that they should be allowed to teach their courses again, even in the face of unfavorable reviews.

A second example of this general dilemma involves learners rather than employees. Are there ever times when confidential reviews of learners' achievements are ethically justified? For example, doctoral programs in adult education generally require a comprehensive examination of their students before these students are allowed to register as doctoral candidates. The results of these examinations—beyond a simple verdict as to whether the student concerned has passed or failed—are sometimes kept private to the professors judging learner performance. Can there be a valid justification for not informing learners as fully as possible of the nature of their performance, particularly in a field of study that so often stresses collaborative, democratic methods and values?

Another version of this dilemma, which also involves learners, occurs when adult educators judge that the results of an evaluation are so potentially devastating to a learner that they should not be revealed to that person. Here, the argument in favor of keeping data private is that the learner concerned would be dissuaded from further learning by knowing of an evaluation that was highly critical of his or her performance. Adult learners frequently have precarious egos to begin with where their performance in a student role is concerned, without their self-esteem being destroyed by an unfavorable evaluation. With particular groups who are unused to formal educational settings (for example, adult nonreaders), the effect of an unfavorable evaluation may be to stop them from engaging in any purposeful formal learning.

It seems to me that, whatever the operational realities, keeping private the results of evaluations of learners' performances is ethically unjustifiable. In the three examples cited of this general dilemma, it seems that the manner and medium through which instructors and learners learn of their evaluations are crucial. Critical verdicts should, as far as possible, be given tactfully and sensitively, preferably leavened by positive comment. If it is impossible to find any saving graces in a learner's activities, then it may be kinder in the long run to advise the person concerned that he or she is in for an unbroken period of anxiety, self-doubt, and painful struggle by remaining in the program.

One of my own most difficult ethical dilemmas is whether, and how, to tell people that the graduate program in which I work as a faculty member is beyond their capacities. Viscerally I feel this offends every principle of democratic accessibility and openness that adult educators hold so dear; yet intellectually I know that the institutional standards and constraints are such that to allow them to continue is to ensure for them several years of misery, struggle, and eventual failure, during which time their image of themselves as capable learners will gradually be whittled away.

If I err on the side of optimism and decide to withhold my assessment of their unsuitability for the program, it may be that my action will be justified by their moving well beyond their current levels of ability. In this case, the consequences of my optimism are positive. But if my optimism is misplaced, I am guaranteeing that their period of graduate study will be an earthly purgatory, an almost wholly dispiriting and depressing experience. On the other hand, if I err on the side of pessimism and attempt prematurely to "counsel them out" (to use the most common euphemism for academic firing) in opposition to their determined desire to stay in the program, I may be destroying forever their desire to grow intellectually. My judgment and prescience concerning learners' likely abilities and performances are frequently fallible, and I have seen many people improve out of recognition over time. I have to live with the knowledge that giving people the full version of an unfavorable evaluation and advising them of their unsuitability for the program may result in their turning their backs on any future attempts to learn. Presenting learners with my assessment and allowing them to make the decision about whether to stop or continue in the program does not work, since most learners conclude that they are only passing through a phase of temporary difficulty that will be followed by continued success.

Dilemma #3. Should evaluators ensure that the criteria of success being used to judge a program's accomplishments are always made public at the outset of the evaluation, so that participants know against what standards they are being judged?

Those who subscribe to the "goal-free" school of evaluation (Scriven, 1972) believe that it is in the best overall interests of a program for participants to be unencumbered by any knowledge of its declared outcomes. They urge that evaluators themselves not be informed of a program's declared goals so that the evaluation study will focus on the actual accomplishments of a program, rather than being distorted by a preoccupation with "official" purposes. In the absence of declared terminal outcomes or objectives, goal-free evaluators are simply to record what appear to them to be the major consequences, effects, and achievements of a program.

This approach seems to me to have some very real merits. It avoids the danger of evaluators' missing important achievements that are unrelated to the declared program goals. Using the phrase *side effects* in reference to unanticipated outcomes is to render these irrelevant. It is to imply that they are of no consequence and innately inferior to the stated program goals. In fact, as those with experience as facilitators and learners know, it is precisely these unanticipated aspects of educational encounters that are frequently the most valuable and important. My own most dramatic critical incidents in learning have been those times when I stumbled, in an accidental and apparently serendipitous manner, on a wholly unexpected insight. Embracing this serendipitous spontaneity and being willing to risk venturing into uncharted intellectual terrain are to me marks of real self-confidence and security in learners and teachers.

On the other hand, there is a clear and convincing case on the grounds of democratic accountability to be made for always informing participants of criteria against which their performance is to be judged. This is particularly true when the consequences of poor evaluations are so serious as to threaten livelihoods. In my own case, not to be informed of the criteria governing decisions that were made on my reappointment, promotion, or tenure would outrage me. Indeed, not to inform me of these would be institutionally self-defeating, since I might otherwise concentrate my energies in areas that are organizationally irrelevant.

Dilemma #4. Should evaluators report only on matters that program organizers have previously identified, or are evaluators responsible to report distressing or harmful practices they observe that are not covered by their evaluative responsibilities?

Ethically, there is no question on this matter. Evaluators do have a duty to report such activities. If they observe learners being abused (psychologically as well as physically), bullied, intimidated, stereotyped, ignored, or racially slurred, then they should bring these to the attention of program organizers. The only conceivable reason for not doing so would be because of the threat to the evaluator's livelihood, in which case economic concerns would outweigh moral considerations. The brevity of discussion on this point should not be interpreted by readers as an indication that it is somehow less weighty than the other dilemmas identified. It is simply that there appear to be no arguments that can be marshaled to argue in favor of not reporting abuses, making extended analysis unnecessary.

Dilemma #5. Are internal evaluators duty bound to respond to evaluative comments in the terms in which these are phrased by learners?

One of the most frequent complaints offered by participants in an evaluation study is that their comments, reactions, and suggestions are ignored by those conducting the evaluation. Why, they ask, bother to conduct an evaluation if you are not going to act upon our recommendations? Do not evaluators and participants essentially enter into a contractual relationship when participants are asked to rate a program according to such indices as its relevance, pacing, format, and usefulness? What is the point of securing this data if you are not going to act upon it?

These are fair questions. Nothing is more irksome than to spend time completing an evaluation only to find that none of one's suggestions have the slightest effect on the way a program is run. It certainly appears that not acting upon participants' comments in their evaluations runs counter to the democratic, collaborative ethos that adult educators generally attempt to foster. The problem arises when those in charge of a program believe that participants' comments do not always reflect these people's best interests or do not take into account broader contextual factors. Some examples from my own practice may make this dilemma more clear.

In end-of-course evaluations I receive from learners, perhaps the most frequent suggestion for change that I receive concerns their wish that I be more directive and dominate the classes more with my own contributions. For example, in a learner-centered, collaboratively determined course I offer on "Adult Education for Social Action" (Brookfield, 1986, pp. 108–112) comments are typically received that run along the lines "more chance to hear Stephen's thoughts on a number of issues," "reduce the amount of time listening to group reports and increase S.B.'s involvement," "question a bit the relevance and value of self-assessment and participation portfolio—you be the judge," "more intervention needed by instructor," and "more sharing of instructor's knowledge and experiences in the form of a lecture."

Since the whole purpose of this course is to encourage participants to develop curricula based on their own perceived needs and experiences and to help them take control for the design, conduct, and evaluation of their learning, I try deliberately to place the responsibility and onus for these activities onto participants themselves. Were I to follow their evaluative suggestions, the course would resemble a much more traditional graduate study experience. It would, for example, certainly relieve them of making difficult evaluative judgments regarding their own work and that of their peers; yet it is in the making of such judgments that they come to ask penetrating questions regarding the nature of educational worthwhileness and to develop powers of critical analysis. Were I to assume the sole responsibility for deciding content, method, and evaluative criteria, then the chances of their developing self-directed learning capacities would be substantially reduced.

A similar situation arises when learners in my courses resist my attempts to encourage them to become critically reflective regarding their practice of adult education. A major tenet of my practice as a professor of adult education is to assist educators to become aware of, and to analyze critically, the assumptions underlying their practice. I think it is important for them to make explicit their ideas regarding how adults learn, the criteria by which they judge whether or not they are succeeding as educators, and how they place the efforts within the context of their wider society.

Frequently, however, learners question these purposes and insist that it is more important for them to acquire practical skills, such as how to conduct needs assessments, how to assess the range of learning styles within members of a new learning group, or how to match learning goals with appropriate methods. While I believe these to be important skills for practitioners to possess, I do not think that graduate study is the appropriate context for their development. Hence, even though learners may complain in evaluative comments that these components are missing and that they should replace the purposes that I feel are important, I remain fully committed to my vision of what adult education should be accomplishing.

There is, obviously, frequent scope for negotiation on these matters, and most courses turn into a transactional encounter in which I heed their comments, try to make clear my own beliefs, and attempt to frame my own purposes in a manner closer to their wishes. Sometimes, however, a clear discrepancy emerges between my own philosophy of adult education and learners' stated preferences. In this situation it is more honest to face these discrepancies openly than to pretend they do not exist. It is also best to admit that a power relationship exists within credit adult education and that the educator's wishes are granted (in learners' eyes) a disproportionate credibility.

In these two situations I see little choice other than for me to explain as fully as possible why the course is arranged as it is and to make it wholly clear to potential participants how the course operates and what responsibilities they will be expected to assume if they join. I explain that were I to change my conduct to become more directive and to assume the responsibility for deciding curricula, methods, and evaluative criteria on their behalf, then I would be denying some of my most fundamental beliefs concerning the nature of adult educational encounters. I make it clear that developing critical reflection regarding one's assumptions and the assumptions governing the actions of others is, for me, the central purpose of graduate adult education.

Perhaps the most crucial dimension in these situations is whether or not my own assumptions, purposes, methods, and criteria were stated clearly to learners at the outset of the educational encounter. If this is not the case, then I am on much shakier ethical ground regarding my response to their evaluative comments. Learners can then make a claim that they contracted into an educational encounter under false assumptions.

Dilemma #6. Are evaluators ever justified in depriving control groups of important services in the cause of research accuracy?

This dilemma arises in situations where an experimental group in a study enjoys the benefits of a certain kind of service that the control group does not. For example, imagine an institution has been awarded a grant to develop centers of educational advice and counseling for adults and to assess the value of this service. A project head may decide that the best way to assess the usefulness of this provision for adults is to find two communities of similar socioeconomic and ethnic composition. One community (the experimental group) would be the site of an extensive publicity campaign and program development effort focused on the opening of new centers of educational counseling for adults in that area. The other community (the control group) would not receive any of these benefits. After a period of, say, five years, the researchers would study whether adults in the experimental group were more likely to engage in higher education, career change, or some form of retraining in comparison to adults in the control group. If this were shown to be the case, then the network of educational counseling services for adults established in the experimental community would be replicated in other communities, including the control community.

As a research approach, this experimental design is derived from the natural science, positivist paradigm of controlled inquiry. Within this paradigm the researcher alters a variable affecting one substance or relationship between substances, while keeping another example of the substance or relationship stable. This hypothetico-deductive method is an excellent way of advancing knowledge about the physical world. The ethical problems only arise when human subjects are involved rather than chemical substances, as is the case in medical science and across the broad spectrum of social and behavioral sciences, of which educational research is a subcategory.

In the example of the community-based counseling service for adults mentioned above, the positivist experimental approach requires that one group be deprived of a service offered to another group in the cause of research accuracy. This is a difficult position to maintain if the service offered is, by consensual judgment, beneficial. Most adult educators would agree that providing adults with greater information regarding the range of educational possibilities open to them is a good thing. It would be regarded as a given;

that is, as a common-sense, taken-for-granted assumption about what it means to be a properly functioning adult educator.

Aside from the consensual condemnation that may result from using an experimental/control group study where adult learners are involved, there is also the question of appropriate evaluative methodologies. In studies of the effects of a new form of adult educational provision on learners it may well be unrealistic to use the experimental approach. This approach is founded on two faulty assumptions where adult education is concerned. First, it assumes that two exactly similar groups of adults can be located in the first place. When one takes into account the breadth of idiosyncratic configurations of inherited abilities, experiences, developed capacities, personalities, and cultural conditionings represented by even one small learning group, it is hard to imagine ever being able to find two communities of sufficient similarity to be suitable for the hypothetico-deductive method.

Second, it assumes that the effect of one individual variable can be isolated from the milieu within which it is located. In the example cited, even if the experimental community did exhibit a more frequent use of educational services at the end of the experimental period, how could a researcher conclude with any definitive accuracy that this was due solely to the introduction of the counseling service? There are so many other variables that could account for this increased educational take-up that isolating one is highly dubious. The change could be due to population movement (an influx of well-educated adults moving into the area), to a media campaign emphasizing the benefits of educational participation, to plant closures (leaving a body of workers eager for retraining), or to program developers being uniquely talented at judging which programs are most likely to attract participants. A community does not exhibit the artificially controlled environment that can be created in a laboratory, so evaluation studies using this approach must be scrutinized carefully and skeptically.

Conclusion

In terms of the dimensions of ethical practice identified by Brockett in Chapter 1 of this volume, the kinds of ethical dilemmas identified are related both to the personal values of educators and to the multiple responsibilities and loyalties evaluators feel to the different parties involved in the evaluation drama. Dilemmas one, two, three, five, and six clearly involve the conflict of loyalties an evaluator is likely to face. Dilemma four is most obviously grounded in the evaluator's sense of personal values, though this same consideration also informs the other five dilemmas in various ways.

As is probably the case with most ethical dilemmas, there are no easy solutions to any of the examples posited. Decisions are likely to be contextual and to take into account the personalities involved and the consequences of different courses of action. Aside from dilemma four, there are no ready rules of conduct to be followed. The development of an evaluative code of ethics will help produce general guidelines in cases such as these, but it is unrealistic to expect that this code can be operationalized in a clearly unambiguous manner. Adult educational programs are complex psychosocial dramas, and the learning that occurs within them is complex and variegated. Evaluating program achievements and individual learners' progress is an ambiguous exercise, both methodologically and ethically.

It is my hope that this chapter will at least bring recognition of this ambiguity into the public domain and generate some discussion of how such ambiguity might be faced and tolerated. All evaluators of adult education have probably faced at least one or two of the dilemmas identified above, yet discussion of how these are faced are remarkable for their absence in the literature of our field. It almost seems as though our professional insecurity is such that we are afraid to admit to ambiguity or ethical qualms in our efforts. The sooner we learn to speak and write openly about these dilemmas and qualms, to make our private knowledge public, the sooner we will be taken seriously as a professional group.

References

Brookfield, S. D. (1982). Evaluation models and adult education. *Studies in Adult Education, 14*, 95–100.

Brookfield, S. D. (1986). *Understanding and facilitating adult learning.* San Francisco: Jossey-Bass.

Forest, L. B. (1976). Program evaluation: For reality. *Adult Education, 26*(3), 167–177.

Guba, E. G., & Lincoln, Y. S. (1981). *Effective evaluation.* San Francisco: Jossey-Bass.

Kinsey, D. (1981). Participatory evaluation in adult and nonformal education. *Adult Education, 31*(3), 155–168.

Lindeman, E. C. (1955). Adults evaluate themselves. In *How to teach adults* (pp. 45–48). Washington, DC: Adult Education Association of the U.S.A.

Nottingham Andragogy Group. (1983). *Toward a developmental theory of andragogy.* Nottingham: Department of Adult Education, University of Nottingham.

Scriven, M. (1967). The methodology of evaluation. In R. M. Gagne, M. Scriven, & R. W. Tyler (Eds.), *Perspectives on curriculum evaluation* (pp. 39–83). Skokie, IL: Rand McNally.

Scriven, M. (1972). Pros and cons about goal free evaluation. *Evaluation Comment, 3*(4), 1–4.

Stakes, R. L. (1981). Conceptualizing evaluation in adult education. *Lifelong Learning: The Adult Years, 4*(8), 4–5, 22–23.

Stufflebeam, D. L. (1975). Evaluation as a community education process. *Community Education Journal, 5*(2), 7–12, 19.

Tyler, R. W. (1949). *Basic principles of curriculum and instruction.* Chicago: University of Chicago Press.

CHAPTER SEVEN

Ethical Dilemmas in the Teaching of Adults

ROSEMARY S. CAFFARELLA

THE major purpose of this chapter is twofold. First, it will be argued that ethical dilemmas are inevitable when teaching adults (Baumgarten, 1982; Tom, 1984). Second, it will be suggested that we, as adult educators, should model ethical behavior and practice in our teaching (McGovern, 1985). Questions of rightness and wrongness and good and bad can be found in the teachers' own belief system about adults as learners, their roles and responsibilities as teachers, and the way teachers implement the teaching process.

Teaching is often spoken of as an art and a craft (e.g., Knowles, 1980; Tom, 1984). The teaching process involves careful assessment of students' learning needs, the ability to design and carry out appropriate strategies and techniques, and the skill to evaluate fairly what an individual has learned. When people take on the role of teacher it implies that they have an adequate knowledge base in whatever content area they are teaching. There are also those illusive qualities that make teachers really good—natural enthusiasm for their subjects, respect and caring for their students, and commitment to helping students learn.

A person who takes on the responsibilities of a teacher is often faced with numerous ethical dilemmas related to that role. Reviewed in this chapter are some of the more salient issues. The chapter is organized according to the following areas: (1) ethical questions related to the personal belief systems of teachers about the nature of adults as learners; (2) ethical issues found in the multiple responsibilities that teachers of adults have; and (3) ethical dilemmas teachers face in the practice of their craft. These three sections mirror the model of the dimensions (personal value system, consideration of multiple responsibilities, and operationalization of values) of ethical practice in adult education, as outlined by Brockett in Chapter 1.

Teachers' Beliefs About the Nature of Adults as Learners

Individuals' basic values and beliefs affect both the way they teach and, in some cases, even what they teach (Apps, 1979; Tom, 1984). This can be illustrated by hypothetical scenarios that describe two very different teachers, Joyce C. and Bob R., who teach the same subject to students with very similar backgrounds.

Joyce C. teaches an English as a second language (ESL) class in a medium-sized city in the Southwest. Her classes are highly structured, with specific lessons planned for each weekly session. Students are expected to prepare at home each week for the next week's lesson. The actual class time is spent in reviewing the material via lecture and drill-and-practice exercises in one large group. Joyce prefers to call on class members in a random fashion, so that she can make sure they have completed their homework and are really listening in class. Joyce often interjects into her teaching what she considers to be information about how to be a good citizen. For example, she discourages students from speaking their native language at home and with friends, and she hosts elaborate celebrations around major U.S. holidays, such as Thanksgiving and George Washington's birthday. In addition to her regular bimonthly tests, she also gives short pop-quizzes. Joyce believes this is the only way she can really get the class members to work. Though a number of her students have asked to bring other family members to class, she has not allowed this unless they are fully registered for the course.

Bob R. teaches an ESL class in that same city, but in a different program. His classes are highly individualized, with students working at their own pace. Bob has developed a core of peer tutors—volunteers from his previous classes and the community at large—who assist him in his weekly classes. When students first start the program, he works with them to see what they know and what their motivation is for learning the English language. For example, he has one woman who would like to obtain a childcare position, whereas a second person just wants to communicate better with family members who have lived in the United States for a number of years. Based on their present knowledge level and their reasons for becoming involved in the program, he individualizes the curriculum as much as possible for each student, without losing sight of the basics that need to be learned. Bob has developed a number of learning packages over his three years of teaching that address the motivations most often expressed by his students (e.g., obtaining a job, communicating with one's children, shopping). The students work individually with Bob, the peer tutor, and/or in small groups as appropriate. Self-check tests are given as each module within a specific unit is completed. If students do not do well on the tests, they are asked to review the parts that they missed, usually with the help of the tutor. Bob has tried to make the classroom as comfortable as possible. He even convinced the director of the program to allow him to have a pot of hot water for coffee and tea. Bob has also encouraged his students to bring other family members to class, especially if the student appeared very timid and shy.

It is obvious that Joyce and Bob view adult learners very differently. Joyce's values are grounded in the mechanistic view of human beings, while Bob is more humanistic in his outlook. This is demonstrated through their teaching methods and the ways they have chosen to structure their classrooms. Joyce's class is highly structured, with specified group lessons planned for each session. She primarily uses lecture and the drill-and-practice method; she maintains control over the content and interaction of the class at all times. Bob, on the other hand, has structured his class primarily in an individualized mode, with the emphasis on student-directed learning. He uses a variety of methods, including one-to-one tutoring, small group interaction, and a variety of audiovisual materials and learning packages.

The actual content that Joyce and Bob teach is also quite different, though both cover the basic material for a sound ESL program. Joyce's content focuses primarily on learning spoken and written English, with a heavy emphasis on proper grammar and correct pronunciation. She also believes her class is a good place to help "Americanize" these people. Although Bob also stresses the basic concepts of the spoken and written English language, he develops his content in the context of the students' everyday lives. This is reflected in the individualized learning modules he has designed. He firmly believes that he should build on the specific needs and cultural background of each student.

In observing Joyce further in the classroom, it is noted that she sometimes becomes very frustrated, though she tries not to show it, with her students' progress. Though Joyce is a committed teacher, she has voiced her concerns at staff meetings about whether some of the students, especially the older ones, can really learn to speak and write the English language properly. She has had a firm belief throughout her teaching career that younger adult students are easier to teach. Joyce has also found that she derives greater enjoyment from teaching those students who really want to "Americanize" themselves. As Joyce says, it is difficult to teach an old dog new tricks.

In observing Bob, something quite different is seen. Bob is delighted when his students make even the smallest progress, and he works hard to enourage those who are having great difficulty. Bob believes all adults can learn, no matter what their age and background, if only they can tap into their needs and interests. Bob seems to teach to the strengths of his students, while Joyce appears to emphasize their deficiencies.

As illustrated by Joyce and Bob, what teachers believe about the nature of adults as learners may influence how they teach, what they teach, and the way they interact with their students. Areas of their value and belief systems that are most salient include their general views on the nature of human beings (Apps, 1979); whether they believe adults can learn, regardless of their age (Knowles, 1980; Kidd, 1973); and whether they should emphasize students' learning deficiencies or their strengths. In addition, teachers' values will reflect whether they will extend equal treatment to students regardless of their race, gender, ethnic origin, or creed (Scriven, 1982; Wilson, 1982).

The Multiple Responsibilities of Teachers of Adults

Teaching adults is rarely a full-time occupation. Rather, the role of teacher is usually submerged into a multiplicity of other roles and responsibilities (Darkenwald & Merriam, 1982; Scriven, 1982). For example, though Linda R., the director of continuing education for a small college located in an urban area, does some teaching as part of her job responsibilities, she spends most of her time on program planning and the administration of the division. For Linda, teaching maintains her "sanity," and thus she looks forward to the few hours a week when she can work directly with students in a formal class or workshop. She does a great deal of preparation for these classes and is a very enthusiastic and energetic instructor. However, even Linda, at times, is not what she considers to be fully prepared for class, especially at those times where her workload as director of continuing education is especially heavy, such as budget preparation time.

Linda has encountered, in her tenure as director of continuing education, three other types of teachers who have much less of a commitment to their role as teacher. The first type of teachers, who are usually members of the full-time faculty at the college, are indifferent to their role as teachers (Dill, 1982). These teachers understand that teaching is a part of their professional responsibility and thus are always prepared for class, but they would rather be doing research or working on a grant proposal. The attitude portrayed by these individuals is that teaching intrudes on their more important roles as scholars. Adult students really resent this type of instructor, and Linda has worked closely with department chairpersons, not always with success, to ensure that these individuals teach continuing education classes rarely, if at all. Linda always has a twinge of guilt when one of these teachers is continually assigned to her division for teaching, despite her requests to the contrary. Yet she knows that it is the policy of the college to use available in-house faculty first, prior to hiring adjunct teachers. This has been a dilemma for her, one for which she has not yet found a solution.

There is a second type of teacher, again usually a full-time college faculty member, whom Linda will not allow a second teaching assignment within the division. This type of teacher is openly hostile to adult students (Dill, 1982; Kidd, 1973). These teachers do not value their role as teachers of adults and make this abundantly clear to all parties involved. They may like teaching the traditional day students, but expect to be home by five o'clock each day, or earlier if possible. Needless to say, the adult students do not respond well to this type of teacher and usually either drop the class or become openly hostile themselves. Linda makes sure she thoroughly documents the behaviors these teachers exhibit to ensure they will not be assigned to an evening class again.

Linda has also observed, mostly with her part-time or adjunct instructors, a third type of teacher. This person, the manipulative type, values the role of teacher for the indirect benefits received (Dill, 1982; Kidd, 1973). These teachers like the extra money or the prestige they receive by being a part of the program. This second motivator, prestige, is especially seen in adjunct faculty who believe it increases their status in the professional community to be teaching college-level courses. These teachers, though not necessarily committed to their role as teachers of adults, may be excellent instructors, especially if they are concerned about their image and standing in the community. On the other hand, if they are just interested in the money and/or their image, this type of instructor may do just enough preparation to get by. The adult students may sense these instructors' major motivations for teaching and resent the fact that they are an "afterthought" in the whole process. Linda has had a difficult time working with the manipulative type of teacher. It has been especially hard at times to figure out whether to ask them to teach again for the division, especially as many of them have knowledge and skills that the full-time faculty at the college do not possess. It may also be hard to locate another adjunct instructor with the same background, especially in some of the high-demand areas, such as educational computing and special education.

Even concerned and committed teachers, as noted earlier, may have problems at times in carrying out their multiple responsibilities, especially if teaching is not a central role in their lives. For those teachers who are employed full-time in other jobs, their other tasks may get in the way of preparing for class or grading papers in a timely fashion. For a person whose primary responsibility is home and family, children get sick or a child may be having major difficulties with school, and thus the time needed to get one's teaching materials together just may not be available. Even committed teachers have to allocate their time and loyalties (Scriven, 1982) to various daily tasks, and the teaching role may not be of high priority at a particular moment in time.

Ethical Dilemmas in the Practice of Teaching Adults

This section focuses on how teachers practice their craft. The primary roles of teachers of adults, specifically those of content specialist and facilitator, and the ethical problems arising from these roles are discussed. In addition, the section highlights ethical dilemmas inherent in the design and management of the teaching situation. A challenge is then given to adult teachers to model ethical behavior as part of their teaching interactions.

Primary Roles of Teachers of Adults

Teachers of adults have two primary roles: to be content specialists and/or to be facilitators of the learning process (Knowles, 1980).

Content specialists believe their most important task is to impart knowledge. Facilitators, on the other hand, view themselves as enablers in the learning process (e.g., Apps, 1979; Knowles, 1980; Baumgarten, 1982). They wish to assist learners in becoming more responsible for their own learning. Each of these primary roles can pose ethical dilemmas in relation to how teachers function in these roles.

George C.'s situation provides an example of the dilemmas faced by teachers who function primarily as content experts. George, a technical training specialist, has just been asked to teach a three-week short course on interpersonal skills to new, entry-level supervisory personnel. He does not really know the subject matter very well, nor does he have the time to prepare to teach the course. Also, George is not really interested in the course content, though he has taught it once before. He is not a firm believer "in all of this communications stuff" anyway—supervisors just need to be tough-minded to be good. He is tempted just to tell his boss that he will not be able to do it, but he knows this decision will not be looked upon favorably by his supervisor or his fellow trainers, as one of them will then have to do the program; thus George decides to do the program himself. After all, he can use his old notes from three years ago, and since this interpersonal skills training is just the "fluffy-stuff" anyway, he can use a lot of structured experiences. George vaguely remembers that the reaction to these exercises was not too good with the prior group, but perhaps this group will be different.

George's actions demonstrate three primary ethical questions faced by content specialists:

1. Should teachers agree to teach subject matter with which they are for the most part unfamiliar? If yes, should they pretend to know this content better than they actually do so that the learners believe they are "getting their money's worth" (Wilson, 1982)?
2. Should teachers present content that they have not updated in a number of years, especially when they know the content really should be updated (Scriven, 1982)?
3. Should teachers with prejudicial beliefs about a specific content area teach that particular subject? If yes, should they explain their biases upfront to the learners (Kidd, 1973)?

Teachers who choose to be primarily facilitators of the learning process also may have to deal with a number of ethical dilemmas.

The situation of Sharon J. provides us with some examples of these dilemmas. Sharon is a community college instructor of English. She strongly believes that one of her major goals as a teacher is to help her students become more self-directed in their learning. She has used learning contracts as one of her teaching strategies with mixed results. Sharon has also tried to foster collaborative learning between and among her students and herself, and thus has viewed herself primarily as a catalyst in the learning process. Some of the students have resented her classroom methods, protesting vehemently that they have paid good money to be taught American literature and she was not doing her job as a teacher. Sharon has often thought she should abandon this way of teaching and go back to the traditional style of the lecture and test format, but a good percentage of the students have really responded favorably to her classes and appear to have learned a great deal. Unfortunately, her division chair has also been dropping some not-so-subtle hints that she is overdoing it in the area of student freedom and choice.

A number of ethical principles and values are at issue in Sharon's situation. Three primary sets of questions that can be raised are:

1. If teachers choose their primary role to be that of facilitator, how can they ensure that the learners really do become more responsible for their own learning (Apps, 1979)? How do teachers know if students are following their course requirements of self-directedness just to get through the course, or whether those students have really developed some new knowledge, skills, and/or attitudes that could assist them in being more self-directed in their learning?
2. Should teachers foster self-directed learning skills at the expense of fulfilling specified learning outcomes (Singarella & Sork, 1983)? If teachers focus on learners taking more responsibility for their own learning, might they in reality be abdicating their role as instructors?
3. Can teachers of adults be only catalysts in the learning process or do the catalytic actions have consequences themselves and, thus, influence the learners' behavior and actions (Kidd, 1973)?

The Design and Management of the Teaching Situation

The process of teaching involves conducting learner needs assessments, developing and using learning objectives, applying instructional methods and techniques, and evaluating learners' progress and achievement. A number of ethical issues and problems can arise in the implementation of this process (Scriven, 1982). The following example illustrates some of the primary ethical questions that can be raised when designing and managing the teaching process.

Wendy P., a faculty member with a School of Nursing, often serves as an instructor for the continuing education division of her school. She teaches both short courses and workshops to R.N. nurses who work in area hospitals and other health care facilities. Wendy usually develops her own course materials, but she has also used learning modules and activities, selected by other faculty members in her school, that have been prepackaged by outside consultants.

In her teaching Wendy tries to match what she is teaching to the learning needs of her students. This has not always been possible, especially with the "canned programs" she is at times expected to use. She has often wondered how the choice was made to buy some of these instructional packages. Though the programs are usually well designed, they do not seem to fit any expressed learning needs she has heard of. This raises the issue of whether or not prestructured programs, especially those that are "canned," should be used without matching the learning objectives and activities to the needs of the learners (Clement, Pinto, & Walker, 1978). Should instructional needs assessment be a prerequisite to teaching adults? If so, from whose perspective should the needs assessment be undertaken: the learners, the organization, and/or society (Apps, 1979; Singarella & Sork, 1983)?

Prior to teaching most of her classes or workshops, Wendy has collected preassessment data. This has helped her to better plan her instruction and the instructional evaluation process. Lately, the director of the program has been pressuring Wendy to report this data back to her for the purpose of overall program evaluation. Wendy really does not want to do this, since she believes it would be a violation of the learner's confidentiality, especially as she has told her students that the data would be used for class purposes only. The question then arises as to who owns the needs assessment data. Is it violating the students' right to privacy to give this type of data to others without prior permission (Clement et al., 1978; Davies, 1981)? If the data are released, who should be allowed to examine them—other instructors in the school, the director, or perhaps even work supervisors? This issue is not unlike concerns raised by Brookfield in Chapter 6.

Wendy has used learning objectives as part of her teaching. Just recently, through her own graduate studies, she has come to realize that there is an implicit assumption in setting forth the objectives before the learning activities take place. The assumption is that learning outcomes should be known by the teacher (Apps, 1979). Is this always desirable, and, if not, how does a teacher judge when and when not to use learning objectives? When it is judged appropriate to use learning objectives, from whose point of view should they be written: the learners', the teacher's, and/or the organization's (Tom, 1984; Houle, 1972)?

There has also been an expectation that all learning objectives should be stated in behavioral terms, and Wendy has met this expectation without ever questioning the practice. Again, through her own further studies, she has come to understand that not all learning can be measured in behavioral terms. While there are certain kinds of learning, such as skill building, that are facilitated by behavioral objectives, the use of behavioral objectives for other types of learning, such as developing analytic abilities and sensitivity, may actually inhibit the learning process (Knowles, 1980). This raises the question of what the important outcomes are for learning situations. Is only learning that can be quantified and measured important, or are less tangible learning outcomes also valued (Houle, 1972)? Who should be responsible for making these kinds of value judgments about "the product" of the teaching situation?

As stated earlier, teachers tend to choose instructional methods and techniques that relate to their own belief systems about the nature of human beings and adults as learners. Wendy, like Bob (the ESL instructor mentioned earlier), is more humanistic in her teaching style. She views her students as individuals and as people with prior knowledge and experience. Thus Wendy chooses techniques that allow her students to express their values and points of view, such as small group discussions and class consultation teams.

Wendy has noticed two specific practices of other instructors who teach for the division that she would like to see changed. The first is exemplified by the teacher who uses a wide variety of techniques and is highly entertaining, yet never seems to address the subject matter. Should these teachers, no matter how good they are at their craft, be allowed to continue teaching when they obviously are not helping their students learn the needed material (Wilson, 1982)? And by whose standards should these judgments be made?

The second type of practice that concerns Wendy is seen in the teacher who knows the subject matter but really does not have a useful repertoire of teaching methods and techniques. The typical comment heard from participants after this type of teacher conducts a short course is that the individual knew the material, but the class time was very disorganized and at times boring. Should these teachers be required to improve their instructional practice prior to being allowed to teach again in the continuing education division? If so, how should acceptable instructional practice be judged, and by whom?

Wendy firmly believes the instructional evaluation policies and procedures should be fair and clearly explained at the beginning of the instructional program (Scriven, 1982). As noted earlier, she has often used the pre- and posttest form of assessment and evaluation. Along with the assessment data she has collected, the director of the continuing education division would also like to have the evaluation data reported to her. Again, Wendy does not want to do this, since she believes it violates the privacy of the individual student. Thus the same questions apply here as for the needs assessment data. Is it violating the students' right to confidentiality and privacy to share this type of data with others without prior permission (Clement et al., 1978; Singarella & Sork, 1983)? If the data are to be released, who should be allowed to utilize the results?

Wendy has also observed that cheating and plagiarism have been handled in an inconsistent way in the division. She has tried to develop, with two other colleagues, a division policy for handling these problems but has met with resistance from the director and some of the other instructors. Wendy herself believes such violations should be handled in an objective and rational manner, with consistent punishments. Some of her colleagues, on the other hand, believe each case should be treated individually within the context of a particular situation. Should the consequences for such actions (e.g., cheating) be based on universal rules and expectations? If so, should the punishments be the same for all or be applied on an individual basis (Strike & Soltis, 1985)?

In doing the evaluation, Wendy has observed that some teachers make the learners feel badly about their work or even bully some students to try to get them to do better (Tom, 1984). She shared these observations at a division faculty retreat, and some lively discussions have ensued. How should teachers tell students they are doing poor work? When and where is the best time to do this, especially for those learning activities that are of short duration and for which no individual time with the learner is built into the activity? How should teachers react when learners respond that it is the teacher's instruction that is the problem and not the learner's poor progress or work?

Modeling Ethical Behavior in Teaching

Teachers of adults should model ethical behavior as a regular part of their teaching interaction (McGovern, 1985). Modeling ethical behavior requires all participants in the learning activity, teachers and students alike, to be willing to question what is being taught and how the subject matter is being addressed. This could include questioning of the content itself in terms of ethical issues related specifically to that content, such as whether the material being reviewed is biased in terms of its source. In addition, when discussing the applications of that content to real-life situations, part of that discussion could be structured to ensure that questions of an ethical nature are raised. For example, in learning how to do an educational needs assessment, not only should students review and discuss the various models and techniques of needs analysis, but they should also focus on the ethical questions and issues that surface as part of most needs assessment processes. Such questions as who is qualified to define the needs of any given population, and what criteria should be used in determining which needs should be given top priority, are not only procedural questions; they are questions related to the values and beliefs of those conducting the needs assessment.

Modeling ethical behavior as part of the teaching process could be done in a number of ways, from integrating this questioning process throughout the learning activity to the scheduling of a specific time slot for discussing the ethical issues and problems related to the content at hand. Some brief illustrations of how this could be accomplished in different types of adult teaching situations are outlined below.

ESL Classes. Teachers could help students examine which of the cultural norms and standards of the host country would be appropriate for individual students to adopt. They could also help students examine the issue of when the English language should be used in their lives, versus when it would be better to communicate in their native language. This type of self-examination and questioning could be an integrated part of the regular classroom activity.

College-Level Learning. Adult students should be encouraged to be critical thinkers as part of all regular classes. This should involve helping students learn how to question what they are taught and the process upon which the knowledge base was built. Activities like small group discussions and formal class debates could be used to facilitate this type of activity.

Training Activities in Business and Industry. Trainers could design their training programs to address both the practical day-to-day problems confronting the organization as well as having participants question the rightness and wrongness of the ways chosen to deal with those problems. This is especially important in management-level training, where the content often focuses on how to motivate, direct, and evaluate employees. This could be done as part of a formal group training activity and/or be integrated into the "coaching behavior" of supervisors as they work one-to-one with their subordinates.

Continuing Professional Education. More and more professional groups are hosting special seminars and workshops on ethics as they relate to the practice of a specific profession. This type of activity should continue to be encouraged, in addition to integrating the ethical questions related to professional practice into other types of content-specific offerings, such as formal college-level courses or professional seminars.

One of the keys to this modeling of ethical behavior is the teacher's willingness to encourage learners to question, from an ethical perspective, the content and the relationship of that content to practice. This may be easier said than done. Teachers may have to help students learn how to raise and then respond to these kinds of questions. In addition, teachers must be willing to engage in this type of questioning as part of their practice of teaching. This includes being continually able to question both what and how they are teaching. This is difficult for some teachers, especially if they believe that their role as teacher is one of imparting knowledge as truths. It is a learned skill to model ethical behavior in teaching, a skill that must be practiced and used as an integral component of one's teaching behavior. Teachers must also believe that the modeling of ethical behavior is a necessary and legitimate part of their practice of teaching.

Conclusion

As noted in the numerous examples given in the chapter, ethical dilemmas, or the question of rightness and wrongness and good and bad, are inevitable when teaching adults. Discussed in-depth were the ethical questions related to the personal belief systems of teachers about the nature of adults as learners, ethical issues found in the multiple responsibilities that teachers of adults have, and ethical dilemmas teachers face in the practice of their craft. It was suggested that it is important for teachers of adults to model ethical behavior in their teaching activities. This requires that teachers and students be willing to question what is being taught and how the subject matter is being addressed. This modeling of ethical behavior can be done in a number of ways, from integrating this questioning process throughout the learning activity to the scheduling of a specific time slot for discussing the ethical issues and problems related to the content at hand.

References

Apps, J. (1979). *Problems in continuing education*. New York: McGraw-Hill.

Baumgarten, E. (1982). Ethics in the academic profession: A Socratic view. *Journal of Higher Education, 53*, 282–295.

Clement, R., Pinto, R., & Walker, J. (1978). Unethical and improper behavior by training and development professionals. *Training and Development Journal, 32*(12), 10–12.

Darkenwald, G. G., & Merriam, S. B. (1982). *Adult education: Foundations of practice*. New York: Harper & Row.

Davies, I. (1981). *Instructional technique*. New York: McGraw-Hill, pp. 231–234.

Dill, D. D. (1982). The structure of the academic profession: Towards a definition of ethical issues. *Journal of Higher Education, 53*(5), 255–267.

Houle, C. O. (1972). *The design of education*. San Francisco: Jossey-Bass.

Kidd, J. R. (1973). *How adults learn*. New York: Association Press.

Knowles, M. S. (1980). *The modern practice of adult education* (rev. ed.). New York: Association Press.

McGovern, T. (1985). Personal interview.

Scriven, M. (1982). Professional ethics. *Journal of Higher Education, 53,* 307–317.

Singarella, T. A., & Sork, T. J. (1983). Questions of values and conduct: Ethical issues for adult education. *Adult Education Quarterly, 33,* 244–251.

Strike, K. A., & Soltis, J. F. (1985). *The ethics of teaching.* New York: Teachers College Press.

Tom, K. (1984). *Teaching as a moral craft.* New York: Longman.

Wilson, K. E. (1982). Power, pretense, piggybacking: Some ethical issues in teaching. *Journal of Higher Education, 53,* 268–281.

CHAPTER EIGHT

Educational Advising and Brokering: The Ethics of Choice

MICHAEL J. DAY

ALTHOUGH often not the apparent goal of a large number of adult education undertakings, choice may indeed develop as a major accomplishment once a learning activity is completed. In this chapter, an attempt will be made to present "choice" as an outcome in adult education activities that, though certainly desirable, is laden with consequences and that raises certain ethical issues for the adult educator. These observations will address how choice-related ethical issues pertain specifically to the role of educational broker, though much of what is written seems also to apply to teachers, trainers, administrators, and other facilitators of adult education programs.

This chapter will first consider what is meant by *choice* and describe various associations we have with the idea of choice. Then a few works from popular literature and film will be presented to illustrate the darker side of learning experiences that yield an increase in choice and options. Against this backdrop some basic functions of the educational broker will be identified, and a number of ethical issues pertaining to the role of broker will be presented. The final section will discuss a few ways educational brokers may address the consequences of choice with their clients.

118

Choice

Definition and Associations

What is meant by *choice?* The second college edition of the *American Heritage Dictionary* (1985) defines *choice* as "The power, right, or liberty to choose; option. . . . Choice implies broadly the freedom of choosing from a set of persons or things." As noted earlier, this freedom entails a certain capacity to choose for oneself from a set of possible alternatives. It is assumed, then, that the individual is not merely a being whose fate rests either with the gods or with behavioral engineers. Choice may indeed be nothing more than a figment of one's imagination, fabricated, perhaps, to make one's existence more lofty and bearable; if so, it is a mistaken belief shared by a very large number of people. Even if one's sense of choice is marked more by desire than by fact, the sensation of choice or the desire to have choice is indeed a common experience.

When associated with adult education, choice suggests a number of linkages. In adult education writings choice has been linked to themes such as independence, empowerment, and voluntary participation. In the work of Allen Tough (1971, 1982), for example, emphasis is placed on the realization that adults do control and often direct the path of changes in their lives, including changes that necessitate new learning. Independence of thought as a goal of adult education is a theme developed repeatedly in the writings of "liberal" adult educators such as Everett Dean Martin (1926), Robert Hutchins (Merriam, 1984; Moreland & Goldenstein, 1985), and Mortimer Adler (Gross, 1982).

This same independence theme—dressed as empowerment— applied to bringing about societal change is woven throughout the work of Paulo Freire (1970, 1973, 1985). Freire implies that choice is linked to a more critical approach to life, one which recognizes that the individual is not only the custodian of culture but the maker of culture. The choice-as-empowerment theme is visible as well in the work and writings of scores of other socially conscious adult educators, such as Jane Addams (1910) and Myles Horton (Adams, 1975). And in numerous program development manuals and treatises on self-directed learning, such as those authored by Malcolm Knowles (1975, 1980, 1985), the association of choice with increased selections in educational offerings and with increased options in the design, implementation, and ownership of adult education activities is made.

A hallmark of the legacy of the adult education movement in the United States and elsewhere is the voluntary nature of this form of education. It was commonly believed that the adult learner chooses, without compulsion, to attend a lecture, read a particular book, or stroll the halls of a particular museum. Today, many adults find themselves participating in educational programs not by choice but by force, that is, they find themselves compelled to participate due to the courts, recertification requirements, job stipulations, and the like. Though much of this is to be expected in a society fixated on protecting the interest of business and government and, at times, the interest of the general citizen, it is still sad to witness the dismantling of the bequest of voluntary learning. As noted a few years ago in the Report of the AEA Task Force on Voluntary Learning:

> Franklin, Thoreau and numerous others have left us a noble legacy. They demonstrated that the totality of life, not merely its parody in institutions, is educative; institutions have no monopoly on learning. Mandatory continuing education negates this legacy. We soon forget that learning is much more than the program which we are coerced to attend. We forget that learning is voluntary; we have neither the freedom to choose what we wish to learn nor the opportunity to reject what we do not wish to learn. (Day, 1980, p. 5)

The Consequences of Choice

The conscious facilitation of choice may then appear as both a noble and proper goal for the organization of adult education experiences. But as presented here, I am not advocating any naive boosterism of choice that does not also address its consequences. It is primarily through a discussion of the consequences of choice that certain ethical issues arise.

To view the consequences of choice, one need not be conversant with the literature addressed to the adult educator. Indeed, as Brockett suggests in Chapter 1 of this volume, relatively little has been written about ethics in the adult education literature. Instead, one is encouraged to consider literature and film. Four works come immediately to mind: *Oedipus Rex, Martin Eden, Pygmalion,* and *Educating Rita.* Each will be briefly discussed.

Oedipus Rex. The story of Oedipus depicted in Sophocles' tragic *Oedipus Rex,* written in ca. 430 B.C., tells of a man's attempt to question and resist fate. Oedipus believed that his destiny was not completely controlled by the gods. Therefore, when told by a prophet of Apollo, one of the Greek gods, that he would kill his father and marry his mother, the youthful Oedipus flees his home and vows never again to see his parents. Oedipus exercised what he considered to be choice. Those familiar with the story of Oedipus might recall the strange circumstances that both precede and follow this decision. After fleeing his home Oedipus travels to Thebes. During his travels he quarrels with an old man and kills him—the man is Laius, King of Thebes, Oedipus' father. Once in Thebes he battles wits with the infamous Sphinx, which held the city hostage. Defeating the Sphinx, Oedipus is hailed as the savior of Thebes and given the hand of the widowed Queen Jocasta—his real mother. The prophesy had been fulfilled.

As the play continues, Oedipus' new home is troubled once more, this time by a terrible plague. Oedipus is told, again through prophesy, that to end the disease he must avenge the death of Laius. So Oedipus begins slowly to unravel the truth behind Laius' death. In a climactic moment Jocasta realizes what all the gathered evidence is indicating and pleads with Oedipus to stop his search, "For God's love, let us have no more questioning! Is your life nothing to you? My own is pain enough for me to bear" (*Oedipus Rex*, in Witt, Brown, Dunbar, Tirro, & Witt, 1980, p. 59). But Oedipus continues his search and eventually realizes that the hand that killed Laius was his own.

Up to this point, Oedipus has made a number of decisions in his attempt to stifle fate, yet one might convincingly argue that choice for Oedipus was truly nothing more than an illusion. But Oedipus' belief in the idea of choice was not unfounded. In the final moments of the play, after blinding himself with brooches from the gown of his mother, Oedipus speaks out:

> Apollo. Apollo. Dear
> Children, the god was Apollo.
> He brought my sick, sick fate upon me.
> But the blinding hand was my own!
> How could I bear to see
> When all my sight was horror everywhere?
> (*Oedipus Rex*, in Witt et al., 1980, p. 63)

"But the blinding hand was my own!" Oedipus is not to be robbed of his belief in choice, nor of control over his destiny. The consequence of his choice is indeed terrible. But the principle of critical free will to choose remains. For similar illustrations of the dangers imposed upon those who, like Oedipus, cherish the belief that they are decision-making beings, one need only observe the adult education practice of Myles Horton and Paulo Freire.

Martin Eden. The eventual consequence of Martin Eden's bout with choice is suicide. *Martin Eden*, a very pertinent novel by Jack London, questions the myth that creativity, learning, hard work, discipline, and active inquiry lead to either self-actualization or happiness. The story reminds one that what results from a commitment to education and self-knowledge may as likely be despair as joy.

   Martin Eden is the story of a young, rough, seafaring, working-class man who critically evaluates his life and decides to better it. Part of the impetus for this transformation is a young woman named Ruth, whom Martin meets and falls in love with rather early in the story. Ruth represents a class well above Martin's, a class Martin soon aspires to join. Initially, Martin is content to be tutored by Ruth in reading, writing, and manners. Through hours, weeks, and months of disciplined study, Martin rapidly develops and refines both his thinking and writing skills. He soon begins to interpret literature for himself; this interpretation is much more critical than either Ruth's or that of her middle-class friends. During this time Martin also begins to write, and soon, writing becomes his passion.

   Much of the novel then focuses on Martin's frustration as he attempts to have his writing published. Finally, after four years of emotional and economic struggles, years marked by humiliating rejection of both his writings and his class, Martin achieves success. He becomes recognized as a writer of major worth and is supported handsomely for his efforts. But success for Martin Eden was not without its toll. While he no longer sensed a connection to the values of the working class, he could not adopt the values of an upper class. All Martin wanted from himself and from his world was the best one's potential could produce. "I want the best of every man and woman I meet" (London, 1909, p. 288). He wanted to be around intelligent and tolerant people who shared his passion for learning. Instead, the acquisition of material goods, not knowledge and understanding, had become the general quest of those around him, regardless of class. At the height of his success Martin found little consolation in either people or his work. He once more yearned for the sea. And it was the sea that finally gave him lasting comfort:

> Down, down, he swam till his arms and legs grew tired and hardly moved. He knew that he was deep. The pressure on his ear-drums was a pain, and there was a buzzing in his head. His endurance was faltering, but he compelled his arms and legs to drive him deeper until his will snapped and the air drove from his lungs in a great explosive rush. The bubbles rubbed and bounded like tiny balloons against his cheeks and eyes as they took their upward flight. Then came pain and strangulation. This hurt was not death, was the thought that oscillated through his reeling consciousness. Death did not hurt. It was life, the pangs of life, this awful, suffocating feeling; it was the last blow life could deal him. (London, 1909, p. 482)

Martin Eden had embarked upon an education that lifted him from the happy-go-lucky naivete of his youth and then rested him upon the ocean's floor. Does this mean, then, that blame for Martin's final decision can be placed on Ruth and those involved in Martin's education? Did they educate poorly or too well? What the story of Martin Eden does bring to the fore is that learning has consequences, most of which an educator with the best of intentions has little final control over. It also quite clearly suggests for me that learners be encouraged to analyze some of the possible consequences of the decisions they might make prior to committing themselves, realizing, of course, that not to change is also a choice. In the next two illustrations the consequences of choice are neither as dire nor as final as for Martin Eden.

Pygmalion and *Educating Rita.* These two works will be presented together because they both address a similar theme: working-class woman elevates herself through education. The two plays, *Pygmalion* by George Bernard Shaw and *Educating Rita* by Willy Russell, are relatively optimistic where the educations of the two leading characters—Eliza Doolittle and Rita—are concerned, though each character experiences moments of doubt and despair. In the end, however, each of these characters manages to resolve the dilemmas brought about by her new learning. Both *Pygmalion* and *Educating Rita* can, in fact, be read or viewed as odes to the importance of learning opportunities that enhance the possibility of choice.

Eliza Doolittle, in *Pygmalion,* is a poor flower girl who becomes the object of a bet between a phonetics scholar, Henry Higgins, and a kindly gentleman who finances the undertaking, Colonel Pickering. Eliza dreams of becoming a "lady" and someday working in a fine flower shop. She accepts an invitation from both Higgins and Pickering to participate in a learning experience, the goal of which is to teach her to behave and, especially, speak as a lady; Higgins bets Pickering that in six months he can take Eliza to Buckingham Palace and pass her off as a lady. Eliza agrees to Higgins's stipulations that she come live with him and his housekeeper, work extremely hard, and obey his every request as a teacher.

Eliza does win Higgins's bet for him but in the process experiences more than she had bargained for. As with Martin Eden, and later Rita, Eliza's new education alienates her from many of the values of her own class. The six months spent studying and living with Higgins dramatically change her life. Once her lessons are over, the bet won, Eliza cannot imagine returning to the streets, yet where is she to go? In a dramatic moment she confronts Higgins with the question, "What's to become of me?" (Shaw, 1916/1983, p. 100). She admirably illustrates the often painful process of choice and change.

By the end of the play, Eliza has nearly completed her transformation. What began for her as lessons in phonetics has ended in new ideas regarding her relationship to her world. She now views herself as a conscious, decision-making being and possesses the strength of independent judgment. She informs Higgins that she is unsure of her next step. Perhaps she will come back to him, perhaps not; she might marry another gentleman, or find employment in a flower store, or teach phonetics herself. But whatever decision is made, she will be the one who makes it.

The background for the story of Rita is quite similar to those of Eliza and Martin. Once more the reader is presented with a youthful member of the working class who desires to better her lot in life. Rita, a 26-year-old hairdresser, enrolls in a literary criticism course through the British Open University. Her assigned tutor is a rather burned-out poet and lecturer named Frank. Like Eliza's and Martin's, Rita's venture into education is viewed by family and friends with suspicion; her husband and father think she should begin having a family instead.

What begins as a critique of literature for Rita soon becomes an examination of her life and future. As the relationship with her tutor matures, the relationship with her husband disintegrates;

they finally separate. Rita endures and is strengthened by the discipline, pain, and doubt of her education. And toward the end of the play, after taking the course examination, she speaks in support of the link between choice and education.

> RITA: You think you gave me nothing; did nothing for me. You think I just ended up with a load of quotes an' empty phrases; an' I did. But that wasn't your doin. . . . I wanted it all so much that I didn't want it to be questioned. I told y' I was stupid. . . . (After a pause) I sat lookin' at the question [Suggest ways in which one might cope with some of the staging difficulties in a production of *Peer Gynt*], an' thinkin' about it all. Then I picked up me pen an' started.
>
> FRANK: And you wrote, "Do it on the radio"?
>
> RITA: I could have done. An' you'd have been proud of me if I'd done that and rushed back to tell you—wouldn't y'? But I chose not to. I had a choice. I did the exam. . . . An' it might be worthless in the end. But I had a choice. I chose, me. Because of what you'd given me I had a choice. (Russell, 1981, pp. 50–51)

From this brief allegorical excursion into the effects of specific learning activities on the lives of a few fictional characters emerge some themes that should be kept in mind when considering ethical issues surrounding choice as an educational outcome:

1. We are decision-making beings and are ultimately responsible for the decisions we make
2. Our participation in a learning activity cannot be viewed in isolation from the wholeness of our lives, that is, what we learn affects what we feel and what we do
3. The idea of increased choices and options may indeed serve as a powerful motivator for participation in learning activities
4. The results of our learning experiences may as likely lead to discontent as to a state of well-being
5. Generally speaking, learning produces consequences

The links between education, choice, and consequence are important. Throughout the previous illustrations, education, resulting in and supporting increased choices, is strongly associated with both freedom and consequences. It is now suggested that those responsible for adult education view their roles as educators in like manner. The idea of providing for choice and addressing its consequences is an important task for all adult educators. It is especially important for the educational broker.

Educational Brokers and Personal Choice

What is an educational broker? An educational broker acts as an agent, or instrument, for uniting individuals with learning opportunities. They serve a community primarily through linkages and advocacy. The major clients of these specific brokers are those who desire to learn. Through such brokers, clients are linked to various available learning opportunities. As advocates, brokers assist their clients in numerous ways to bring about desired learning outcomes. According to Heffernan (1981, p. 25), core brokering functions should enable individuals to:

1. Define goals for their personal and working lives
2. Set objectives for further education and training
3. Select learning experiences to attain competencies and certification
4. Gain access to the appropriate learning opportunities

Educational brokers, then, are both a resource and an ally. Unlike general teachers or administrators of adult education, who often must balance their concern for the adult learner with such other responsibilities as the dissemination of information or program development and marketing, the brokers' *raison d'être* is the adult learner (Day, 1985). Working closely with their clients, brokers attempt to fuse learning objectives with available resources. Together with their clients they select what seem to be the most appropriate learning experiences for desired objectives. At times brokers are called upon to take an active part in the linkage process between resource and client—sometimes making a few calls for the client to assess the likely fit between resource and objective, sometimes assisting the client with the completion of forms, and sometimes accompanying the anxious client to an initial meeting with his or her learning resource.

Illustration

In such a clearly client-centered, helping role, what are some of the ethical issues that may surface? In considering these issues it may be useful to utilize the following illustration.

John is a 26-year-old single parent. He has a high school education and has been employed at a local railroad tie plant since leaving high school. But a shoulder problem caused by a severe skiing accident a year ago has hindered his performance on the job. It has been suggested to John that he consider other forms of employment, but he continues to work at the plant, though, at times, with much discomfort. John married shortly after high school. He has a son, now 6 years old; his wife deserted them both three years ago. John's parents live nearby, and he continues to receive a great deal of emotional and economic support from them. The reason, or trigger, for his visiting the educational broker is a rumor that the plant may be relocating to another state; thus John may lose his job.

The journey to the learning center to meet with the broker was not undertaken without a great deal of trepidation. John's high school experience left him with many doubts about his learning ability. But the broker soon assured John that he had little to fear. John's feeling of dread was soon replaced by a sense of excitement over finding someone who appeared to understand his educational history and who was neither shocked nor disappointed by his performance. Together John and his learning broker examined career interests and options as well as general interests and concerns. Based on meetings with the broker, John decided to register for an introductory class in accounting at the local community college. It seems that John had always enjoyed working with numbers but was not aware of the many careers that involve their manipulation. Because John felt rather in awe of the community college, his broker accompanied him to the admissions office, introduced him to a few of the people he would visit with later, toured the campus with him, and helped him complete the necessary paperwork. John's course in accounting was to meet two evenings a week, allowing him to continue at his current job. At the end of his course, he and his education broker planned to meet again to evaluate the accounting experience and explore further options.

Ethical Issues

In an encounter such as that described above, what ethical issues arise? What are acceptable and unacceptable principles of "right" practice for the educational broker? Certainly any listing of such principles would include the following:

1. *Respect for the client*—respect for the client's history, concerns and wishes, future goals, and privacy
2. *Familiarity with resources*—having a strong sense of the re-

sources available, individual as well as institutional, regional as well as local

3. *Competence at working with assessment tools*—which might include tools in areas such as career, aptitude, and learning style preferences

4. *Willingness to address the client's educational fears and familiarity with techniques to address these fears*—dealing with the scars of past educational experiences

5. *Setting realistic objectives*—keeping in mind some long-term desires but dealing with short-term goals

6. *Acting as a liaison between the learning resource and the client*—providing nonthreatening bridges between the learner and resource and being willing and available to assist in the process of initiating a learning experience

But the ethical issue that probably takes precedence over all the others and the one that may commonly be neglected—one already hinted at throughout this discussion—is the one that pertains to dealing with the consequences of the choices considered. Should brokers encourage their clients to address the consequences of the choices they may make? I certainly believe so. How, then, do brokers address the issue of consequence?

Addressing the Consequences of Choice

Certainly the easiest way to address the consequences of choice is to encourage clients to discuss what the results of their current decisions are. Brokers may begin by looking at the general consequences of the numerous actions taken by their clients each day. They might, for example, suggest that clients keep a daily log of the decisions they make, the actions that follow these decisions, and the consequences that follow the actions. Having clients understand the results of choices made, or not made, in their daily lives may facilitate the projection of consequences for future choices.

Once clients are familiar with the patterns of the actions arising from the decisions they make, they may more realistically look at what new decisions may portend for the future. If, for example, John senses that his decision to watch four hours of TV each weekday evening is made more from habit than from need or desire, then he may find some comfort in a decision to replace some TV-watching time with class time. And if, given the choice between working in a group or working alone, John consistently opts for working alone, then he will quite likely wish to find out whether studying initially through some form of individualized instruction is available at the college.

Another useful and simple tool educational brokers can use when discussing consequences of choice with clients is one suggested by Howard McClusky's margin theory. Margin is

> a function of the relationship of Load to Power. In simplest terms Margin is surplus Power. It is the Power available to a person over and beyond that required to handle his Load. By Load we mean the demands made on a person by self and society. By Power we mean the resources, i.e. abilities, possessions, positions, allies, etc., which a person can command in coping with Load. (McClusky, 1970, p. 82)

Day & James (1984) have noted that if adult educators are to be more effective in helping adult learners (and this is especially the case in the emerging role of the educational broker), it is imperative that these educators communicate that learning normally involves such factors as some restructuring of commitments and responsibilities as well as various societal and personal expectations and pressures—collectively viewed as adult learners' margin.

Brokers might encourage their clients to identify components of margin—sources of load and power—and to observe the often delicate balance between the two in their lives. Many individuals, quite unconsciously, make subtle adjustments to their margin daily. John, for example, made an adjustment to his margin when he decided to use some of his free time (time spent watching TV) to attend classes; in the future he will need to find additional time to deal with the other demands of classroom study. The resource of time serves to counter the additional load of returning to school. But John's time is not his only resource or source of power. Emotional and financial support from his parents are major resources, as is income from his job. Components of load would include the bills he must continue to pay and certainly his responsibilities as a father. Also, a major initial source of load for John was his fear of school and his negative view of his ability to learn. But that, with the assistance of the broker, has already been minimized.

What the concept of margin, as a tool, provides brokers is a medium for describing to clients the normal consequences of any decision they make. Deciding to initiate a learning experience has consequences and must alter in some way the clients' existing margin. A learning endeavor will make certain demands on clients, demands they should be prepared to address through some re-alignment of existing resources or utilization of new resources. Again, brokers are actively engaging their clients in an analysis of the consequences of the choices they consider.

Conclusion

Any examination of the principles that constitute ethical norms for the practice of adult education might begin with a consideration of some of the concerns that adults commonly evince when they involve themselves in an organized learning activity. The most apparent concern quite likely centers around the content of the activity, though as observers such as Houle (1961), Boshier (1977), and Boshier and Collins (1985) have suggested, this apparent interest may mask other, more immediate matters, such as a quest for companionship, a sense of civic responsibility, or an occupational mandate. But there are frequently other concerns. Repeatedly, adult learners desire to be treated as adults—treated with respect, with dignity, and as capable of directing their own learning (Knowles, 1975, 1980, 1985; Tough, 1971, 1982)—and treated as critically knowledgeable problem solvers (Freire, 1970, 1973, 1985). And, quite possibly, a good number of adult learners hope that the activity will somehow expand their options and provide a suitable foundation for continuing inquiries on their own; in other words, provide them with choice. Of the concerns just listed, it is the last—choice—that may be the most significant personal achievement in any learning activity.

If those involved in adult education value the idea of choice, then the previous discussion should have some relevance. It is not enough to increase the options of adult learners; adult educators must also encourage adult learners to address critically the consequences of the choices made. This is especially true for those whose occupation is that of educational broker. For these individuals, dealing with and providing choice options for adult learners is a major responsibility.

References

Adams, F. (1975). *Unearthing seeds of fire: The idea of Highlander.* Winston-Salem, NC: Blair.

Addams, J. (1910). *Twenty years at Hull-House.* New York: Phillips.

American heritage dictionary (Second College Edition). (1985). Boston: Houghton-Mifflin.

Boshier, R. (1977). Motivational orientations re-visited: Life-space motives and the education participation scale. *Adult Education, 27*(2), 89–115.

Boshier, R., & Collins, J. B. (1985). The Houle typology after twenty-two years: A large-scale empirical test. *Adult Education Quarterly, 35*(3), 113–130.

Day, M. (1980). On behalf of voluntary adult education. In T. W. Heaney (Ed.), *Task force report: AEA task force on voluntary learning* (pp. 5–6). Chicago: AEA Task Force.

Day, M. (1985). The educational broker: An emerging role for adult educators. In G. J. Conti & R. A. Fellenz (Eds.), *Dialogue on issues of lifelong learning in a democratic society* (pp. 89–92). College Station: Texas A&M University.

Day, M., & James, J. (1984). Margin and the adult learner. *MPAEA Journal of Adult Education, 13*(1), 1–6.

Freire, P. (1970). *Pedagogy of the oppressed.* New York: Seabury.

Freire, P. (1973). *Education for critical consciousness.* New York: Seabury.

Freire, P. (1985). *The politics of education: Culture, power, and liberation.* South Hadley, MA: Bergin & Garvey.

Gross, R. (Ed.). (1982). *Invitation to lifelong learning.* Chicago: Follett.

Heffernan, J. M. (1981). *Educational and career services for adults.* Lexington, MA: D. C. Heath.

Houle, C. (1961). *The inquiring mind.* Madison: University of Wisconsin Press.

Knowles, M. S. (1975). *Self-directed learning: A guide for learners and teachers.* Chicago: Association Press/Follett.

Knowles, M. S. (1980). *The modern practice of adult education: From pedagogy to andragogy.* Chicago: Follett.

Knowles, M. S. (1985). *The adult learner: A neglected species* (3rd ed.). Houston, TX: Gulf.

London, J. (1909). *Martin Eden.* New York: Macmillan.

Martin, E. D. (1926). *The meaning of a liberal education.* New York: Norton.

McClusky, H. Y. (1970). A differential psychology of the adult potential. In S. A. Grabowski (Ed.), *Adult learning and instruction* (pp. 80–95). Syracuse, NY: ERIC Clearinghouse on Adult Education.

Merriam, S. (Ed.). (1984). *Selected writings on philosophy and adult education.* Malabar, FL: Robert E. Krieger.

Moreland, W. D., & Goldenstein, E. H. (Eds.). (1985). *Pioneers in adult education.* Chicago: Nelson-Hall.

Russell, W. (1981). *Educating Rita.* London: Samuel French.

Shaw, G. B. (1983). *Pygmalion.* London: Penguin Books. (Original work published 1916)

Tough, A. (1971). *The adult's learning projects.* Toronto: Ontario Institute for Studies in Education.

Tough, A. (1982). *Intentional changes: A fresh approach to helping people change.* Chicago: Follett.

Witt, M. A. F., Brown, C. V., Dunbar, R. A., Tirro, F., & Witt, R. G. (1980). *The humanities: Cultural roots and continuities* (Vol. 1), pp. 44–66. Lexington, MA: D. C. Heath.

CHAPTER NINE

The Adult Educator
and Social Responsibility

PHYLLIS M. CUNNINGHAM

THE process of education is powerful, since, especially in its institutionalized form, it is an apparatus for social control. The role schooling plays in reproducing existing structures, practices, and social relationships has been well documented (Bowles & Gintis, 1976; Giroux, 1983).

Many adult educators tend to think of themselves as being outside of schooling, since very little adult education is done as a major activity of schools. What is not recognized, however, is that modern forms of adult education are highly institutionalized. Adult education is a function, either highly integrated (e.g., cooperative extension) or marginalized as an ancillary function (e.g., human resource development in an industry). In either case it is institutionalized.

Institutionalization, by its very nature, can make adult education "schooling" in that both the overt and the hidden curriculum reproduce the dominant culture. For example, cooperative extension can be seen as the highly successful educational invention that helped create the most productive farming enterprise in the world; looking at its darker side, however, it can be seen as the invention that gave successful farmers added help to put less successful farmers out of business, thus maintaining and strengthening existing social and power relationships. This type of comparison indicates why ethics must be a day-to-day topic in the practice of adult education: many practitioners do not critically examine the darker side of adult "schooling." In fact adult education is usually conceptualized and mythologized as a nonschool activity having a very different agenda than schools.

"Friends teaching friends" is one mythical definition of adult education taught to graduate students, but, in fact, this idea is rarely considered as appropriate activity in the everyday work world. The concept of adult education as an activity primarily concerned with helping adults become responsible, participating citizens in a democratic society is another myth. This "apple pie and motherhood" ideal of North American adult education as reported in our histories may once have been the norm, but development of responsible citizens does not occupy the "professional" adult educator's present-day literature, conferences, or daily activity.

Adult education as practiced in most of North America by those persons who identify themselves as adult education professionals is, for the most part, simply technology that can be bought in the marketplace by the highest bidder. Any ethical concerns expressed by these professionals as a group are tightly framed within "standards of practice" and "codes of ethics" whereby the starting points of the arguments assume that the way the world is organized is natural and the appropriate role of educators is to use their knowledge and skills in behalf of that order. In many cases motivations for producing these codes and standards are self-serving. The code-of-ethics issue is addressed by Carlson in Chapter 11 of this volume.

Institutionalized adult education is rapidly becoming what McKnight (1978) calls a disabling profession. That is to say, through mystification (e.g., "scientific needs analysis") a technology is developed that forces the public to be dependent on the professional. McKnight suggests that the chronicling of "needs" by professionals for their "clients" (not partners) in essence is a chronicling of the needs of the professional. The professional needs a pool of clients, better pay, a steady occupation. Clearly these "needs" can be met by "disabling clients," so that they become incapable of helping themselves and are dependent on professionals.

The ethical dilemmas and hopes for adult education and social change proceed from its structures. Adult educators must become more critically aware so as to be able to distinguish between education and schooling, myths and reality, educational professionalism and education as emancipation. Because it is less institutionalized, less professionalized, and more voluntary, the education of adults may be distinguished in degree, if not in kind, from the education of children. This, then, frames the ethical problem and the potential of socially responsible behavior by adult educators.

The Social Construction and Reconstruction of Reality

How much responsibility do adult educators have to actively promote constructive societal change through their work by promoting the ideals of a democracy (i.e., full citizen participation, freedom, equality, and justice)? To respond to that question, we will examine two prior questions. What is the nature of society? How can participation in education bring about change? Only then can we look at the field and see how ethical practice is presently engendered and what might be a better way of practicing adult education.

The Nature of Society

The idea that our world is not preordained but is constructed within our minds from our daily activities and projected outward to form an objective reality and that, in turn, the objectified world interacts with our subjective selves is not new (Berger & Luckmann, 1966). Each of us constructs our own reality. What we assume to be true becomes a frame for making sense out of the world we experience. This is regularly demonstrated by comparative anthropologists. What is unique is that we have difficulty seeing how we ourselves have constructed our world. Put in a succinct way by Mao Tse Tung, "Fish don't know they are in water."

The ethical role of educators is to provide environments that allow people to examine critically the water in which they swim. For example, if racism is seen as a socially constructed mechanism to control groups of people who can be easily identified physically, then we can reconstruct our society to eliminate such an unjust social apparatus. If sexism is experienced as a means by which one gender establishes dominance and power to control another gender through psychological, biological, economic, and social elaborations that become "norms" and "oughts," then only by counteracting "norms" and "oughts" can this inappropriate social apparatus be reconstructed.

Accordingly, if one accepts the premise that we do produce and can change our social reality, then it logically follows that our social apparatuses are invented to provide some function. Again, logically we can argue that historically the function of social control has been one of the pervasive issues for society. And we see how many of our apparatuses are concerned with social control. The family is a social invention to provide social control, since it clearly is not needed for biological survival. This social control provided by families may be seen by some as a positive mechanism to provide for optimum social integration—something all societies need. However, in a democracy, racism and sexism and limited popular control over resource distribution can be distinguished as inappropriate mechanisms of social control even as we make judgments to promote the family and its control function.

It is these critical ethical decisions that become important in socially transforming a society. Should we simply ignore an unjust social apparatus? Many would choose to do so, because, if we destroy these oppressive social inventions, our own personal social reality would be very different. People of color would be respected as equals; the women of the world would lay half their burden down; the underclass would disappear. We in the United States would have to view the whole world differently. We could not be content with a world where simply being white or male results in one's having better pay, better food, better housing, and more power and status. Many "perks" go to the dominant portion of society.

This may explain why some adult educators claim to be apolitical. It is a professional way of making one of the most political statements one can make. Because what one says when one declares neutrality (or objectivity) is that one is quite satisfied with the present organization of social relationships and the distribution of resources in the society. Those who "have" in society rarely see the need for change as clearly as those who "have not." Accordingly, one could argue that we professionals invent such ideas as scientific objectivity and professionalism to sanitize our basic desires and tendencies to maintain inequality, racism, sexism, and classism since we are satisfied, on balance, with our "share of the pie."

Participation and Change

If we accept the premises of the social construction of reality, as addressed in the previous section, then, clearly, what we make we can unmake. But the further question is, can social change be accomplished through education? Many would say no. They argue that by definition schools are agents of maintaining and conserving what is. The recourse (and the place for ethical choice) for those who think like this lies in studying the "resistance" that schools engender. Schools may exist to maintain the status quo. However, within the school, students, teachers, and other personnel resist and counterattack its systematized curriculum directed toward marginalizing competing bodies of knowledge (Giroux, 1983).

Unfortunately, most of the persons who study schools and schooling limit themselves to the compulsory schools of the young. We do not know if schooling for adults is qualitatively the same as for children, but we do know that by fostering resistance and by resisting within our institutions we can promote change. And, clearly, in para-educational systems for both children and adults education can be practiced more freely than in public schools. With this freedom, adult educators can develop programs that encourage the full, active participation of adults building up an opposing body of knowledge to confront the official knowledge, which has as its raison d'être the maintenance of the system. Let us examine knowledge and participation more carefully, as well as how these concepts can guide ethical social choices.

Like our social reality, knowledge is produced and interpreted by us. However, all bodies of knowledge are not equal. The knowledge that supports the dominant paradigms in a culture is systematically produced, disseminated, and reified so as to become common sense to the average citizen (Gramsci, 1971). Other knowledge is not official, yet clearly reflects the reality of the nondominant cultures that produce it. To the extent that adult educators can assist individuals in creating, disseminating, legitimating, and celebrating their own knowledge (including cultural knowledge), social change can occur—for two reasons. First, the participant-produced knowledge competes with, confronts, and forces change onto the official knowledge; second, the participants, in recognizing that they have produced and celebrated their own view of the world, empower themselves. This exercising of power through creation of their own knowledge can produce interdependence and informed critical thinkers, as opposed to a dependent and "coping" underclass. This fundamental distinction as to why we develop programs suggests a clear ethical choice. Education either domesticates or it liberates (Freire, 1972).

Participation in Adult Education

Adult educators from Lindeman (1926) to Freire (1972) have stressed the importance of informed citizen participation in a democracy. The argument proceeds from the notion that voluntary participation by adults in the social fabric of society indicates the health of a democratic republic. Thus such writers as David Horton Smith (1980) link participation with democratic values. Participation must not be merely economic, but social and cultural as well (Bordieu, 1977). Swedish public policy researchers demonstrated how organized adult education can be used as a means of increasing voluntary social participation in the greater society (Rubenson & Höghielm, 1980). To the degree that adults voluntarily participate in a society, one can argue that there is a parallel commitment to and a responsibility for the society and its shared values. Thus meaningful participation prevents alienation.

Democracy involves equality and justice and must by definition be moving toward these goals. To do so one must have a critically informed citizenry if participation is to be meaningful. Habermas (1974) calls for the use of the highest level of thinking, that is, emancipatory knowledge as contrasted with instrumental reason or interpretive understanding. Freire (1972) links the education of adults with the ability to be critically conscious. These ideas are based on the notion that people must exercise control over their own decisions by being able to critique their environment. How can this occur and how do adult educators facilitate learning that will bring it about?

To encourage critical thinking in others, one must be able to think critically oneself. One must be able to permeate the ideological envelopes that encompass each of us. If we accept the idea that the participation of critically aware citizens is basic to a democracy, then the development of critically aware persons who are in charge of their own education would be a norm for adult education programs in a democratic society. Further, we would understand that this means far more than running a course on public affairs.

If adult educators are to uphold a responsibility to contribute to a healthy democratic society by developing critically conscious adults, then they themselves must be capable of emancipatory thinking, or critical consciousness. This ability allows one to examine ethical issues in ways that promote equality and justice on a daily basis in everyday work; it prevents one from making these concepts so abstract that one can ignore unequal and unjust behavior in one's own world of work.

Ethical Choices in Practice

We now turn to the field of practice to illustrate some ethical concerns. The views being suggested here turn the model proposed by Brockett in Chapter 1 on its head. Brockett's model starts with personal values as a base upon which we as educators rationally consider our competing roles. Further, in actual practice our choices are made by some decision-making model optimizing one set of values as against another; thus, the process of making ethical decisions is seen as a rational activity. But it is inappropriate to apply rational discourse to a political activity. I argue that ethics is being socially defined in the political arena of practice. Our personal values, our social roles are socially constructed and defined by our socially constructed reality. The reality, or water in which we swim, is defined and controlled by the groups that are dominant. As a result, the structural hegemony that controls our interpretation of our personal values and our social roles does not provide an adequate basis for making ethical decisions. It is informed emancipatory practice that helps adult educators and their partners, adult learners, to forge new understandings of social roles and relationships through dialogue and to bring to life and to practice the personal values that are congruent with a democratic society. It is in the politics of practice that the question of ethics is confronted. The political nature of ethics makes it conflictual; similarly, the political nature of our roles and personal values engenders conflict. Accordingly, we must always keep the dialogue open and critical in nature. Let us illustrate this point of view in practice.

Are Some Ethical Decisions More Basic Than Others?

Adult educators in North America appear to organize themselves around their technology. The organizing, implementing, and evaluating skills attached to program planning (which also takes into account the needs and learning styles of participants) are very important in providing useful adult education programs of high quality. But this is not enough; an educator is more than a technician. Processes or means may not deny ends. Yet graduate programs, continuing professional development, and in-service training activities are almost entirely organized around the technology of adult education and give little concern for emancipatory thinking and ethical concerns. Issues concerning the purposes education should serve are rarely considered. If an *ought* is raised, as in "adult educators *ought to*," there is an immediate concern for objectivity and a desire to keep away from normative statements. In fact, the scientific paradigm is invoked in a normative manner to deny the use of normative statements without most persons noticing the incongruity.

The level of abstraction at which ethical concerns are raised is critical. Ethical decisions that are confined to our technology, important as they are, are not the basic questions. Yet many educators of adults base their "ethicalness" in their technology, thus never having to come to grips with the purposes of that technology. Two basic ethical questions that should be discussed are (1) who has the power to make decisions on the nature of adult education programs, and (2) who do these programs benefit? To make this point at the basic ethical level in practice is to decide whether our resources should, for example, be addressed to questions regarding andragogy or racism; self-directed learning or sexism; models of evaluation or the emergence of a permanent underclass in our democracy. Ethical concerns are embedded at both levels, but in each case the latter represents a more basic dilemma.

Is the Education of Adults Neutral?

The issue of whether or not basic ethical issues should be made explicit has its starting point in the nature of the activity. If planning and implementing educational programs is an objective exercise of a professional (technician), then ethical concerns are logically limited to the technology. But the evidence shows that the education of adults is not neutral but is a highly political activity. Consider some examples of that evidence.

First, adult education as now practiced in the United States is elitist by nature, contradicting democratic principles of equity. Research indicates, over and over again, that the best predictor of participation in adult education is the level of education of the potential participant (Courtney, 1983). Thus those with more education get more education, but the cost of this education is often paid for by the public. Those who have more get more, and their education is paid for, in part, by those who have less. This result is not just an artifact of a neutral needs assessment showing that only those who are educated want more education. Rather, it is an institutional bias and is reflected in judgments educators make about what programs to offer and what funding to seek. Even when federal intrusion occurs through public policy to promote more equitable programming, educators are quite often adept in seeing to it that definitions are gerrymandered to fit the guidelines, insuring that the institution's public or its activity is not changed.

Further evidence of the political nature of adult education is revealed in the training of adult educators, which is organized around the "technology" of education—"how to do it." If one compares the existing graduate programs in adult education one notes the homogeneity of the professional curriculum. A foundational history course consists of a study of institutionalized adult education beginning with the Mayflower (Knowles, 1977) or Aristotle (Grattan, 1955). In this historical study, Western civilization is celebrated and competing histories are nonexistent. There is no history of black educators of adults, of female educators of adults, of socialist educators of adults. Neither does this history account for peoples here before the Mayflower. So much for rational scientific discourse.

The bias on behalf of the majority culture can be illustrated in other subjects as well. For example, the psychology of individual deficit becomes the basis for explaining social phenomena, with little mention of the oppressive structures in which people live. Program planning based on needs analysis and evaluation based on objectives is posited as scientifically neutral rather than acknowledging that value positions must be taken in the everyday practice of these activities.

And, finally, the voluntary nature of adult education is being eroded. In some areas there are unmasked coercive forces mandating the education of adults (Ohliger, 1981). More subtle, and perhaps far more intrusive, is the social pressure exerted covertly within the culture as a norm. Thus, phrases such as "learning never ends," "the learning society," and "lifelong learning," which in and by themselves appear harmless, become changed to unconscious normative imperatives regarding institutional education. The notion that one should be involved in institutionalized education as a lifelong pursuit becomes an internalized "ought" and thus subconsciously detracts from the voluntary nature of the educational activity. Courtney (1983) offers an extensive review of participation demonstrating that most researchers study participation almost entirely within the institutionalized forms of adult education, with the notable exception of Allen Tough. Goodnow (1982) combined analysis of participation with market theory to show how educational institutions could capture the market. The language here is intriguing. Where are the ethics in defining participation? Participation conceptualized as marketing for one's institution is a far cry from participation as a critical, knowledge-producing, empowering activity for marginalized groups.

Ethics as Everyday Activity

It is not surprising that little is written about ethics in educational literature or that the subject is seldom discussed at education conferences. Many would mystify ethics as an abstract field of study that is objective, scientific, and metaphysical—not an everyday activity engaged in by all persons. Ethics as a scientifically mystified field, available only to professional philosophers, thus becomes one more apparatus of social control.

It is only when we educators realize that we are not neutral, and that being a capable program planner is not *the* only endeavor, and that choices permeate our everyday world, that we confront our responsibility for ends as well as means. To know that *all* adult educators have choices and make decisions means that power is available to all. While the rational scientific world tells us that power is limited, our social reality teaches us that power, through critically accessing knowledge, is ubiquitous and can be appropriated by all (Foucault, 1972).

Once we recognize that there are choices and that our job is not simply that of a technician, then we can make a conscious decision to enter this ambiguous world. Adult educators exhibit several professional levels of awareness:

1. Those who are critically unaware and thus ethically naive
2. Those who have become aware but have limited that awareness, since it is not in their own self-interest to operationalize it
3. Those who are beginning to be critically aware intellectually but have not matured to the point that their analysis systematically affects their practice
4. Those who have well-developed mechanisms of critical analysis and put into practice the results of that analysis

A responsibility of the field is to make professionals critically aware and to encourage practical strategies for making the education of adults work to foster critical awareness in the citizenry.

What are the principles available that could guide our daily work and promote an evolving discourse in our practice? The following list could be a starting point for such a dialogue. Adult educators would:

1. Be strong proponents of voluntarism, voluntary learning, and voluntary participation in all institutions of society. The extent of voluntary participation in a society is an indicator of the strength of the democracy.
2. Promote basic and critical literacy. This means encouraging expression by the individual through dialogue, writing, and public expression. Individual expression requires reading, listening, and computing skills but does not stop with passive activity. Rather, it is important to promote use of basic skills in creating knowledge and action.
3. Make sure that the content of programs is open to competing ideas. Representation of ideas from nondominant cultures would be legitimated—not as an add-on to meet some legislated multicultural guidelines but as essential to the discourse. We would admit to the politics of knowledge.
4. Encourage popular (populist-oriented) education programs, guarding against any usurping of the participants' prerogatives. Community-organized programs should be seen as complementary to rather than as competitive with institutional programs. The sharing of power and the promotion of program independence from the assisting institution could be a priority.
5. Provide professional development programming that includes content that goes beyond nationalist concerns, including such subjects as peace education and global resource sharing.

In summary, adult educators must face up to ethical choices that are defined as everyday activities rather than as mystifying, abstract, elitist concepts. Ethical issues can be identified at two levels, and educators owe it to participants to be concerned with the more fundamental level. Day-to-day choices that make adult education a contributor to social equity and justice are required.

Conclusion

I have made three points in this chapter. First of all, we socially construct our own world. Our world is not an objective, scientific system guided by some unchanging laws. Rather, we live in history and have the opportunity within our historical times to reconstruct our socially constructed reality. Human activity does cause social change.

Second, adult education, which in this historical time has the potential to be a voluntary, life-related, directly relevant activity, can be a mechanism for change. To the extent that adult educators find ways to stimulate the development of critical consciousness and thought, the practice of adult education can contribute to a more equitable, peaceful, and just society.

Third, adult education professionals might move to a more socially responsible stance by creating constructive critical dialogue with their publics. This movement is made possible by recognizing and learning from knowledge that is produced by the experience of all people regardless of their formal education, developing a dialogical stance and an openness to challenge the assumptions of the field and resisting those forms of adult education that, in reality, primarily seek to domesticate participants.

References

Berger, P., & Luckmann, T. (1966). *The social construction of reality.* New York: Doubleday.

Bordieu, P. (1977). Cultural reproduction and social reproduction. In J. Karabel & F. Halsey (Eds.), *Power and ideology in education* (pp. 487–511). New York: Oxford University Press.

Bowles, S., & Gintis, H. (1976). *Schooling in capitalist America.* New York: Basic Books.

Courtney, S. (1983). *Visible means of learning.* Unpublished doctoral dissertation, Northern Illinois University, DeKalb.

Foucault, M. (1972). *The archaeology of knowledge.* New York: Pantheon.

Freire, P. (1972). *Pedagogy of the oppressed.* New York: Herder & Herder.

Giroux, H. (1983). Theories of reproduction and resistance in the new sociology of education: A critical analysis. *Harvard Educational Review, 53*(3), 257–292.

Goodnow, B. (1982). Increasing enrollment through benefit segmentation. *Adult Education, 32*(2), 89–103.

Gramsci, A. (1971). (Q. Hoare, Ed. and Trans.) *Selections from the prison notebooks.* New York: International Publishers.

Grattan, C. H. (1955). *In quest of knowledge.* New York: Association Press.

Habermas, J. (1974). *Theory and practice.* Boston: Beacon.

Knowles, M. (1977). *A history of the adult education movement in the United States* (2nd ed.). Huntington, NY: Krieger.

Lindeman, E. (1926). *The meaning of adult education.* New York: New Republic.

McKnight, J. (1978). Professionalized service and disabling help. In I. Illich (Ed.), *The disabling professions* (pp. 69–91). Boston: Marion Boyars.

Ohliger, J. (1981). If "learning never ends," does living ever begin. *Second Thoughts, 3*(3), 6–7.

Rubenson, K., & Höghielm, R. (Eds.). (1980). *Adult education for social change—Research on the Swedish allocation policy.* Stockholm: Studies in Education and Psychology.

Smith, D. H. (1980). General activity model. In D. H. Smith, J. Macaulay, and Associates (Eds.), *Participation in social and political activities* (pp. 461–530). San Francisco: Jossey-Bass.

CHAPTER TEN

Ethics in Adult Education Research

SHARAN B. MERRIAM

Rarely discussed at research conferences or in the literature of adult education are ethical issues involved in conducting even the simplest research project. Yet there are ethical concerns related to every step of the research process from conceptualizing the problem, to collecting and analyzing data, to reporting the findings. The purpose of this chapter is to explore the ethical concerns inherent in the production of knowledge through research. Specifically, this chapter is divided into ethical considerations regarding (1) goals of research and the nature of knowledge; (2) procedures used in conducting an investigation; and (3) dissemination of research findings.

As Brockett and several others have pointed out in earlier chapters, ethics can be both a theoretical and a practical endeavor. As a branch of philosophy, ethics investigates moral behavior by asking what is good or bad, right or wrong within a specific culture and time. Practical ethics is the process of taking one's understanding of "good" or "right" behavior and applying it to the decisions one makes in everyday life. Beliefs and values are inextricably woven into one's ethical standards. Acting ethically, or making an ethical decision, is the operationalization of what one considers to be the correct, right, or best way to behave. In the research process, there are many decision points that involve operationalizing one's beliefs; these then become ethical decision points.

The Goals of Research and the Nature of Knowledge

The way in which a researcher structures an investigation has a lot to do with his or her notion of the overall purpose of the endeavor. "The questions asked and the problems studied are the ones considered interesting, worthwhile, and important. The criteria that determine what is interesting, worthwhile, and important are often based on ethical values" (Robinson & Moulton, 1985, p. 52). Research is systematic inquiry, but systematic inquiry for what purpose? A common answer to the question is that research is undertaken to discover or produce knowledge. The so-called knowledge base of adult education has been developed and continues to expand through the contributions of research as well as the experiences of practice. Questions arise, however, when one begins to assess the extent to which knowledge production (based upon the questions one asks) is a function of contemporary social concerns, cultural values, political ideologies, or financial exigency. Debates in the literature center on the questions of how "valid" is the knowledge produced, how "neutral" is that knowledge, and how much responsibility one has for the consequences of research.

In the traditional research paradigm, the more control one can effect in an investigation, the more chance there is for "valid" knowledge to be produced. Validity rests with the methods available to achieve internal and external control. In qualitative and participatory modes of research, valid knowledge is established through the meanings those being studied attach to the phenomena. As Reason and Rowan point out, validity in this context "must concern itself both with the knower and what is to be known; valid knowledge is a matter of relationship" (1981, p. 241). Valid knowledge is not that discovered by controlling for confounding variables; rather, it is that which emerges from the shared experiences of those involved in the phenomenon under investigation.

Neutral Knowledge

Closely entwined with the question of valid knowledge is the extent to which knowledge produced through research is "neutral." Early research in adult education and the social sciences imitated traditional scientific models wherein it was thought that scientists dispassionately and objectively investigated the world in order to explain, predict, and control. While this might be more possible in the physical sciences, where one is dealing with inanimate objects (although even this notion is being challenged by quantum physics), achieving any objectivity with human beings in human society is highly debatable. In the last few decades, in fact, there has been a decline in the value-free image of scientific inquiry. Diener and Crandall (1978) present several reasons why value-neutrality in research is impossible. First, social forces often determine what topics are of importance at a particular point in time; governmental support then influences what research is done. At this particular time, for example, literacy is a social priority. In the 1960s job training was prominent in adult education research. Second, personal beliefs, experiences, values, and the disciplinary orientation of the researcher determine how problems are conceptualized and what questions are asked. Third, the philosophy of science has questioned the notion of one objective reality; some posit the idea that the external world cannot be known in any absolute sense; rather, there are many realities dependent upon one's culture and perceptions. Finally, research findings are "powerful social forces in themselves" (Diener & Crandall, 1978, p. 185). There is an inevitable interaction of research findings with the context from which they were drawn and to which they are applied, possibly affecting, among other things, the direction of predicted change. Studying identified barriers to participation in adult education, for example, may alter the nature and/or strength of those barriers for some students.

Most social science researchers acknowledge the fact that knowledge production is both subjective and value-laden. Some even say it is, and should be, a political act. In practice, most researchers recognize the subjectivity of their activity, while at the same time attempting to minimize bias in collecting and analyzing data.

Consequences of Research

The consequences of research is another area of ethical concern, one that can be traced as far back as Socrates, "who was sentenced to death because his inquiries were claimed to have threatened social stability" (Robinson & Moulton, 1985, p. 49). Just producing knowledge, most feel, does not release one from some responsibility for the ways in which that knowledge gets used. The consequences of certain areas of scientific research, such as in nuclear physics, biochemistry, or genetic engineering, have obvious ethical implications. Findings from research in the social sciences and education can also be used in unethical ways or have unanticipated consequences. Discovering, as Tough (1979) did in the early 1970s, that 90% of adults are engaged in learning on their own could be used by legislators *against* appropriating funds for adult education. Or suppose it were discovered that most adult nonreaders have learning disabilities not amenable to educational intervention. What might be the consequences for the thousands of literacy programs in operation, for the adults who are successfully learning to read, or for the disabled illiterates themselves?

In summary, research does not begin in a value-free vacuum, nor do the results of research get used in value-free ways. Engaging in research in adult education is not a simple matter of producing knowledge. The questions deemed worthy of investigation are linked to an investigator's stance on the nature of knowledge, the production of knowledge, and the uses of knowledge.

Conducting Adult Education Research

Ethical concerns in the actual conducting of an investigation can be explored first from the perspective of the adult learners and settings, and second, with regard to particular methodologies employed. Societal agencies that monitor ethical concerns inherent in the research process are also discussed.

Adult Research Participants

The major ethical issues in adult education research are issues common to all social science research. The protection of subjects from harm, the right to privacy, the notion of informed consent, and the issue of deception are the dominant ethical dilemmas in conducting research in the social sciences—research that investigates the behavior of people and their interaction with the social institutions that they create.

Ideally, adults should enter research projects voluntarily, understanding the nature of the study and the dangers and obligations that are involved. It is also expected that participants will not be exposed to risks that are greater than the gains that might be derived from the study. While these seem to be very sensible guidelines, when applied to actual situations they are far from simple. Take, for example, a situation in which a researcher would like to test an experimental approach to learning English as a second language. Potentially it might be the most effective method yet developed for helping adults learn English. On the other hand, it may turn out to be ineffective with certain adults and may even be harmful in that the technique could block future learning. How does one assess these risks ahead of time?

A particularly complex problem in conducting research deals with the individual's, versus society's, right to know. If adults are told they are part of a study, it could very well affect the results, since they may perform differently because of being in a study and not because of the variables in question. For example, if supervisors were told that they were being observed to determine what effect the gender of an employee had upon merit ratings, their behavior might be different from what it would have been had they not been told the purpose of the study. To not inform subjects of their participation, or, more likely, to not inform them of the specific goals of the research, is deceptive and weakens the notion of informed consent. These concerns, though, must be weighed against the advantages and disadvantages of the research for the greater society.

These issues of protection, informed consent, privacy, and deception cannot be considered in isolation. A profession's position in the form of a code of ethics, or an individual researcher's judgment throughout the research process, reflects various ethical ideologies. Forsyth (1981) has identified four ideologies, each of which corresponds to an area of philosophical thought: *absolutism*, where one believes that the best possible outcomes will be achieved if universal moral principles are followed in all situations; *exceptionism*, which also adheres to moral absolutes but admits exceptions based upon the nature of the consequences; *situationism*, which argues that morality should focus on the specific situation or context; and *subjectivism*, which posits that moral standards are valid only in reference to one's own personal behavior. Depending upon which of these positions a researcher holds, there might be, for example, four resolutions to the research issue of deception—that is, to what extent it is permissible to conceal the real intent of an experiment if revealing the intent will result in invalid responses. Is deception always wrong? Are there exceptions? Should each situation be judged separately? Does the answer lie with the investigator's own perceptions, values, and attitudes? Should it? Solutions to the ethical dilemmas inherent in conducting adult education research evolve from very fundamental ethical ideologies.

As noted earlier in the chapter, however, adult education researchers are involved in the very practical application of ethical principles in their day-to-day concerns. Reynolds (1982) suggests three strategies for resolving moral dilemmas: one can decide what to do based upon (1) respect for individual rights as defined by society, (2) an evaluation of the costs and benefits of the research, and (3) the personal treatment of others. Most researchers are guided by common sense in dealing with human participants. Specifically,

1. Respondents should be told the purpose of the research and how the data they are being asked to provide will be used.
2. Respondents should be informed of the nature of the research before data are collected and should be allowed to withdraw at any given point.
3. There should be no unpleasant or damaging effects on the individual, the setting, or others close to the participant either during or subsequent to the research.
4. The investigator must respect the privacy of the respondents and, whenever possible, ensure anonymity or confidentiality.
5. There should be no unprofessional behavior required of the participants.
6. The participants should be given an opportunity to learn from the research. (Fox, 1969, pp. 384–386)

Overall, the problem of the ethical treatment of adults who participate in research studies can be guided by common sense. "At the very least," reasonable measures should "be taken to ensure the safety of participants, that subjects be treated by the researchers as if the researcher were a subject, that the respondents give their consent to participate, and that all information be kept confidential" (Merriam & Simpson, 1984, p. 66). In most studies, participants are presented with a written description of the study and how the results are to be used and are asked to sign a consent form. Furthermore, institutions that employ people who do research have established procedures for reviewing and approving proposals.

Ethical Concerns Related to Research Design

The most basic distinction in research design is between experimental and nonexperimental. Experimental research assumes that the researcher can manipulate the variables of interest; that is, there is a high level of control over the research situation. Experimental research is also identified by its major intent—to investigate cause and effect. In order to determine cause and effect, randomization of subjects to experimental and control groups is essential. Ethical concerns are perhaps most dramatic in experimental research, which, but its very nature, requires the manipulation of variables and intervention in the natural process of events. Participants are more likely to be affected in experimental research; thus the questions about privacy, deception, and harm are of major concern.

Whether conducted in a laboratory or in social settings and institutions, experimental studies are permeated with ethical concerns. Studies on memory and cognitive functioning, for example, are often conducted in a laboratory, a setting that handicaps the performance of older adults who are less familiar with, and perhaps intimidated by, the situation. Negative effects in laboratory experiments in general "may include being deceived, physical discomfort, psychological stress, or unpleasant self-knowledge" (Reynolds, 1982, p. 30). Participants may also "realize a number of positive effects, such as involvement in an interesting activity, altruistic satisfaction at contributing to science, new and valuable self-knowledge, knowledge about research procedures, or cash payments, academic credits, special privileges, and the like" (Reynolds, 1982, p. 30).

As in the laboratory, in a social experiment there is a treatment or intervention of some sort. Potentially harmful side effects may not be known ahead of time. On the other hand, a treatment that may improve the condition of the experimental group is withheld from the control group. Suppose, for example, a new method for teaching adults math skills is to be tested in an experimental study. Adults in math classes are randomly assigned either to the new method or to a traditional instructional intervention. The new method may fail completely, and in fact so confuse participants that they are set back in their math learning. On the other hand, the new method may be wildly successful in advancing the students' knowledge. Valuable time has thus been wasted with the control group, who would also have benefited from the instruction. Reynolds (1979) summarizes the ethical dilemma in experimental research:

> The same research techniques that provide the greatest confidence that a causal relationship between variables can be established also maximize the investigator's responsibility for the impact on participants. . . . The dilemma is minimized when the benefits of the new knowledge are substantial, the negative effects (especially for participants) are minimal, and there is clear evidence of consideration for the rights and welfare of the participants (such as the use of full informed consent procedure and post-research surveillance to determine and correct negative effects). (pp. 156–157)

Nonexperimental research is often labeled descriptive research. Its goal is to examine events or phenomena, to characterize "something as it is, though some descriptive research suggests tentative causal relationships. There is no manipulation of treatments or subjects; the researcher takes things as they are" (McMillan & Schumacher, 1984, p. 26). Data in descriptive research are collected primarily through surveys, interviews, and observation of the phenomenon under study.

In surveys and interviews, individuals are asked questions about their background, experiences, attitudes, beliefs, and so on. Such information may be combined with measures of particular characteristics and analyzed in relation to one another. For example, a scale measuring self-esteem may be related to certain hypothesized factors, such as income, education, or gender. Ethical concerns arise when participants are asked embarrassing questions, when their privacy is invaded, or when public disclosure of sensitive information has negative effects. In-depth interviewing may have unanticipated long-term effects, negative or positive, on the interviewee. For example, what are the residual effects of an in-depth interview with a displaced homemaker who articulates, for the first time, anger and hostility about her condition? Or the part-time teacher of adults who becomes aware of a lack of career options through participation in a study of such? Or the adult student who is probed to identify reasons for failing to learn to read? On the other hand, an interview may actually improve the condition of interviewees, when, for example, they are asked to review their lives, share coping strategies, articulate grief, and so on.

Written questionnaires, telephone surveys, and interviewing are used in the great majority of adult education research. In a sense, the less personal contact the researcher has with respondents, the less problematic are ethical concerns. Recipients of written questionnaires simply need not respond; a telephone call may invade someone's privacy, but there is usually more anonymity, and the person called maintains control; face-to-face interviews pose the most problems, and informed consent is usually obtained for them.

The observation of behavior, whether it be directly or indirectly through unobtrusive measures, presents special ethical problems of its own. Here, those being observed have almost no control in participating. If data gathering is totally disguised, such as through hidden microphones or cameras, or through the examination of materials from files, archives, or other sources, subject privacy has been invaded, "with privacy defined as the individual's right to decide what of himself he will expose, to whom, and in what circumstances" (Bower & de Gasparis, 1978, p. 35). Observation, especially as a participant in the activity, often involves deception about the real purpose of the researcher's presence. In such situations it is feared that the researcher "might actively entrap the subject into the expression of attitudes, or confessions of sins, or displays of behavior that he would otherwise withhold" (Bower & de Gasparis, 1978, p. 35). Of course, data gathering through observation has its advantages. In addition to circumventing "artifacts created by direct interaction of researcher and subject, such as respondents' error in self-reporting or distortions created by reactions to the interviewer or the interview situation," the process avoids "undue coercion to participate, embarrassment caused by sensitive questions in an interview, or impositions on time" (Bower & de Gasparis, p. 35). If disguised observation is deemed the best way to obtain data, Diener and Crandall (1978) suggest incorporating the following safeguards:

1. Deceive as little as possible.
2. Enter private spheres with the maximum informed consent consonant with the research goals. Consider obtaining informed consent post hoc whenever possible.
3. Plan procedures that absolutely guarantee subject anonymity, especially in published reports and where sensitive information is reported.
4. Review the potential influences of the observers on the group and rework the study if any negative consequences are foreseen.
5. Fully inform research assistants about the research, giving free choice whether to participate.
6. Consider whether the study could cause indignant outrage against social science, thus hampering other research endeavors.
7. Consult colleagues and request their suggestions for minimizing ethical problems. If possible, consult representatives from the group to be studied. (pp. 125–126)

There are at least two potential problems when collecting data through observation. One is that the mere act of observing may change what is being observed. This is, of course, particularly true if one is a participant observer, but it has even been advanced as happening in the physical sciences, with the physicist Heinsenberg stating that observing a subatomic particle may alter it (in Diener

& Crandall, 1978, p. 185). Anthropologists and other field researchers who go and live in a setting in order to study it cannot but help to affect, in some way, the phenomenon being observed.

The other problem with collecting data through observation is that the investigator may observe behavior that causes him or her ethical problems. Suppose, for example, inappropriate physical contact is witnessed while observing a first-aid training program? Or if, while reading documents related to a continuing education program, it becomes clear that funds have been misappropriated? Or if, in gathering background information on program personnel, it is discovered that someone has a criminal record that was not revealed when being hired? In any of these situations, what action should be taken by the investigator, and when? The answers reside in the individual researcher's attitudes, values, and ethics. Decisions will reflect the ideological position of the investigator, which, as mentioned earlier, can range from an absolutist to a subjective standard for moral decision making.

Outside Monitoring of Research

Early research in the physical and social sciences paid little heed to the ethical issues discussed above. The autonomy of the researcher/scientist was left unquestioned, and the results of research were viewed as essential to the enhancement of the human condition. Nazi concentration camp experiments, the nuclear bomb, and more recent publicized abuses of research subjects have called into question both the autonomy of researchers and the application of knowledge produced through research. Means of monitoring the investigator and the research process have emerged through professional associations, government regulations, and legal precedents.

Professional monitoring occurs through professional training, in review committees that can revoke an individual's right to practice, and in professional codes of ethics, aspects of which deal with research. Unfortunately, there are few guidelines that one can consult when confronted with some of these ethical issues in conducting research. Some fields, adult education included, have no code of ethics that covers research. Codes of ethics, in fact, are relatively new, dating back to the Nuremberg military tribunals in 1945. The Nuremberg Code established basic principles that researchers are obligated to respect in conducting experiments that involve human subjects.

Disciplines closely related to adult education that do have codes of ethics addressing research are psychology, sociology, anthropology, and several health fields. Anthropology's code addresses relations with those studied, responsibility to the public, responsibility to the discipline, responsibility to students and to sponsors, and responsibility to one's own government and host government. Principles in psychology's and sociology's codes deal with weighing the costs and benefits of an investigation, with safeguards to protect the rights of participants, and with ethical considerations in the presentation of research findings (Diener & Crandall, 1978).

Since the issues in adult education research are no different from the issues in these disciplines, the field of adult education might well fashion its own code of research ethics from these models. That is not to get into the debate about establishing a professional code of ethics discussed by Carlson (Chapter 11) and others in this volume. Rather, it is to suggest that researchers could well benefit from guidelines established by the profession in this area. Such a code would, of course, be based upon ideological assumptions, which may or may not be congruent with elements of the specific research situation and the investigator's subjective reaction to the research problem. They would be *guidelines,* and as such could do no more than guide researchers in resolving particular research-related ethical dilemmas.

A second form of monitoring, beyond that which an individual researcher exerts, exists in the form of federal procedures for review of studies involving federal funds. In one author's opinion, such procedures are "dramatic evidence of the failure of associations to convince the public that either their members are to be trusted as individuals or that the associations are to be trusted to control them" (Reynolds, 1982, p. 103). Before any money can be awarded for research, proposals are rigorously reviewed, and "full, complete informed consent from the participants" must be obtained (Reynolds, 1982, p. 103).

The legal system represents a third mechanism of control of research. This is somewhat more indirect than professional or governmental monitoring, but ultimately more influential, since legal resolutions to ethical dilemmas are backed by an enforcement component lacking in professional or governmental sanctions. Reynolds (1982) points out four issues associated with social science research that the legal system has grappled with: "individual rights that may be affected by research, the criteria for legally valid informed consent, rights of investigators (both individuals and governments), and special legal privileges for investigators (to maintain the anonymity of participants)" (1982, p. 113).

Thus, in conducting adult education research, ethical issues emerge in the consideration of research participants and in the particular methodologies employed. Informed consent, privacy, protection of subjects, and deception permeate to some extent all studies that seek to uncover knowledge about human beings and their interaction with their environment. The choices of study design and data collection techniques involve equally difficult questions. Professional guidelines, governmental regulations, and legal opinions are being used today to help researchers resolve some of the dilemmas.

Dissemination of Findings

The last section of this chapter deals with ethical considerations in the dissemination of research findings. If research is going to contribute to the knowledge base and/or improve the practice of adult education, findings need to be distributed to those who are in positions to make use of them. Unfortunately, much research never finds its way into print because authors underestimate the time and discipline needed to carry out this important last step of the research process. For those who do feel an obligation to disseminate research findings, ethical issues center on protecting those involved, honesty in reporting data, and questions of authorship.

There are many mechanisms for disseminating research results, including conference presentations, journal publications, press conferences, visual displays, and so on. Regardless of how results are made known, it is the investigator's responsibility to ensure that such revelations will not cause problems for the participants or for future interactions with the group or institution involved. In anthropological field studies or case studies in adult education where thick description is used to convey a holistic picture of the phenomenon, protecting the identity of the participants or the setting is especially problematic. Informed consent and participant assistance or agreement with how the data are interpreted are strongly recommended. Subjects' identities should be protected, and anonymity should be extended to both written and oral reporting of information. Bogdan and Biklen further advise that "the researcher should not relate specific information about individuals to others and should be particularly watchful of sharing information with people at the research site who could choose to use the information in political or personal ways" (1982, p. 50). This issue, of course, is not as acute in experimental or survey research, where data are aggregated and not reported in the rich descriptions of ethnographies or case studies. Even so, care must be given to disguise specific sites where experiments were conducted or surveys were administered.

A second concern in disseminating findings is with honesty and accuracy. There have been some startling cases of fraud within both the natural and social sciences. Perhaps the most famous is the Piltdown hoax, where falsified "discovery" of the so-called missing link in evolution set physical anthropology back decades. Other fabrications have been uncovered in parapsychology, intelligence testing, and medical research (Robinson & Moulton, 1985). The reward system in higher education and other institutions that employ researchers contributes in part to the problem. "Finding and publishing significant results will partly determine employability, salary, promotions, and national reputation. Without impressive research findings, the young researcher may lose his job, the older scientist may not be promoted" (Diener & Crandall, 1978).

There is, of course, no justification for ouright fraud in the reporting of research results. The development of knowledge in an entire field may be disrupted or set back by the publication of falsified data. More subtle forms of dishonesty, such as altering statistical analyses, ignoring contradictory data, or biasing results by how one conceptualizes the study or collects data, can also be damaging. Sometimes such biases are not readily apparent to the researcher, nor is it always clear what the "ethical" answer is to some dilemmas. Imagine, for example, in reporting to practitioners the results of an evaluation, that the overall findings of the study were not statistically significant, but that one could support certain desirable findings with frequencies. Such situations involve decisions on the part of the investigator. Diener and Crandall (1978) present perhaps the best summary to guide one's decisions:

> There is simply no ethical alternative to being as nonbiased, accurate, honest as is humanly possible in all phases of research. In planning, conducting, analyzing, and reporting his work the scientist should strive for accuracy, and whenever possible, methodological controls should be built in to help experimenters and assistants remain honest. Biases that cannot be controlled should be dis-

cussed in the written report. Where the data only partly support the predictions, the report should contain enough data to let readers draw their own conclusions. (p. 162)

A third area in dissemination where ethical issues arise is in the determination of authorship. As noted above, the pressure to publish often causes questionable decisions to be made as to who should be given credit for the research. It is apparently a common practice in the physical sciences, though not the social sciences, for the director of a laboratory or head of a research team to be an author on any work done by those who work in that setting (Robinson & Moulton, 1985). This situation has been problematic, especially in cases of fraud. General questions about authorship arise when determining who is the first author, how to list co-authors, the order of multiple authors, whether to include all who contributed, and so on. The American Psychological Association designates as authors those who have made "major contributions of a professional character" (quoted in Robinson & Moulton, 1985, p. 69). The question becomes how to determine what a major professional contribution is.

Diener and Crandall (1978) suggest two criteria for determining scientific contribution—(1) conceptualizing and designing the study and (2) writing the article or report. How substantial the contribution is in each of these areas can help determine the ranking of publication credit. Possibilities range from being sole author, to being first author among others, to being acknowledged in a footnote. Guidelines such as these are subject to individual situations in which the assigning of authors may still be difficult to determine. Such is often the case with student/faculty research, especially with doctoral dissertations. A professor may have made major contributions to the study, but in a sense, it is supposed to be an independent piece of work that "qualifies" the student to enter the profession. In responding to this problem, the American Psychological Association has recommended that major professors not claim *senior* authorship on publications from student dissertations (Fields, 1983).

In summary, disseminating research findings is an important part of the research process and, like the rest of the process, involves ethical issues the investigator must grapple with. Ensuring for anonymity of subjects and site, honesty in the collection, interpretation, and reporting of data, and fairness in assigning authorship must be attended to in the disseminating of research findings.

Conclusion

This chapter has examined some of the ethical problems involved in adult education research. While the issues are common to social science research in general, an attempt was made to illustrate some of the problems with examples from the field of adult education. First discussed was the fact that one's ethical ideology affects how one views the goals of research and the nature of knowledge. What is valid knowledge that researchers produce, and how neutral is that knowledge? And what is one's responsibility for the use of the knowledge produced through research? Thoughtful adult educators who examine these issues are engaging in "practical" ethics.

The major portion of the chapter explored ethical issues in actually conducting research. Protection, informed consent, privacy, and deception were discussed as major concerns relating to the involvement of adult participants in research studies. Resolutions to dilemmas raised by these issues hinge, to some extent, upon the researchers ethical ideology, which can range from an absolutist position to a subjectivist orientation. These same issues of protection, informed consent, privacy, and deception were found to interface with types of research designs. Protection, for example, is a primary concern in experimental research, while privacy is a more prominent issue in survey research. Research codes of ethics developed by professional groups, and governmental and legal forms of monitoring research, were also discussed in this section.

Finally, ethical concerns in the dissemination of research findings were briefly reviewed. Regardless of how findings are disseminated, an overriding concern is with protecting the anonymity of the participants and the site of the research. Like other ethical problems, there are times when this is difficult to do and when the best of intentions are not good enough. Honesty in reporting research was addressed briefly as another ethical concern, as was the designation of authorship.

Thus ethical concerns permeate the entire research process from conceptualizing the problem to disseminating the findings. The first step for adult educators in dealing with the ethical issues is to be aware of the concerns and to know at which junctures in the research process they are likely to emerge. Equally important is for the adult education researcher to have examined his or her own philosophical stance vis-à-vis these issues, for it is still primarily the individual researcher who determines how ethical the search for knowledge will be.

References

Bogdan, R. C., & Biklen, S. K. (1982). *Qualitative research for education: An introduction to theory and methods*. Boston: Allyn and Bacon.

Bower, R. T., & de Gasparis, P. (1978). *Ethics in social research: Protecting the interests of human subjects*. New York: Praeger.

Diener, E., & Crandall, R. (1978). *Ethics in social and behavioral research*. Chicago: The University of Chicago Press.

Fields, C. (1983, September 14). Professors' demands for credit as "coauthors" of student research projects may be rising. *Chronicle of Higher Education*, pp. 7, 10.

Forsyth, D. R. (1981). A psychological perspective on ethical uncertainties in research. In A. J. Kimmel (Ed.), *Ethics of human subject research* (pp. 91–100). San Francisco: Jossey-Bass.

Fox, D. J. (1969). *The research process in education*. New York: Holt, Rinehart & Winston.

McMillan, J. H., & Schumacher, S. (1984). *Research in education*. Boston: Little, Brown.

Merriam, S., & Simpson, E. (1984). *A guide to research for educators and trainers of adults*. Malabar, FL: Krieger.

Reason, P., & Rowan, J. (1981). Issues of validity in new paradigm research. In P. Reason & J. Rowan (Eds.), *Human inquiry: A sourcebook of new paradigm research* (pp. 239–250). New York: Wiley.

Reynolds, P. D. (1979). *Ethical dilemmas and social science research*. San Francisco: Jossey-Bass.

Reynolds, P. D. (1982). *Ethics and social science research*. Englewood Cliffs, NJ: Prentice-Hall.

Robinson, G. M., & Moulton, J. (1985). *Ethical problems in higher education*. Englewood Cliffs, NJ: Prentice-Hall.

Tough, A. (1979). *The adult's learning projects*. Austin, TX: Learning Concepts.

CHAPTER ELEVEN

A Code of Ethics
for Adult Educators?

ROBERT A. CARLSON

ARGUMENTS in behalf of a code of ethics in adult education, taken at face value, would seem unassailable. How can one dispute the need for a high standard of moral conduct in the practice of adult education? Don't all respected professions have a code of ethics to protect their clientele from charlatans, quacks, and shysters? Surely, it is argued, adult education needs to emulate this aspect of other professions and at least begin the process of developing a professional code of ethics.

This chapter will analyze the case for a professional code of conduct in adult education and put the argument into the perspective of the realities of adult education practice. It will provide, as a context, examples of professional practice in various fields, examples that may speak generally to the issue of professional codes of conduct. The chapter will also present challenges to the seemingly unassailable. It will inspect the issue of a code of ethics from a point of view, a theoretical framework, that questions the public advantage of professions and their trappings. This framework will then be applied to the developing field of adult education.

Advocates of a code of ethics in the field correctly point out that adult educators tend to be drawn from a wide range of professions and vocations. They include nurses and welders, clergy and military personnel, agriculturalists and carpenters, school teachers and business practitioners, and many others. Some of these professions and vocations, it is argued, have developed written codes of ethics or unwritten codes of craftsmanship that could be seen as aiding their practitioners in the proper conduct of adult education. Others of these fields of practice offer no such consensually arrived at ethical standards. Theoretically, only the warning of *caveat emptor*, let the buyer beware, stands as protection between the person served and the practitioner providing the service.

Proponents of a code of ethics in adult education contend that a process should be in place that would seek to ensure at least a minimum consensus of ethical principles among adult educators, whatever their backgrounds (Shores, Sork, Davenport, & Carlson, 1983). Few would question the underlying concern that adult education be practiced in an ethical way. The issue is whether a code of ethics for adult educators will achieve the sort of ethical practice desired.

Codes of Ethics: How They Work

Consider how professional codes of ethics actually operate. Medicine is an important profession with a highly regarded code, yet a Canadian surgeon felt he had to speak out on an ethical issue that was not being dealt with under the professional code of conduct. The surgeon was no longer able to keep quiet about the way he believed anesthetists were lining their pockets by moving back and forth between two ongoing operations and rendering full billing for their attendance at each. Early in the 1970s he publicly challenged what he believed was unprincipled action by his colleagues. As a result of his ethical concerns, he was prevented from practicing his craft (*Star-Phoenix*, 1975). In his work, he had to rely on general practitioners for referrals. He no longer got those referrals because he had sinned against the unwritten code of the "professional culture" (Bledstein, 1976; Wright, 1970). He had challenged accepted professional practice in public.

What was the role played in this case by the Canadian Medical Association's high-sounding, written code of ethics? Apparently, none whatever. The professional elite, fearing controversy and the loss of income and prestige, was able to silence the concerned practitioner with impunity. Indeed, it was the higher quality of his personal ethics in speaking out that resulted in his informal banishment from practice by those adhering to narrow professional ethics.

In theology, the distinction between the sword and the scepter has long been acknowledged in the Roman Catholic Church—the church acts in things spiritual, and the state operates in things secular. It is part of the professional ethic. Yet in 1982, when six parishioners in Stellarton, Nova Scotia, knelt while receiving communion in church, the clergy denied the spiritual basis of the act and called in the civil authorities, who packed the parishioners off to court, where they were convicted of creating a "disturbance." What they had disturbed, of course, was not the peace but professional authority. They had defied the directives of bishop and pastor to foresake the old way of kneeling for the professionally approved innovation of taking communion while standing (*Chronicle Herald,* 1983; Dunwoody, n.d.; *Star-Phoenix,* 1985). The professionals were acting *for* God, as they saw it, or *as* God, as consumers of services are beginning to interpret a number of the actions by professionals.

The code of ethics advocated for adult education, however, does not rely on informal or traditional values. What is called for is a black-and-white document arrived at by consensus. It is the sort of written code Joan Wright described in her 1970 study of the professionalization of practitioners in adult education (Wright, 1970). She indicated that such formalized codes often include a variety of elements, but always two universals: that a fee or salary for services should be the sole remuneration and that no advertising should be done by any member of the profession. As the Canadian Medical Association puts it: "Remember that integrity and professional ability should be your only advertisement" (Canadian Medical Association, n.d.).

Canadian lawyers provide another example of the invocation of a written code of professional ethics. They were quick to apply it in what was to them a matter equal in seriousness to the situations that faced medicine and the church. A few lawyers in British Columbia and elsewhere began to offer the public lower fees than those set by their bar associations and to advertise their competitive rates. In accordance with its code of "ethics," the Law Society of British Columbia took disciplinary action to prevent such practice, practice clearly in the interests of the public but a threat to both professional authority and income (*The Globe and Mail,* 1982; *Vancouver Sun,* 1982).

A Critical Theory of Professionalism

The question is whether these examples reflect a basic problem with professional ethics or are merely unrepresentative isolated incidents. A body of literature has developed in recent years suggesting that these examples do reflect the reality of professionalism. Growing out of this literature is a theory indicating that professional codes of ethics are rhetorical facades of public service erected to preserve and enhance a profession's independent and monopolistic control over an area of social interaction (e.g., Illich, 1970, 1973, 1975; McKnight, n.d., 1977; Ralph, 1983).

Analysts like John McKnight, Diana Ralph, and Ivan Illich have challenged the assumption that professions are good for the people they allegedly serve. They accuse professionals of engaging in "the service business." This is the business of creating client needs to which the professionals then cater with services they have researched, developed, and manufactured to meet their own professional needs of status and increased income. Prestigious technological processes, such as the heart transplant, are destined for use among the wealthy, yet they tend to take precedence in medicine over public health initiatives that would be controversial but might decrease the need for such processes as transplants and improve the health of all. Expensive research, conducted by school professionals, documents the obvious but reports the findings in esoteric language that instigates one costly fad after another in the schools—to the detriment of the children in the care of the school officials. Yet, it is charged, the professionals use these fads—from behavioral objectives to what Thomas Armstrong calls "the learning disabilities scam"—to advance their own careerist ambitions. Such action not only *exists* throughout the professions; according to the critics, it *dominates* the modern-day professions.

The results of schooling and medicine that Illich reports— namely, higher expenditure on the schools in conjunction with less learning, increased funding of the medical profession in conjunction with the development of more and more illness—are neither ironic nor unintended. Illich shows that dropouts are taught to blame themselves rather than the system for their "failure" in school and then in life, a situation predetermined by their social and economic class. Consumers of health care, blinded by the mystique of modern medicine, seldom question the social function of the medical establishment.

The health professions, in fact, have become a significant part of the apparatus required for the preservation of an unjust society. In her book *Work and Madness: The Rise of Community Psychiatry*, Diana Ralph (1983) argues that industrialization of our society has resulted in a wide range of oppressive situations, including job dissatisfaction, lack of job security, unemployment, and economic stress. It is in the interests of employers and their governments to maintain the ability of the worker to cope, she wrote, and therefore they have supported the proliferation of community psychiatry. The mental illness profession diagnoses such individuals as ill and treats their symptoms with mood-altering drugs, behavior modification, and electroshock—treatment she says avoids dealing with the reality of the patients' alienated situations. Instead of prescribing expensive medical treatment to adjust individuals to alienating conditions, she writes, it might be more effective to encourage these people to analyze and change the conditions. But that does not appear to be in the interests of those in power or of the profession that caters to the powerful. Increasing worker productivity, keeping a lid on social unrest, and upholding private profits are at the root of the "madness business," according to the analysis by Ralph. Indeed, she argues that psychiatry actively cooperates with the police and public education in seeking to maintain social control of the population on behalf of the existing power structure.

The situation, the critics contend, is a concomitant of the professionalization process. It is a process they claim begins with the stated aims of better serving the public and protecting it from shoddy practices. It winds up defending special interest, privilege, monopoly, conspiracy to set prices, and the legal crushing of ethical dissenters within the professions. The Supreme Court of Canada, a body consisting in large part of lawyers, put the rationale this way in sustaining objections to advertising by lawyers and in upholding the defense of price fixing by the legal monopoly: "The general public is not in a position to appraise unassisted the need for legal services or the effectiveness of the services provided in the client's cause by the practitioner, and therefore stands in need of protection" (*The Globe and Mail,* 1982). It would seem that the concerns currently motivating advocates of a code of ethics in adult education are the very ones that have led other vocations down a slippery path.

The slippery path of professionalization leads to the monopoly by an elite over a particular area of practice. The state grants power to the elite to govern the right of its members to practice the profession. This power generally comes to be exercised by a politically oriented subgroup of professionals, an even more powerful elite, through a professional association like the medical or bar association. They utilize certification, accreditation, relicensure, mandatory in-service continuing education, codes of ethics, and discipline to maintain a stranglehold on their respective fields of practice and thereby elevate the economic and political power and the social control of their professions over the public. The political nature of professions is a crucial factor in understanding why their codes of ethics fail to achieve high standards of moral conduct.

Codes Political, Not Ethical

The development of norms of professional practice is not an ethical undertaking. It is a political undertaking. Law and medicine may have reached the top of the professional ladder by dedication and hard work. But it was by dedication and hard work primarily in the political arena. In his history of professionalization, Kenneth Imhoff (1980) shows how one vocation after another sprang up to create and/or meet public needs unmet by established practitioners. These newcomers then fought to achieve a position for their occupations equally as privileged as that of the existing professions. Successful in this effort, they, too, became elites. Imhoff uses the dramatic example of the flight of the privileged physicians from London during the plague of 1665. This self-serving act provided an opening into the medical business for the lowly apothecaries who had little choice but to remain in the city. Their aid to the physicianless afflicted gained acceptance for the apothecary vocation, which gradually but effectively engaged in the professionalization process to become a new elite termed "general practitioners." Soon the new profession was acting like the old. Historically, Imhoff writes, the primary motivation of professionals has been the "desire to protect their own positions in society, often with seemingly callous disregard for the welfare of the public" (1980, pp. 108–109).

The social fallout of this self-serving professionalization behind the facade of protecting the public has been to make people, the laity, increasingly dependent upon the professions. Efforts are made to pass laws forbidding the individual to install his or her own electrical wiring, and the "licensed electrician" starts on the way to professional status. The medical doctors started in a similar way, gradually increasing their power and hegemony. For years they used their influence in society in behalf of laws that weakened their competitors. They labeled practitioners of such alternative healing arts as chiropractic, acupuncture, and reflexology as ineffective quacks. The monopoly of the medical elite in most jurisdictions is still such as to cause legal trouble for unlicensed individuals who dare to prescribe alternative remedies. By their monopoly and their political power, a series of professional elites have seized the initiative from the people. Increasingly, people are forbidden to help each other. They must report for help to legally constituted helpers who will "service their needs." Self-confidence and independence are supplanted by feelings of inadequacy and dependency upon power groups, the professions (Ohliger, 1974).

All these unfortunate results accrue from approaches advocated in the interests of protecting and caring for the public. No one wants the individual to electrocute himself or herself. No one wants people to be lulled into a false sense of receiving proper advice if it is unsound quackery. But the critique challenging professionalization, as well as the real-life examples noted, would suggest that a professional code of ethics, written or otherwise, ultimately results in narrow, self-serving, professional ethics that are a travesty of true ethical action.

Clemenceau is said to have quipped that "military justice is to justice as military music is to music" (Sherrill, 1971). He could see that the structure of the military is such that neither justice nor music can flourish as such within the military system. They become instrumental to the interests and ends of the military profession. The same is true of professional ethics. Professional ethics are to ethics as military music is to music. They serve the narrow interests and ends of an elite. As such, professional ethics are the antithesis of real ethics.

Professional Ethics Codes in Adult Education: The Implications

If this analysis is correct, what are the implications of efforts to develop a code of ethics in adult education? Turning again to Wright's study (1970), she found that a number of concepts tend to appear in formalized codes of ethics of the various professions. While the only universals are to require fee-for-service remuneration and to forbid advertising, other professional values, norms, and symbols often appear in such codes, including:

1. The professional's belief in his or her authority based on expertise

2. The professional's belief in a professional monopoly based on that authority
3. The maintenance of the professional's monopoly of authority by admonition against his or her transfer of professional skills to clients

Are these the standards of behavior to be required by a code of ethics in adult education? The very opposite of such professional behavior would be more appropriate to adult education. But to seek to enforce any code of ethics on adult education would be falling into the professionalization trap and accepting the professional ethic, which is based on expertise, authority, monopoly, and mystification. "In an adult educator," former Fund for Adult Education Vice-President Robert Blakely wrote, "such an arrogance would be a fatal flaw . . ." (Blakely, 1966, p. 156).

It would be a fatal flaw because of the importance to Western liberal-social democracy of a pluralistic adult education open to involvement by the public. Adult education is the means whereby such a form of democracy can exist in a welter of competing interests and ideologies. It allows competing organizations and ideologies to engage in educational campaigns in favor of opposed alternatives (Carlson, 1980). Anyone can participate. No professional monopoly of adult educators can prevent efforts to educate that are deemed by the profession to be inappropriate. No volunteer can be ruled ineligible by an elite of professionals. As a result, there seems to be less need than in some other societies for labor camps for dissenters, less need for police-state methods, and less need for armed revolt. Adult education is a key element in the open society, a society that rejects totalitarianism.

"Principles of Good Practice in Continuing Education"

Despite the importance of an open adult education to an open society, efforts to impose professional codes of ethics have appeared in adult education. Brockett, in Chapter 1 of this volume, alludes to an existing set of "principles" in the field of adult education that he sees as at least similar to a code of ethics. These so-called "principles of good practice in continuing education" and their relationship to a code of ethics need analysis.

The "principles" were launched upon adult education in 1984 by means of a meeting that gathered 60 professionals, academics, business representatives, and government officials at a prestigious conference center in Wisconsin (Council on the Continuing Education Unit, 1984b). The meeting was a key part of an effort begun three years earlier by the major proponent agency of the "principles," the Council on the Continuing Education Unit (CCEU). Like any propagators of any faiths utilizing modern promotional processes, the Council was prepared to monitor "endorsement"—philosophical agreement with the "principles"; "adoption"—official promises by adult education organizations to use the "principles" within their institutions; and "implementation"—actual use of the "principles" by those organizations (Council on the Continuing Education Unit, 1984b). It also published a 30-page brochure and extensively advertised it and its contents to adult educators in an effort to achieve the desired hegemony of these "principles" throughout the field of adult education (Council on the Continuing Education Unit, 1984a).

"Principles," Codes of Ethics, and Ideology

A linkage can certainly be made between these alleged "principles of good practice in continuing education" and the concept of a code of ethics. In many ways, the pattern followed in the continuing effort to impose these "principles" on the field of adult education has been similar to attempts to impose codes of ethics on other vocations. There is a major difference, however, in that the advocates of these particular "principles" seem to be "true believers" in a dogma rather than pragmatic, politically oriented professionals seeking the lowest common denominator, the more traditional pattern of those working for professional ethics codes and professionalization generally.

"*Principles* calls for providers to define 'learning outcomes' for each offering," the ERIC Clearinghouse succinctly reported soon after the conference, "so that students will know exactly what they will learn, when, and how" (ERIC, 1984). This is indeed a "principle," even an ethic. But it is only one ethic among several; one creed in a pluralistic adult education.

It was quickly and rightly challenged by a practitioner of a different creed, Jack Mezirow, a professor at Teachers College, Columbia University. He characterized the "principles" as "more an April Fool's deception and a snare for the unsophisticated than a truth, law, rule or essence to be taken seriously" (1984, p. 28).

The Mechanistic Ideology

Indeed, the knowledgeable practitioner riffling through the "principles" document (Council on the Continuing Education Unit, 1984a) could quickly identify its ideological nature:

> The continuing education provider has clear and concise, written statements of intended learning outcomes for the continuing education program/activity. (p. 8)
> The agenda of the continuing education program/activity clearly specifies when each learning outcome will be addressed. (p. 13)
> Learning outcomes are sequenced so that learners are able to recognize their progress toward achieving the stated learning outcomes. (p. 13)
> Continuing education programs/activities are evaluated through assessment of learners' performance in terms of intended learning outcomes. (p. 18)
> Outcome is defined as "a specified change that is measurable or observable." (p. 8)

These ideological statements are clearly based on positivist philosophy and behaviorist psychology, the rock of the mechanistic dogma of schooling.

Faith in such dogma is equivalent to faith in the Trinity and the virgin birth, sectarian doctrines in Christiantity. While these Christian concepts were life and death matters some years ago, today only the most fanatical devotees would dismiss as non-Christians Unitarians and others who may reject such dogma.

Yet, the advocates of the document, *Principles of Good Practice in Continuing Education*, would impose their sectarianism upon a traditionally pluralistic field of practice. They would proscribe the ethic of adult education that allows free range for the Holy Spirit and individual initiative to determine, on an apparently ad hoc basis, what is learned, when, and how. They would deny as heresy the allegation that virtually all (or even some) meaningful learning experiences in people's lives are those beyond the pale of "defined learning outcomes." They would use their sectarian "principles" as the ethical and ideological criteria for an Inquisition directed at the adult educator who claims that "specified learning outcomes" tend to trivialize adult education or to turn it into indoctrination. They would dismiss, as unethical, charges that their "principles" of tight control and careful packaging are more appropriately utilized in manufacturing a product of standardized quality like a box of crackers than in achieving meaningful education (Mezirow, 1984).

The Costs of a Professional Code

Whether true believers or those seeking the lowest common denominator eventually impose a code of ethics on adult education, it is hard to visualize any gain to the society from such a code. At the same time, the loss to the individual and to the society under an imposed ethical code would be staggering. Under the *Principles of Good Practice in Continuing Education,* freedom to learn would be dramatically diminished. Joy in learning would suffer the same fate as joy at the workplace when the assembly line was introduced to improve standards of quantity and quality of production.

Efficient evaluation advocated by the *Principles* would ensure that tyros who did poorly in Introductory Ballroom Dancing would not be eligible for Intermediate Ballroom Dancing, even if the learner wanted to take it and the adult educators were willing. Mastery of the basics would be required under the code of ethics. No longer could adult education be ethically utilized for the unstated goals of individuals, goals that would be seen as open to abuse by unethical adult educators. No longer would lonely persons who failed to master Dance I be allowed to move on to Dance II with the friends they had made. It would be an unethical act by an adult educator to allow an unspecified outcome, the friends made in Dance I, to determine "promotion." The adult educator's pecuniary self-interest, moreover, encourages promotion to Dance II, since the lonely "failure" will likely drop out rather than repeat the class with a new set of strangers. Such pecuniary self-interest of the practitioner, one of the major unstated reasons for a professional code of ethics, could ironically be prevented by the code from operating in this instance in the interest of the learner. To be ethical, in the religion of mechanistic education, the practitioner would have to prevent enrollment in Dance II or ensure that the goal of making new friends is specified at the beginning of Dance I, degrading and embarrassing the lonely person at the outset.

It is important to recognize that the ramifications of questionable decisions and recommendations, even of outright fraud, are different in adult education than, for example, in medicine. A recommendation for removal of the tonsils, appendix, or uterus is more serious than promotion of the "unqualified" dancer to the next level of instruction to be with his or her newly won friends. Yet what medical code of ethics has prevented a high incidence of medical advice in behalf of such operations, surgery often deemed by professional peers to have been unnecessary? Even in such life-and-death matters, economic enhancement of the professional has taken precedence at times over the interests of the client. One wonders just how much "protection" the learner would achieve from the implementation of the *Principles of Good Practice in Continuing Education*. The learner may well lose not only freedom and joy, but also money and independence, from an enhancement of the prestige and power accorded to adult educators operating as "professionals" on such a code of ethics.

Codes of ethics and their concomitant professionalization, it would seem, are more oriented toward narrowness, profit, and totalitarianism than toward enlightenment, client protection, and democracy. Associated with such codes are politically arrived at party lines of "professional ethics," professional monopoly over the vocation by force of law, centralized control through licensure and relicensure, a concentration of power in the hands of an elite of politically oriented professionals who control the majority of prac-titioners, and increased dependency upon the "profession" by the public. This is the fruit of the apparently well-meaning desire to ensure a high standard of moral conduct in the practice of a vocation. It would appear that the attempt to protect the individual is bought at too high a social price. The effort to protect individual participants by allowing adult educators to emulate the ways of other professions is simply too dangerous to countenance in a democratic society.

Participant Self-Defense Better Than Professional Codes

Even without a professional code of ethics for protection, the individual participant in adult education can still take defensive action. The individual can look for practitioners of adult education with personal standards as high as those held by professionals persecuted through the years by the elite and its "professional ethics." Ethical individuals exist in adult education, as in other vocations. The intelligent participant can find and work with such individuals whose personal and societal values he or she regards. If this is *caveat emptor*, the concept might be more appropriate than many have recognized. Most people do find ways of utilizing the marketplace to their advantage and of avoiding at least the worst of the plunderers. Professional codes of ethics, on the other hand, are smokescreens thrown up to cloud the good sense of those who would be better off heeding *caveat emptor* than relying on the good faith of any professional "in good standing."

This concept of defensive action against the professions and their practitioners is consistent with what Martin Carnoy (1974a, 1974b) has called "defensive education." "It makes . . . sense," Carnoy wrote, "to speak of *defensive* education for most people of the world; an education that helps children and adults defend themselves against exploitation by dominant classes in thier own societies and in the industrial societies" (1974b, p. 58). And what more dominant classes are there in these times than the professional classes?

The major safeguards for democracy, client protection, and significant learning in adult education would appear to be participants sensitized to the dangers of professionalism and practitioners with perspective on their work and commitments to considered sets of personal values. Brockett's discussion of his model, "dimensions of ethical practice in adult education," in Chapter 1 is relevant here, but only to underline the relative importance of the personal value systems and the relative insignificance of what he calls multiple responsibilities and operationalization of values. These latter aspects are simply the context in which personal values are practiced. It is compatible personal and social values that the participant must look for in practitioners when seeking to engage an adult educator.

Conclusion

Instead of trying to institutionalize adult education with a professional code of ethics, practitioners would be better absorbed in developing their own personal values and in gaining an understanding of the historical and philosophical foundations of their work. Leslie Gail Rothaus (1981) was on the right track when she wrote that adult education "must come to terms with the sharp contrast between the original intentions of the field to stimulate grass roots policy-making and social action . . . [and] the current movement to create and empower trained experts, whose instrument is simply prescriptive policy formation through bureaucratic information-gathering and dissemination systems" (p. 20).

Perspective and commitment to humane values by practitioners can retard the forces of institutionalization, professionalization, and dehumanization of adult education. A professional code of ethics, whether an imposed ideology or the lowest common denominator of a series of competing ideologies, is an attempt to institutionalize and standardize values. It is a false friend of the participant and the society, a ploy to further the political and economic self-interest of an aspiring profession.

Ethics functions when the individual makes personal choices, not when the decisions are imposed by a politically motivated professional code. Ethical issues arise in all areas of adult education practice: in program planning and evaluating, in marketing of programs, in administering or advising or teaching, in deciding to use or not to use some instrument of technology, in participating or not participating in action for social change, in conducting research in the field. In adult education all too often concepts, technologies, and techniques that are rife with moral implications are presented as though they were devoid of ethical import. No standardized professional code is likely to change this situation. Indeed, such a code is more likely to legitimize the absence of personal moral judgments in the field of practice.

The question is whether you, the adult educator, have a perspective and a personal value system that enable you to see the underlying assumptions and that alert you to the fact that you are faced with an ethical issue requiring choice. Do you believe, for example, in the authority of the adult educator's expertise, or do you try to demystify adult education? Do you favor a professional monopoly based on the authority of the adult educator's expertise, or do you encourage co-learning and an egalitarian exchange of knowledge between practitioner and participant in adult education? Do you seek to maintain a professional monopoly of authority by refusing to transfer professional skills to clients, or do you share your expertise with learners, putting yourself truly in the service of the laity (Rothaus, 1981)?

What is important for participant and practitioner alike in adult education is to recognize that there are choices to be made. It is experience and sensitivity in making such choices—not politically inspired, standardized, professional codes of ethics—that will lead to a high standard of moral conduct in the practice of adult education. There is no need to develop a professional code of ethics. Indeed, considerable evidence suggests advantage in avoiding this move. What is needed is a recognition of the choices facing us and a will to base these personal choices on reasoned and humane values.

References

Blakely, R. J. (1966). Is adult education developing as a profession? *Continuous Learning, 5*(4), 153–158.

Bledstein, B. (1976). *The culture of professionalism.* New York: Norton.

Canadian Medical Association. (n.d.). *Code of ethics.* Ottawa, Ontario: CMA Communications Department.

Carlson, R. A. (1980, November 2). *An alternative policy to that of the professionalization of adult education: A response to the address of John McKnight on professionalism.* Speech presented at the annual meeting of the Commission of Professors of Adult Education, St. Louis, MO.

Carnoy, M. (1974a). *Education as cultural imperialism.* New York: McKay.

Carnoy, M. (1974b). Learning to be—Consensus and contradictions. *Convergence, 7*(3), 53–60.

Chronicle Herald. (1983, February 16). Halifax, Nova Scotia, p. 5.

Council on the Continuing Education Unit. (1984a). *Principles of good practice in continuing education: Report of the CCEU project to develop standards and criteria for good practice in continuing education.* Silver Spring, MD: Author.

Council on the Continuing Education Unit. (1984b). *Principles of good practice in continuing education.* Report of the conference at the Wingspread Conference Center, Racine, Wisconsin.

Dunwoody, G. (n.d.) *Professions in society: Implications for adult education.* Unpublished paper, University of Saskatchewan, Saskatoon.

ERIC. (1984). *Principles of good practice.* (Brief report of the CCEU conference in Racine, Wisconsin, reproduced in the Canadian Association for Adult Education news package, *circa* May, 1984, no page number.)

The Globe and Mail. (1982, August 10). Toronto, Ontario, pp. 1, 2.

Illich, I. (1970). *Deschooling society.* New York: Harper & Row.

Illich, I. (1973). *After deschooling, what?* New York: Harper & Row.

Illich, I. (1975). *Medical nemesis.* London: Calder & Boyars.

Imhoff, K. J. (1980). *Professionalization: Implications for Canadian adult educators.* Unpublished master's thesis, University of Saskatchewan, Saskatoon.

McKnight, J. (n.d.). *The professional problem.* Unpublished manuscript.

McKnight, J. (1977). Professionalized service and disabling help. In I. Illich et al. (Eds.), *Disabling professions* (pp. 69–91). London: Marion Boyars.

Mezirow, J. (1984). Review of *Principles of good practice in continuing education. Lifelong Learning: An Omnibus of Practice and Research, 8*(3), 27–28, 31.

Ohliger, J. (1974). Is lifelong adult education a guarantee of permanent inadequacy? *Convergence, 7*(2), 47–59.

Ralph, D. (1983). *Work and madness: The rise of community psychiatry.* Montreal: Black Rose Books.

Rothaus, L. G. (1981). The conspiracy against the laity. *Setting the Pace, 1*(3), 16–26.

Sherrill, R. (1971). *Military justice is to justice as military music is to music.* New York: Harper & Row.

Shores, L., Sork, T. J., Davenport, E., & Carlson, R. (1983). *A code of ethics for adult educationists—Our common bond?* Paper presented at the annual meeting of the American Association for Adult and Continuing Education, Philadelphia.

Star-Phoenix. (1975). Saskatoon, Saskatchewan, July 29, p. 4; July 30, p. 4; August 1, p. 13.

Star-Phoenix. (1985, March 15). Saskatoon, Saskatchewan, p. A10.

Vancouver Sun. (1982, August 10). Vancouver, British Columbia, p. A14.

Wright, J. W. (1970). *The professionalization of practitioners in the institutionalized occupation of adult education.* Unpublished doctoral dissertation, Cornell University, Ithaca, NY.

CHAPTER TWELVE

Translating Personal Values and Philosophy into Practical Action

ROGER HIEMSTRA

THE appearance now of this book in adult education's literature base is probably more a reflection of the field's maturity than of any other factor. In fact, as is pointed out in previous chapters, a variety of ethical issues are currently under discussion. Standards of practice, certification issues, ethical dilemmas faced daily by many adult educators, and even discussion about the need for a professional code of ethics are all indicators of a field's natural evolution, maturity, and growth in professionalization.

Whether or not a reader agrees with some of the dilemmas presented in other chapters, I believe it is very healthy to think about such issues and to reflect critically on our personal actions as adult education professionals. Reflection and questioning as precursors to thinking about and assuming responsibility for one's action should be superior to the "seat-of-your-pants" management of daily chores that can become a way of life for the very busy professional.

This chapter's purpose is to engage readers in an analysis of personal values and philosophy in terms of their professional action as adult educators. As Brockett points out in his Chapter 1 model, a personal value system serves as a basic stepping stone to ethical practice and behavior. Kasworm, in Chapter 2, also addresses the process of developing personal values in terms of adult development theory. This recognition of personal values, beliefs, and the various changes a person undergoes throughout life, if combined with a personal philosophy statement, can result in foundational tools useful as guides or mirrors for subsequent professional actions and ethical decision making.

This chapter will discuss why a professional should have a philosophy, summarize various philosophical frameworks, and talk about the potential of such frameworks for understanding adult education practice and for use as guides for personal decisions. In addition, my statement of philosophy as a teacher and how I translate this into professional action will be discussed as an example of how one person has wrestled with applying personal philosophy to practice. Readers will be shown how and encouraged to construct a personal philosophy statement. Finally, some discussion of philosophy in relation to the preparation of adult educators in a graduate program setting will be included.

Why Have a Philosophy?

Why should an adult education professional even worry about philosophy or having a personal statement of philosophy? Elias (1982) perhaps best states an answer to this question when he notes that "philosophers of every age have offered explanation of freedom and determinism, individual and societal rights, good and evil, and truth and falsehood" (p. 3). I write this chapter based on the premise that most professionals are desirous of at least working toward a personal understanding of such explanations.

From my experience I believe that there are at least four reasons for an adult education professional to be able to explicate a personal philosophy:

1. A philosophy promotes an understanding of human relationships
2. A philosophy sensitizes one to the various needs associated with positive human interactions
3. A philosophy provides a framework for distinguishing, separating, and understanding personal values
4. A philosophy promotes flexibility and consistency in working with adult learners

Merriam (1982) also notes that philosophy can inform practice, provide guidelines for policy decisions, and guide administrators, teachers, and counselors in their everyday practice: "Philosophy contributes to professionalism. Having a philosophic orientation separates the professional continuing educator from the paraprofessional in that professionals are aware of what they are doing and why they are doing it. A philosophy offers goals, values, and attitudes to strive for. It thus can be motivating, inspiring, and energizing to the practitioner" (pp. 90–91). Boggs (1981) suggests that philosophy provides "the means whereby adults . . . not only get information but also interpret it, organize it, and use it in making decisions and in taking action" (p. 4).

But being able to state a personal philosophy and use it in making decisions or taking action is not necessarily easy. For example, Cunningham (1982) describes the potential for contradictory and inconsistent views that may be held by a continuing educator: "It is not problematic that inconsistencies occur when a thoughtfully conceived system of values is put into practice. What is worrisome is that continuing educators develop and operate programs without a clearly visualized set of values in which the adult learner and societal well-being are central concerns" (p. 85).

It is this need for a clearly identified set of values that may be most important for the busy professional. Darkenwald and Merriam (1982) describe this need as follows:

> Many adult education practitioners engaged in the daily tasks of program planning, administration, or teaching have little time to reflect upon the meaning and direction of their activity. The educator is generally more concerned with skills than with principles, with means than with ends, with details than with the whole picture. Yet all practitioners make decisions and act in ways that presuppose certain values and beliefs. Whether or not it is articulated, a philosophical orientation underlies most individual and institutional practices in adult education. (p. 37)

Thus the main power of philosophy is its ability to help people better understand and appreciate what they do.

Philosophical Systems for Educators

Many efforts have been made to derive some philosophical guidance for educators. There are a number of scholars who have developed and advocated a single philosophical model. Others have attempted to systematize or separate these models into an array or system for comparison on various factors. Brubacher (1969) perhaps provides the most comprehensive system, or what he refers to as schools of educational philosophy. He identifies no less than a dozen distinct schools of thought, ranging from "pragmatic naturalism" to "democracy."

A useful document presenting a rationale for philosophy's use to adult educators is Apps's (1973) monograph. He describes five categories (essentialism, perennialism, progressivism, reconstructionism, and existentialism) as bases for viewing and understanding the purposes of adult education. The most comprehensive effort to date of examining various models for application to adult education has been carried out by Elias and Merriam (1980). They discuss the difficulties in attempting to understand the various schools of thought and make some sense out of them for adult education: "The problems of classifying different philosophers into schools have long been recognized. Nevertheless, the systematization of the discipline continues and schools of thought develop because similarities and affinities do exist among theorists" (p. 1). They then describe six distinct systems they believe have relevance for study and understanding by adult educators.

Their organizational scheme has received considerable attention among adult education scholars. For example, Podeschi (1986) delineates a number of values prevalent in the United States that appear to cluster around some beliefs central to four of the six systems. Zinn (1983) developed a self-administered, self-scoring, and self-interpreted instrument for measuring the extent to which a person values five of the six systems. Based on a seven-point Likert Scale, 75 items related to such topics as program planning, adult learning, the purpose of adult education, and teaching adults are presented. McKenzie (1985) carried out a study using the instrument and suggests that his findings "could be the basis for the conclusion that many adult educators merely accept patterns of practice (and corresponding theoretical assumptions) to which they have been exposed without testing these patterns critically" (p. 20). He suggests further that adult education practice should include some theoretical reflection and a critical examination of some philosophical grounds for that practice.

Constructing a Personal Philosophy

Learning to reflect critically on practice is something that takes effort. In the graduate program of adult education at Syracuse University, we believe such effort is crucial in the development of highly skilled professionals. We encourage each student to develop a personal statement of philosophy, typically in their first graduate course. Such a statement then can be examined and updated periodically as the person progresses through courses and achieves a heightened understanding of the field and of individual strengths. It would not be unusual for a student to be asked during a qualifying examination one or more questions that in some way relate to a personal philosophy of education. We stress to students the need for a framework of values and beliefs as a foundation for ethical practice as professionals.

When I am helping others develop their personal statements of philosophy I present a set of systems that overlaps five of the frameworks presented by Elias and Merriam (1980) but that also details two additional systems, idealism and realism, as a foundation-building mechanism. During the presentation we talk about how different philosophies or views of human nature affect the professional and ethical decisions a person makes. This typically leads to further discussion about the need for each adult educator to be able to articulate a personal philosophy. Figure 12.1 summarizes the information I present.

Plato's idealism model is based on the notion that life is made up of ideas or truths that should be used for remolding a less than perfect world. Realism, on the other hand, is predicated on the belief that ideals can come only through proven facts and that rationality, observation, and analysis are the keys to improving life. Some adult educators will be able to extract some meaning from either of these models. For example, a person who has considerable affinity for an idealistic view might make an ethical decision that a well-paid expert lecturing to a group of adults would want there to be no questions from the audience and would therefore structure a highly formal setting. A realist who designed an adult course, on the other hand, might require that the teacher or expert back up all assertions with various forms of proof or bibliographic support.

Dewey's pragmatic model suggests that research and scientific problem solving lead to logical interpretations of what successful living is. With this model, the adult education teacher would serve as a democratic guide for any necessary learning and ethically might feel that the student's role in any learning needs to be enhanced. On the opposite side of the coin is the liberalism model that had its beginning centuries ago with the thinking of such philosophers as Socrates and Aristotle. They believed that because humans have a special gift for reasoning, an improvement of intel-

FIGURE 12.1. Philosophical Systems and Education

IDEALISM

Meaning: The overall meaning is in life itself
What is Reality: Divine or absolute truths
Nature of Humanness: Each of us is a part of the meaning
Educational Aims: Tell others the truths
Educational Method: Inductive reasoning; authority lecturing
Educational Content: Life's events; the world of our own mind
Main Criticism: "Truths" may be only in beholder's eyes
Key Proponents: Plato (Cushman, 1958; Taylor, 1926)
Programs/Practices: Some religious education programs

REALISM

Meaning: Empirically proven facts; reality
What is Reality: Natural laws and facts
Nature of Humanness: Awareness is perceiving
Educational Aims: Develop intellectual abilities
Educational Method: Inductive and scientific reasoning
Educational Content: Life's laws and principles
Main Criticism: Empirical facts always subject to change
Key Proponents: Chisholm (1961); Whitehead (1933)
Programs/Practices: Phenomenology; science education

PROGRESSIVISM

Meaning: Concrete facts and interrelationships
What is Reality: Theory is based on truth
Nature of Humanness: Humans are part of the environment
Educational Aims: Development through experiencing
Educational Method: Problem solving; experimental method
Educational Content: Build on people's experiences and needs
Main Criticism: Diminishes traditional role of teacher
Key Proponents: Bergevin (1967); Dewey (1938); Lindeman (1926)
Programs/Practices: Adult Basic Education, community education,
                        Cooperative Extension

LIBERALISM

Meaning: Freedom comes through a liberated mind
What is Reality: Humans endowed with ability to reason
Nature of Humanness: Improvement through intellect and wisdom
Educational Aims: Development of the mind
Educational Method: Critical reading; teacher as expert
Educational Content: History; humanities; the classics
Main Criticism: Past may not relate to modern problems
Key Proponents: Aristotle (Bambrough, 1963); Hutchins (1968)
Programs/Practices: Chautauqua; Elderhostel; Great Books; Lyceum;
                        Center for the Study of Liberal Education
                        for Adults

FIGURE 12.1. (*Continued*)

BEHAVIORALISM

Meaning:	Human behavior tied to prior conditioning
What is Reality:	External forces control human behavior
Nature of Humanness:	Stimulus creates response
Educational Aims:	Behavioral change; develop survival skills
Educational Method:	Conditioning; feedback; practice
Educational Content:	Life skills; basic skills
Main Criticism:	Learning too complex for behavioral control
Key Proponents:	Skinner (1971); Tyler (1949)
Programs/Practices:	Adult Performance Level; behavior modification; behavioral objectives

HUMANISM

Meaning:	Intellect distinguishes humans and animals
What is Reality:	Humans have potential and innate goodness
Nature of Humanness:	Dignity. freedom, and autonomy are sacred
Educational Aims:	Individual potentiality; self-actualization
Educational Method:	Self-direction; teamwork; facilitation
Educational Content:	Any curriculum a vehicle for meeting needs
Main Criticism:	Important societal goals can be missed
Key Proponents:	Knowles (1980); Maslow (1976); Rogers (1969); Tough (1979)
Programs/Practices:	Individualized learning efforts; learning projects; sensitivity training

RADICALISM

Meaning:	People create meaning, history, and culture
What is Reality:	Knowledge leads to understanding of reality
Nature of Humanness:	Humans can change their environment
Educational Aims:	Create change through education/knowledge
Educational Method:	Dialogue and problem solving
Educational Content:	Begin with cultural situation of learners
Main Criticism:	Tends to be idealistic in nature
Key Proponents:	Adams (1975); Freire (1970); Illich (1970)
Programs/Practices:	Community-based literacy; Freire's literacy training; Highlander Center

lect through constant exposure to classical works is the path to an improved world. The arguments of liberal versus vocational emphases have been around for some time in the U.S. literature on adult education.

More a way of doing than of thinking, Skinner's behaviorist model is predicated on the notion that stimulus and response are natural forces for humans as well as animals. Programmed instruction, computer-assisted instruction, and various teaching machines were developed with this model as a basis. For example, as a teacher I incorporate some behaviorist thinking in my use of learning contracts.

Evolution of the humanism model from the thinking of people like Carl Rogers and Abraham Maslow has had a tremendous impact on North American adult education thinking in the past 20 to 30 years. Indeed, much of the current scholarly thinking and resultant programs related to self-direction in learning can be traced to the humanism model. Related ethical decisions adult educators will make center around beliefs that learners must have considerable freedom and autonomy in educational experiences.

A more recent North American interest in terms of program development has been stimulated by the radicalism model. Programs like the Highlander Folk School and community-based literacy efforts are examples of such interest. Educators in such programs are likely to support or even encourage learners to confront aspects of the environment that are serving to block their development in some way. Whereas someone with the radical framework in mind often will promote confrontations, such behaviors would likely present ethical dilemmas for humanists or progressivists because the latter groups would be in favor of protecting the personal rights of all people.

I present the information described above to students and lead some discussion pertaining to how adult educators have wrestled with issues of philosophy for some time. For example, Bergevin (1967) believes it is important to consider several basic philosophical concepts in building a personal statement, such as issues about differences between children and adults, abilities for lifelong learning, the importance of learner needs or problems, and how learning resources are utilized. Cunningham (1982) talks about contradictions that can occur: "Clearly, human potential programs based on a philosophy emphasizing the autonomy of the learner [such as with the humanism model] are in conflict with empowerment programs [derived from the radicalism model] whose goals are based on altering social arrangements, even though the anti-institutional analyses on which both these practices are based appear similar" (p. 84). Apps (1985) also describes a major problem with examining a list of philosophical frameworks: "They can prevent analysis and original thought. Once one reads through a description of these various philosophers, the tendency is to try to fit one's own philosophy into one of these established philosophies. Once one has done so, the inclination is to become comfortable with this new-found intellectual home and stop questioning and challenging and constantly searching for new positions" (pp. 72–73).

We discuss a variety of related concepts and potential problems, and then I suggest how students might use such information in constructing their own personal philosophy. I point out that, in another source, Apps (1982a) suggests there are at least four phases in a process of analyzing personal beliefs: (1) the identification of beliefs held about adult education or adults as learners, (2) searching for contradictions among the beliefs held, (3) discovering personal, institutional, or social/cultural bases for at least the most important beliefs, and (4) making judgments about any bases for the particular beliefs held. Such a filtering or screening technique usually results in a much clearer understanding of what a person's most important beliefs are.

Then I introduce students to a worksheet (Figure 12.2) that provides headers similar to those used in my presentation on various models. I provide my own statement of philosophy (see the next section) to demonstrate how I used the headers to guide my thinking. Most students will have read the Elias and Merriam (1980) book, and I point out what they offer as possible options in deciding on a philosophy statement: (1) choose a particular model or philosophic framework that best fits with personal values and beliefs, (2) opt for an eclectic approach and choose certain elements to integrate into a personal model, or (3) choose a particular framework upon which a personal statement of philosophy is built (p. 206). The many sources related to philosophy cited by Apps (1982b) are noted for the students' further reading. Finally, I offer to provide feedback and reflection as students create their personal statements. My feedback typically centers around how they think through ways of translating their system of beliefs into practice as professionals and how such beliefs will impact on ethical decision making. Some students also will opt to work together in the development process for the synergistic value of networking.

A Personal Philosophy of Education

The purpose of this section is to describe my philosophy and how I translate such philosophy into a teaching and learning process. The process and my educational philosophy are based on the premise

FIGURE 12.2. Personal Philosophy Worksheet

PHILOSOPHICAL BELIEFS

Philosophical System:

Meaning:

What is Reality?

Nature of Being Human:

PROFESSIONAL PRACTICE

Educational Aims:

Educational Method:

Educational Content:

that adult education students are mature learners who flourish in settings where considerable independence is expected or permissible. Thus the process I use is a dynamic one that actively involves the learner in determining personal learning needs, potential, and capabilities.

Beliefs Associated with Adult Teaching and Learning

I suspect most current day educators carry a certain portion of John Dewey's heritage around in their value system. I certainly have been influenced somewhat by his thinking. His beliefs that education is a continuous process of reconstructing experiences, that students are capable of a greater and more active role in the learning process, that the teacher's role is to guide the process of learning, and that the school is a social institution that should reflect and alter the culture (Archambault, 1964; Dewey, 1916, 1922, 1938) certainly have influenced me.

Behaviorist beliefs also have had some impact on me. The role of the teacher in designing an environment that elicits desired human behaviors is clearly one that I can subscribe to in terms of paying attention to environmental needs, making the best use of media and other learning devices, and providing some type of feedback to learners regarding their personal progress (Skinner, 1971). My use of learning contracts is also based on some behavioral expectations (Knowles, 1975, 1986).

The lifelong learning movement of the 1960s and 1970s and the concurrent beliefs of many educators that learning must be lifetime in nature have had a tremendous impact on me (Cassara, 1979; Cropley, 1980; Dave, 1976; Gelpi, 1979; Gross, 1977, 1982; Hesburgh, Miller, & Wharton, 1973; Hiemstra, 1976a; Himmelstrup, 1980). My research on and work with older learners has convinced me, too, that the potential for learning can increase throughout life if we know how to stimulate that potential (Hiemstra, 1975, 1976b, 1980a, 1985a). Finally, considerable personal scholarship related to self-direction in learning has substantiated beliefs about the desire of learners to assume considerable responsibility for their own learning (Brockett & Hiemstra, 1985; Brockett, Hiemstra, & Penland, 1982; Hiemstra, 1980b, 1982, 1985b).

Perhaps the biggest impact on my philosophy and ethical beliefs has been the humanist movement of the past 30 years. I share with most humanists beliefs in the natural goodness of humankind, in freedom of choice, in the dignity and worth of all people, and in the value of establishing an environment in which the potential inherent in every person can be developed (Rogers, 1969). Thus a person wishing to understand my teaching philosophy must realize that I view the act of learning as a highly personal endeavor in which the teacher serves as a facilitator, helper, and partner in the learning process.

Therefore, I think one must call me somewhat eclectic in terms of my beliefs regarding teaching and learning. As Elias and Merriam (1980) note, "In this approach one chooses certain elements from different theories and operates according to those principles" (p. 206). Centered within my eclectic choosing is a heavy reliance on humanistic belief in the power of each individual learner to discover personal learning needs. My role then becomes that of helping to facilitate both such a discovery and the subsequent learning related to the identified needs.

Statement of Philosophy

Given the set of beliefs described above, I offer to learners in my course my professional statement of philosophy (see Figure 12.3). This statement also serves as a framework for my own decision-making process, and periodically I do haul it out as a reference point when I am faced with some sticky issue. I include it in this chapter in the hope that it can serve as a model for others wishing to develop a personal statement.

My Teaching and Learning Process

The translation of such a philosophical statement into a consistent teaching and learning process was not something I did overnight. What I have attempted to do over the past several years is to become as knowledgeable as I could about the likes and dislikes of the mature adult in a learning setting. I bring to this knowledge the kind of beliefs described above.

Following are some of the specific duties I undertake, therefore, in translating such beliefs and philosophy into a facilitator role with learners:

- Providing direct information on certain topics through lecturing, media, or other learning techniques
- Serving as a resource on certain portions of the course content
- Assisting learners to assess their needs and competencies so that each person can map out an individual learning path

FIGURE 12.3. A Personal Philosophy of Education

PHILOSOPHICAL BELIEFS

Philosophical System: I draw eclectically on several systems. However, the humanism model provides the foundation upon which rests most of what I do as a teacher. I also try very hard to be consistent with the tenets of this foundation not only in what I do as a professional but also in my role as spouse, parent, and community member.

Meaning: I believe that intellect is what distinguishes humans from animals and that we have the potential to expand that intellect throughout life. I also believe that there are a large number of concrete facts basic to our being able to perform as capable adult education professionals.

What is Reality? The reality that I embrace rests on an assumption that all humans are basically good and have potential for continuous growth and development as individuals. This growth can include such features as intellectual improvement, enhanced interrelationship abilities, and expanding civic literacy skills.

Nature of Being Human: I adhere to basic humanistic notions that the dignity of each human being must be respected. I also respect each person's desire for autonomy and independence but recognize that such desire is in a constant state of fluctuation.

PROFESSIONAL PRACTICE

Educational Aims: I believe that educational aims should center around helping adults reach their maximum potential in any learning setting. This should include both the development of personal intellect and the translation of new knowledge into practical skills and behaviors.

Educational Method: I encourage considerable self-direction and student involvement in all aspects of a course. I also use learning contracts as a means for students to plan individual routes through the learning experiences.

Educational Content: I provide learners with some basic parameters of what the course should cover in order to meet professional expectations regarding mastery of the subject matter. However, because there are so many ways of achieving mastery, students are involved in some needs assessment activities at the beginning of the course to help them plan their specific route through the content and to provide me with some input to help in my preparation of curricular material, activities, and experiences for the remainder of the course.

- Providing feedback on various drafts of each person's learning contract
- Serving as a resource locator or securing new information on some of the topics identified during needs assessment efforts
- Arranging for speakers, setting up outside learning experiences, and building a varied collection of learning resources
- Working with learners outside of the classroom as a stimulator or sounding board
- Helping adults develop an attitude about and approach to learning that fosters independence
- Promoting discussion, the raising of questions, small group activity, and a positive attitude about learning
- Managing a learning process throughout the specified time period that includes such activities as rediagnosis of needs, acquisition of continuous feedback, and fostering of learner involvement
- Serving as a validator or evaluator of student accomplishment both throughout and at the end of a course

Thus the teaching and learning process that I use calls for the instructor to serve as a facilitator of the learning process and for students to assume responsibility for their own achievements. When I teach a graduate course, for example, I provide the following statement to class members at the beginning of the course:

> It is the instructor's philosophy that adult students should be actively involved in all learning processes and activities, including assessing the group's and personal learning needs and evaluating the various learning efforts. Furthermore, each adult has considerable potential for self-directed, independent learning on any topic. Thus, each learner will be encouraged to develop a learning contract that represents an individual commitment to obtaining new skills and upgrading existing competencies relative to the course topic through independent, group, and in-class study.

It has been my experience that the mature learner flourishes in a setting in which identification of needs, personal ownership of learning involvement, and use of a wide variety of available resources are integrated parts of the instructional process.

Conclusion

The adult education field has matured to a point where we must understand personal philosophy and ethical behavior. Private entrepreneurship, marketing issues, certification or mandatory continuing education requirements, lifelong education versus lifelong schooling, and worldwide literacy problems are only a few of the dilemmas facing adult educators today. Such problems have been matched by the continual increase in numbers of professionals, programs, and learners. Understanding more about personal roles and responsibilities is necessary if such dilemmas and changes are to be managed. This book will provide a foundation upon which some personal growth and enhanced understanding can take place.

Thus I conclude this chapter by encouraging the reader to attempt the development of a personal statement of philosophy if one does not already exist. Whether the process I have outlined or some other process is used, it should be informative and professionally rewarding to wrestle with an understanding of personal values, beliefs, and ethics. Such a statement can be compared with the philosophy of an employing institution or of other professionals to provide a foundation for future practice.

References

Adams, F. (with Horton, M.). (1975). *Unearthing seeds of fire.* Winston-Salem, NC: John F. Blair.

Apps, J. W. (1973). *Toward a working philosophy of adult education.* Syracuse, NY: Syracuse University Publications in Continuing Education.

Apps, J. W. (1982a). Developing a belief structure. In C. Klevins (Ed.), *Materials and methods in adult and continuing education* (pp. 25–32). Los Angeles: Klevens.

Apps, J. W. (1982b). Sources in philosophy and continuing education. In S. B. Merriam (Ed.), *Linking philosophy and practice* (New Directions for Continuing Education No. 15, pp. 93–101). San Francisco: Jossey-Bass.

Apps, J. W. (1985). *Improving practice in continuing education.* San Francisco: Jossey-Bass.

Archambault, R. D. (1964). *John Dewey on education.* New York: Modern Library, Random House.

Bambrough, R. (Ed.). (1963). *The philosophy of Aristotle* (A. E. Wardman & J. L. Creed, Trans.). New York: New American Library of World Literature.

Bergevin, P. (1967). *A philosophy for adult education.* New York: Seabury.

Boggs, D. L. (1981). Philosophies at issue. In B. W. Kreitlow (Ed.), *Examining controversies in adult education* (pp. 1–10). San Francisco: Jossey-Bass.

Brockett, R. G., & Hiemstra, R. (1985). Bridging the theory–practice gap in self-directed learning. In S. Brookfield (Ed.), *Self-directed learning: From theory to practice* (New Directions for Continuing Education No. 25, pp. 31–40). San Francisco: Jossey-Bass.

Brockett, R. G., Hiemstra, R., & Penland, P. R. (1982). Self-directed learning. In C. Klevins (Ed.), *Materials and methods in adult and continuing education* (pp. 171–178). Los Angeles: Klevens.

Brubacher, J. S. (1969). *Modern philosophies of education.* New York: McGraw-Hill.

Cassara, B. B. (1979). The lifelong learning act—An assessment. *Convergence, 12,* 55–63.

Chisholm, R. M. (1961). *Realism and the background of phenomenology.* Glencoe, IL: Free Press.

Cropley, A. J. (1980). *Towards a system of lifelong education.* Oxford, England: Pergamon.

Cunningham, P. M. (1982). Contradictions in the practice of nontraditional continuing education. In S. B. Merriam (Ed.), *Linking philosophy and practice* (New Directions for Continuing Education No. 15, pp. 73–86). San Francisco: Jossey-Bass.

Cushman, R. E. (1958). *Therapeia: Plato's conception of philosophy.* Chapel Hill, NC: University of North Carolina Press.

Darkenwald, G. G., & Merriam, S. B. (1982). *Adult education: Foundations of practice.* New York: Harper & Row.

Dave, R. H. (1976). *Foundations of lifelong education.* Oxford, England: Pergamon.

Dewey, J. (1916). *Democracy and education.* New York: Macmillan.

Dewey, J. (1922). *Human nature and conduct.* New York: Modern Library, Random House.

Dewey, J. (1938). *Experience and education.* New York: Macmillan.

Elias, J. (1982). The theory–practice split. In S. B. Merriam (Ed.), *Linking philosophy and practice* (New Directions for Continuing Education No. 15, pp. 3–11). San Francisco: Jossey-Bass.

Elias, J. L., & Merriam, S. (1980). *Philosophical foundations of adult education.* Huntington, NY: Krieger.

Freire, P. (1970). *Pedagogy of the oppressed.* New York: Herder & Herder.

Gelpi, E. (1979). *A future for lifelong education* (Vols. 1 & 2). Manchester, England: University of Manchester, Department of Adult and Higher Education.

Gross, R. (1977). *The lifelong learner.* New York: Simon & Schuster.

Gross, R. (1982). *Invitation to lifelong learning.* Chicago: Follett.

Hesburgh, T. M., Miller, P. A., & Wharton, C. R., Jr. (1973). *Patterns for lifelong learning.* San Francisco: Jossey-Bass.

Hiemstra, R. (1975). *The older adult and learning.* Ames, IA: Adult and Extension Education, Iowa State University. (ERIC Document Reproduction Service No. ED 117 371)

Hiemstra, R. (1976a). *Lifelong learning.* Lincoln, NE: Professional Educators Publications. (Reprinted in 1984 by HiTree Press, Baldwinsville, NY)

Hiemstra, R. (1976b). The older adult's learning projects. *Educational Gerontology, 1,* 331–341.

Hiemstra, R. (1980a). *Policy recommendations related to self-directed adult learners* (CEP 1). Syracuse, NY: Syracuse University Printing Service. (ERIC Document Reproduction Service No. ED 198 304)

Hiemstra, R. (1980b). *Preparing human service practitioners to teach older adults* (Information Series No. 209). Columbus, OH: Ohio State University, ERIC Clearinghouse for Adult, Career, and Vocational Education. (ERIC Document Reproduction Service No. ED 193 529)

Hiemstra, R. (1982). *Self-directed adult learning: Some implications for practice* (CEP 2). Syracuse, NY: Syracuse University Printing Service. (ERIC Document Reproduction Service No. ED 262 259)

Hiemstra, R. (1985a). The older adult's learning projects. In D. B. Lumsden (Ed.), *The older adult as learner* (pp. 165–196). Washington, DC: Hemisphere.

Hiemstra, R. (1985b). *Self-directed adult learning: Some implications for facilitators* (CEP 3). Syracuse, NY: Syracuse University Printing Service. (ERIC Document Reproduction Service No. ED 262 260)

Himmelstrup, P. (1980). Introduction. In P. Himmelstrup, J. Robinson, & D. Fielden (Eds.), *Strategies for lifelong learning 1* (pp. 11–23). Esbjerg, Denmark: University Centre of South Jutland.

Hutchins, R. (1968). *The learning society.* New York: Praeger.

Illich, I. (1970). *Deschooling society.* New York: Harper & Row.

Knowles, M. S. (1975). *Self-directed learning.* New York: Association Press.

Knowles, M. S. (1980). *The modern practice of adult education.* Chicago: Follet.

Knowles, M. S. (1986). *Using learning contracts.* San Francisco: Jossey-Bass.

Lindeman, E. C. (1926). *The meaning of adult education.* New York: New Republic.

Maslow, A. (1976). Education and peak experience. In C. D. Schlosser (Ed.), *The person in education: A humanistic approach.* New York: Macmillan.

McKenzie, L. (1985). Philosophical orientations of adult educators. *Lifelong Learning: An Omnibus of Practice and Research, 9*(1), 18–20.

Merriam, S. B. (1982). Some thoughts on the relationship between theory and practice. In S. B. Merriam (Ed.), *Linking philosophy and practice* (New Directions for Continuing Education No. 15, pp. 87–91). San Francisco: Jossey-Bass.

Podeschi, R. L. (1986). Philosophies, practices and American values. *Lifelong Learning: An Omnibus of Practice and Research, 9*(4), 4–6, 27–28.

Rogers, C. R. (1969). *Freedom to learn.* Columbus, OH: Merrill.

Skinner, B. F. (1971). *Beyond freedom and dignity.* New York: Knopf.

Taylor, A. (1926). *Plato: The man and his work.* London: Methuen & Co.

Tough, A. (1979). *The adult's learning projects* (2nd ed.). Austin, TX: Learning Concepts.

Tyler, R. (1949). *Basic principles of curriculum and instruction.* Chicago: University of Chicago Press.

Whitehead, A. N. (1933). *Adventures of ideas.* New York: Macmillan.

Zinn, L. (1983). *Development of a valid and reliable instrument to identify a personal philosophy of adult education.* Unpublished doctoral dissertation, Florida State University, Tallahassee.

CHAPTER THIRTEEN

Ethical Issues: Some Concluding Thoughts

RALPH G. BROCKETT

THE preceding chapters have addressed ethical issues in adult education from a variety of perspectives. Clearly, ethics is a theme that lies at the heart of adult education practice, for an understanding of ethics can help us to reaffirm our responsibilities as educators of adults. The purpose of this concluding chapter is to provide a summary and synthesis of the previous chapters by reflecting on the "dimensions of ethical practice" model presented in Chapter 1 and suggesting ways that the model can be applied in the practice and study of adult education. In addition, several possible directions for future exploration relative to adult education ethics will be identified.

Applying the "Dimensions of Ethical Practice" Model

The model presented in Chapter 1 is not intended to be a "theory" of ethical practice in adult education. Rather, it should be thought of as a guiding framework that may be helpful in identifying concerns relevant to adult education ethics. In order to apply the model, it is important to recognize two basic underlying assumptions. First, as was mentioned in the opening chapter, the model should be seen as a way of understanding the *process* of ethical decision making. It is not a *prescriptive* model intended to offer specific suggestions for how one "should" respond in a given situation. Thus instead of providing prescriptive guidelines for dealing with specific situations, the potential usefulness of the model lies in the identification of different considerations involved in the process of ethical decision making.

Second, the model assumes that ethical decision making begins with the personal values held by individual adult educators. In Chapter 9, Cunningham points out quite correctly that the model views ethical decision making as a rational process. She argues that since ethics is "socially defined in the political arena of practice," a rational framework is inappropriate. My own position is that the personal value system does not develop in a vacuum. It is highly influenced by the specific social context in which the individual exists. Thus the individual and social emphases are not necessarily antithetical. Still, the point Cunningham makes is a crucial one. The extent to which one might be able to subscribe to the "dimensions" model will be influenced by how one views the centrality of individual and social influences.

There are at least three ways in which the "dimensions of ethical practice" model can be utilized in adult education. First, it can be used by individuals who wish to explore their own personal development relative to ethical practice. In addition, it can be utilized as a tool in the critical analysis of adult education programs and practices. Finally, it can serve as a framework out of which research questions can be derived. Each of these applications is discussed further.

Personal and Professional Development

One way in which the "dimensions" model can be used is by individual practitioners in the development of their own views about the nature of ethical practice. The previous chapters contain numerous questions and illustrations of situations in which ethical conflict can arise. Although few specific answers are provided to the questions raised, readers should come away with a greater awareness of the wide range of concerns that can prove ethical in nature.

While the model assumes that ethical decision making is a rational process, it also recognizes that in many instances, behaviors that may be considered unethical are undertaken because an individual has not "realized" the potential unethical consequences of his or her actions. The "dimensions" model can therefore be used in a "consciousness-raising" manner to assist adult educators in gaining new insights into what may be considered, at least in some circles, to be unethical practices. Through this awareness, perhaps one can become better able to act *consciously* and *rationally* in an ethical way.

The chapters by Kasworm and Hiemstra are intended to provide insights into personal and professional ethical development. Kasworm shares perspectives on theory, research, and applications related to moral development in adulthood. Hiemstra points out the potential benefits of developing a working philosophy of adult education, particularly with respect to one's ethical orientation. The process he shares is an approach that can be used to gain greater insight into one's personal value system.

Critical Analysis of Adult Education Programs and Practices

Apps (1985) has recently presented a rationale and process for critically analyzing various aspects of practice in the education of adults. He notes that critical analysis is vital to the improvement of practice in such areas as adult learning, aims of continuing education, the teaching and learning process, program development, and policy formulation and analysis. While Apps tends to focus on critical analysis in a broad way, a similar argument can be made for the use of critical analysis in the process of ethical decision making. The "dimensions" model can be utilized in such analysis.

To illustrate this point, take the hypothetical case of an adult basic education (ABE) teacher whose success in the classroom has declined considerably since being required to adopt a competency-based approach to ABE one year earlier. An administrator seeking to better understand this change might explore the problem from an ethical standpoint and find that the teacher has been struggling with conflict between a personal approach that is largely based in concepts of humanism and the mandate of teaching in a way that is more rooted in behaviorism. For this teacher, the incorporation of the competency-based adult education focus has given rise to an ethical conflict between personal values and organizational mission.

Those individuals responsible for evaluating both the process and outcomes of adult education programs might find ethics to be a valuable source of information. Many of the issues raised in the chapters by Sork, Burns and Roche, Sisco, Brookfield, Caffarella, and Day deal with questions that frequently arise in the day-to-day practice of adult education. In a similar vein, Merriam's chapter addresses concerns related to the study of the field. By critically examining these questions in the context of one's own practice, it is possible to gain information that, as Apps (1985) suggests, can contribute to improved practice.

Generation of Research Questions

A third potential use of the "dimensions" model can be by researchers who wish to explore adult education ethics through a process of systematic inquiry. Since the model distinguishes between individual, organizational, and professionwide concerns, it could be used by adult educators in developing a specific focus for the asking of researchable questions.

Each of the three dimensions of the model holds potential for the generation of research questions. For instance, researchers interested in the "personal value system" dimension might want to look at such areas as personality, moral development, and possible links among teaching/leadership style, adult education philosophy, and one's ethical orientation. Similarly, those interested in the "multiple responsibilities" dimension might choose to explore questions surrounding the meanings that adult educators attach to their practice and how they would choose to deal with situations in which their ethical values are called into question. And in terms of the "operationalization" dimension, questions could range from determining attitudes toward a code of ethics for adult educators, to perceptions of social responsibility in terms of adult educators' roles, to studies of actual, observed unethical behavior, such as was done in the study by Clement, Pinto, and Walker (1978) discussed in Chapter 1. The chapters by Cunningham and Carlson are particularly relevant to the development of research questions related to this third dimension.

Considerations for the Future

The intent of this book has been to introduce readers to a number of ethical issues that can surface in the practice and study of adult education. Since so little has been written to date in this area, it is hoped that the book will stimulate a greater awareness of and interest in the topic, both among those who practice in the field and those who study it. In this way, the book might be viewed as a blueprint for future consideration of ethical questions relative to the education of adults.

Where do we go from here? Clearly, ethics is a topic whose time is long overdue in adult education. This volume has been an attempt to stimulate thought about a number of key issues; yet many more remain unexplored to date. Four such concerns are briefly highlighted below with the hope that they may serve as a point of departure for others who wish to take a closer look at this area.

Ethical Relativism

Do there exist *universal* rights or wrongs in adult education? Or is the rightness or wrongness of a behavior totally determined by the *context* in which the behavior occurs? Those who support the former position might be referred to as absolutists, while those who subscribe to the latter position could be described as ethical relativists. According to Bayless, ethical relativists do "not merely maintain that people have different beliefs . . . but that these different beliefs may all be correct" (1981, p. 17). As one considers the issues raised in the previous chapters, it should be clear that one's response will largely be a product of the degree to which one subscribes to a relativist or absolutist view of ethics. The typology of ethical ideologies by Forsyth (1981), which was mentioned by Merriam in Chapter 10, may hold promise for gaining greater insight into this issue.

Given the diversity of the adult education field, the question of ethical relativism will be essential. For instance, take the question of whether situations exist in which adults should be "required" to participate in continuing education. While many educators will argue consistently either for or against mandatory continuing education requirements, many others are likely to take the position that the appropriateness of mandatory continuing education depends on the circumstances. Here the argument is sometimes proposed that professionals such as physicians and airline pilots, who deal with potentially life-threatening circumstances, should be required to participate in continuing professional development, while other professional groups need not be subject to such requirements. Examination of ethical relativism in adult education will be essential if we are to consider the diversity of contexts and settings where the education of adults is practiced.

Metaethics

As we stated at the outset, the focus of this book has been on normative ethics, or the application of ethical principles to judging the rightness or wrongness of adult education programs and practices. In looking to the future, there is much potential value in looking at ethics from the perspective of philosophical analysis or metaethics. While most adult educators probably do not have extensive background in philosophy, those who *do* possess this perspective are in a unique position to help the field critically analyze the meaning of terms such as *good, bad, right,* and *wrong,* particularly as they relate to the education of adults. Although metaethics has not been a major focus of this book, it is recognized that if the topic of ethics is to gain a greater foothold in the future of adult education, questions of a metaethical nature will need to be explored by those who can successfully bridge philosophy and adult education.

Legal Versus Ethical Issues

In looking to the future, it will be necessary to distinguish between ethical and legal issues. While many issues may simultaneously be of an ethical and a legal nature, ethical issues are often *not* identified as law. Whereas most individuals would agree that it is unethical to discriminate in the hiring of adult education teachers on the basis of race or gender, it is also *illegal.* On the other hand, many practices related to such areas as needs assessment, marketing, and evaluation may not be illegal but might, in fact, be considered unethical by most educators of adults. The interface between law and ethics pertaining to the education of adults is, therefore, a potentially fruitful direction for the future.

The Code-of-Ethics Question

Few issues have divided adult educators more than the question of whether the field should strive toward increased status as a profession. In considering the professionalization of adult education, the question of whether a code of ethics should be developed will be necessary to consider. Houle (1980), for instance, has stated that one of the key elements of a profession is a formalized ethical code. As Cervero (1987) points out, professionalization will continue to be a major issue as the field moves toward the year 2000; however, he suggests that a number of "alternative" models of professionalization might be more appropriate for adult education than the more traditional conceptualizations that characterize most professions today. In these alternative models of professionalization, it can be argued that the case presented by Carlson in Chapter 11 against the development of formal ethical codes gains additional strength. Thus while the question of whether adult education should adopt a formal code of ethics has been considered, either directly or indirectly, in several of the preceding chapters, the question is one that clearly warrants further exploration, for its resolution will most certainly have implications for the future of the field.

Conclusion

Ethics has a definite, vital place in the practice and study of adult education. Adult education is a field that has grown out of a practice tradition. Ethics is a practical endeavor. While ethical concerns are certainly not new to the field, the awareness of these concerns, as reflected in adult education professional literature and conference proceedings, would suggest that ethics has not been a visible topic within the field. As we look to creating the kind of future we desire for adult education, ethics can, and indeed must, play a central role. However, only through greater interest, awareness, discussion, research, and debate will it be possible for this centrality of ethics to become a reality. It is up to each of us to ensure this reality.

References

Apps, J. W. (1985). *Improving practice in continuing education.* San Francisco: Jossey-Bass.

Bayless, M. D. (1981). *Professional ethics.* Belmont, CA: Wadsworth.

Cervero, R. M. (1987). Professionalization as an issue for continuing education. In R. G. Brockett (Ed.), *Continuing education in the year 2000* (New Directions for Continuing Education No. 36, pp. 67–78). San Francisco: Jossey-Bass.

Clement, R. W., Pinto, P. R., & Walker, J. W. (1978). Unethical and improper behavior by training and development professionals. *Training and Development Journal, 32*(12), 10–12.

Forsyth, D. R. (1981). A psychological perspective on ethical uncertainties in research. In A. J. Kimmel (Ed.), *Ethics of human subjects research* (New Directions for Methodology of Social and Behavioral Science No. 10, pp. 91–100). San Francisco: Jossey-Bass.

Houle, C. O. (1980). *Continuing learning in the professions.* San Francisco: Jossey-Bass.

Principles of Good Practice in Continuing Education

Part 1—Learning Needs in Continuing Education

    1.1 Sponsors or providers of continuing education programs/ activities utilize appropriate processes to define and analyze the issue(s) or problem(s) of individuals, groups, and organizations for the purpose of determining learning needs.

Part 2—Learning Outcomes in Continuing Education

    2.1 The continuing education provider has clear and concise written statements of intended learning outcomes for the continuing education program/activity.

    2.2 The statements of intended learning outcomes of a continuing education program/activity focus on learning that can be applied by the learner to situations beyond the boundaries of the learning environment.

    2.3 When a continuing education program consists of several interrelated activities, courses, seminars, and workshops, the contribution of the intended learning outcomes of each to the total program is clearly designated.

    2.4 The agenda of the continuing education program/activity clearly specifies when each learning outcome will be addressed.

    2.5 Learning outcomes are sequenced so that learners are able to recognize their progress toward achieving the stated learning outcomes.

Part 3—Learning Experiences in Continuing Education

    3.1 Learning experiences are designed to facilitate the role of the learner and are organized in such a manner as to provide for appropriate continuity, sequencing, and integration of the program/activity to achieve the specified learning outcomes.

    3.2 The statements of intended learning outcomes of a continuing education program/activity determine the selection of instructional strategies, instructional materials, media and other learning technology, and create an appropriate learning environment.

3.3 Program content, instructional materials, and delivery processes are relevant and timely for achieving intended learning outcomes.

3.4 Instructional staff in continuing education programs/activities are qualified by education or experience to provide quality instruction in the subject-matter area.

3.5 The physical environment for the continuing education program/activity is conducive to learning.

Part 4—Assessment of Learning Outcomes

4.1 Continuing education programs/activities are evaluated through assessment of learners' performance in terms of intended learning outcomes.

Part 5—Continuing Education Administration

5.1 Each continuing education provider has a clearly stated, written statement of its mission, which is available to the publics served.

5.2 The continuing education provider has appropriate, sufficient, and stable *human, fiscal,* and *physical* resources to provide quality programs/activities over an extended period of time.

5.3 The continuing education provider's promotion and advertising provide full and accurate disclosures about its programs, services, and fees.

5.4 The continuing education provider ensures the maintenance of a set of limited-access, permanent records of participants and the provision of documentation for accurate, readily available transcripts.

5.5 The continuing education provider makes available to participants recognition and documentation of achievement of learning outcomes specified for the continuing education program/activity.

5.6 The continuing education provider ensures that appropriate quality control systems are in place and in use within its organization.

Contributors

Ralph G. Brockett is assistant professor of adult education, Center for Adult Learning Research, Montana State University, Bozeman. Previously he was on the adult education faculty at Syracuse University and has worked in continuing education for health and human services professionals. He holds B.A. and M.Ed. degrees from the University of Toledo and a Ph.D. from Syracuse University. A past member of the executive board of the Commission of Professors of Adult Education, he is the editor of *Continuing Education in the Year 2000* (New Directions for Continuing Education No. 36) and has written or coauthored a number of articles, reviews, and manuals. Currently, he serves as book review editor for *Adult Education Quarterly* and is on the editorial board of *Adult Literacy and Basic Education.*

Stephen Brookfield is associate professor in the department of higher and adult education and associate director of the Center for Adult Education at Columbia University, Teachers College in New York City. He is the author of numerous articles and several books, including *Understanding and Facilitating Adult Learning,* which received both the 1986 Cyril O. Houle Award for World Literature in Adult Education and the 1986 Imogene E. Okes Award for Outstanding Research in Adult Education. He holds a B.A. from Lancashire Polytechnic, an M.A. from the University of Reading (England), a Ph.D. in Adult Education from the University of Leicester, and postgraduate diplomas from three institutions. His main research interests have been in the areas of adult learning, community education, comparative adult education, qualitative research, and political/philosophical aspects of adult education.

John H. Burns is manager of education planning and development, Agway Incorporated, of Syracuse, New York. He holds a B.S. in Marketing from Fordham University and a master's degree in Adult Education from Syracuse University. He is a member of the board of directors of the National Society of Sales Training Executives, where he received the 1982 and 1986 Bronze Awards for contributions to the profession.

Rosemary S. Caffarella is associate professor of adult education at Virginia Commonwealth University, Richmond. Her major areas of emphasis in teaching and research are self-directed learning, adult development, and program planning and evaluation. Among her recent major works are a forthcoming book entitled *Planning and Evaluating Training Programs: A Guide for Action*, a critical review of the literature on self-directed learning, and a conceptual paper on faculty development for mid-career faculty.

Robert A. Carlson is professor of adult education at the University of Saskatchewan in Canada. He has also served as visiting professor at North Carolina State University in Raleigh, at Dalhousie University in Halifax, and at Concordia University in Montreal. In 1975 he was a scholar-in-residence at the Open University in England. He has lectured and published throughout North America and in Europe. His most recent publication is *The Americanization Syndrome*, a revised and expanded version of his earlier book, *The Quest for Conformity*, which is being republished by Croom Helm, Ltd.

Phyllis M. Cunningham is professor of adult education at Northern Illinois University. Her research interests lie in popular education, participatory research, and voluntarism. She actively supports the International Council for Adult Education, Basic Choices, Inc., and several local community-based adult education programs. She was co-editor of *Adult Education: A Journal of Theory and Research* for five years and is currently co-editing the *1990 Handbook of Adult Education*. As the primary organizer of a formal exchange program between her university and the Shanghai Second Institution of Education, she has been officially named as "consulting professor" by the Shanghai Institute.

Michael J. Day received his Ph.D. from the University of Michigan in 1981 with specializations in both adult education and the history of art. He currently heads graduate study in adult education at the University of Wyoming. He also has served as chairperson of the faculty senate and president of the Wyoming Adult, Continuing and Community Education Association. His interest and involvement in educational brokering for adult students began in 1974 when he coordinated the field program at the University of Maryland in Wiesbaden, West Germany. He continues to be an advocate for campus and off-campus adult students and to concentrate on questions directed at the role of educational adviser, specifically in the areas of preparation/training, brokering, and ethics.

Roger Hiemstra is professor and chair of the graduate program in Adult Education, Syracuse University, Syracuse, New York. He also directs a project sponsored by the Kellogg Foundation for the international exchange and dissemination of information for educators of adults. He obtained his Ph.D. in Adult Education in 1970 from the University of Michigan and has also served on the adult education faculties at the University of Nebraska and Iowa State University. He is past president of the Commission of Professors of Adult Education, was senior editor of *Lifelong Learning: The Adult Years*, and currently is editor of the *Adult Education Quarterly*.

Carol E. Kasworm is currently the associate vice president for faculty and program development at the University of Houston–Clear Lake. She was formerly on the faculty of the University of Texas at Austin and previously a staff member of the Georgia Center for Continuing Education at the University of Georgia. Her publications include research in the area of adult learning, adult undergraduate students, adult literacy, and self-directed learning. She most recently edited *Educational Outreach to Select Adult Populations* (*New Directions for Continuing Education*, Volume 20).

Sharan B. Merriam is professor of adult and continuing education at the University of Georgia. She has also served on the faculty at Northern Illinois University and Virginia Polytechnic Institute and State University. Her authored or co-authored publications include *A Guide to Research for Educators and Trainers of Adults*, *Philosophical Foundations of Adult Education*, *Themes of Adulthood Through Literature*, and *Adult Education: Foundations of Practice*, winner of the 1985 Cyril O. Houle International Award for Literature in Adult Education. She is particularly interested in adult development, adult learning, and qualitative research methods. *Doing Case Study Research in Education* is due for publication in 1988.

Gene A. Roche is Director of the Career Center at Hamilton College in Clinton, New York. Previously he served on the professional staff of the Boy Scouts of America. He received his master's degree in Adult Education from Syracuse University, where he is currently working toward his doctorate.

Burton R. Sisco is assistant professor of adult education at the University of Wyoming. He holds a bachelor's and master's degree from the University of Vermont and an Ed.D. in adult education from Syracuse University. Previously, he held faculty positions at Syracuse and at Saint Michael's College in Winooski, Vermont, and worked as an administrator of continuing higher education at the University of Vermont. He possesses extensive experience in the field of adult and continuing education, having developed education and training programs at the higher education level and conducted basic research, and is actively involved in professional groups dealing with the education of adults at the local, state, and national levels. His current research interests are in the areas of self-directed learning, cognition and learning effectiveness, and historical foundations of adult education. He is coauthor of *Individualizing Instruction for Adult Learners*, which is slated for publication in 1989.

Thomas J. Sork is assistant professor in the Department of Administrative, Adult and Higher Education at the University of British Columbia. His academic and professional interests focus on program planning in adult and continuing education. He has edited a volume in the Jossey-Bass New Directions for Continuing Education series, entitled *Designing and Implementing Effective Workshops*, and has contributed two recent book chapters on needs assessment. In addition, he co-authored an article on adult education ethics that appeared in the *Adult Education Quarterly* and has contributed a chapter on ethics to the 1987 edition of *Materials and Methods in Adult and Continuing Education*. He has held academic appointments at Colorado State University and the University of Nebraska–Lincoln and has served as an administrator of continuing education programs at three universities. He holds a Ph.D. in Adult Education from Florida State University.

Index